LITERATURE
AS
EXPLORATION

LITERATURE AS EXPLORATION

Fifth Edition

LOUISE M. ROSENBLATT

With a foreword by WAYNE BOOTH

THE MODERN LANGUAGE ASSOCIATION
OF AMERICA   NEW YORK   1995

Foreword by Wayne Booth
© 1995 by The Modern Language Association

Library of Congress Cataloging-in-Publication Data

Rosenblatt, Louise M. (Louise Michelle)
    Literature as exploration / Louise M. Rosenblatt. — 5th ed.
        p.   cm.
    Includes bibliographical references (p.   ) and index.
    ISBN 0-87352-567-1. — ISBN 0-87352-568-X (paper)
    1. Literature—Study and teaching.   I. Title.
PN59.R6   1995
801'.95—dc20   95-38208

Paperback cover and dust jacket design by Dorothy Wachtenheim
Text design by Charlotte Staub
Set in Bembo with Weiss Titling display type. Printed on recycled paper

Jacket and cover art: Georgio de Chirico, *The Double Dream of Spring*,
1915. Oil on canvas, 22⅛" × 21⅜" (56.2 cm × 54.3 cm). The Museum of
Modern Art, New York. Gift of James Thrall Soby. Photograph ©1995
by The Museum of Modern Art, New York.

Published by The Modern Language Association
10 Astor Place, New York, New York 10003-6981

CONTENTS

FOREWORD

I doubt that any other literary critic of this century has enjoyed and suffered as sharp a contrast of powerful influence and absurd neglect as Louise Rosenblatt. Has she been influential? Immensely so: how many other critical works first published in the late thirties have extended themselves, like this one, to five editions, proving themselves relevant to decade after decade of critical and pedagogical revolution? How then can I claim that she has been unfairly neglected? The answer obviously depends on what we mean by "unfair." She has in fact been attended to by thousands of teachers and students in each generation. She has probably influenced more teachers in their ways of dealing with literature than any other critic. But the world of literary criticism and theory has only recently begun to acknowledge the relevance of her arguments to questions like What constitutes a text? and What finally is the point of reading literature? and Why try to improve students' reading?

I confess that as I have reread this book and her later work, *The Reader, the Text, the Poem: The Transactional Theory of the Literary Work* (1978), I have found that I must revise what I said of her about a decade ago in the afterword to the second edition of *The Rhetoric of Fiction*: I hereby change my mealy-mouthed "See the unfortunately neglected works of Rosenblatt" to "See the works of Rosenblatt that *I have sadly neglected*; if I had read *Literature as Exploration* carefully before completing this book in 1961, I could have done a better job of celebrating not just how authors 'make their readers' but how good readers construct and then revise the constructions of the authors they meet."

Like most participants in most critical movements over the nearly six decades since Rosenblatt's work made its initial splash, I failed for too long to see that it was not just a valuable guide to pedagogy in secondary teaching; it was a necessary antidote to the excesses that result when this or that element in any rhetorical transaction is turned into an exclusive center.

One way of seeing why her work has survived with generation after generation is to think of her as standing to one side of our various fashionable movements and repeating, quietly but persistently, "Yes, *of course*, but don't you see? You have caught only a fragment of the whole picture." Demanding that teachers think constantly of "the relationship between the individual student and the book"—that is, of the *transaction* between potentially powerful texts and readers whose emotional engagement should be "read" as closely as the text itself—Rosenblatt offered corrections, too often ignored for too long, of the exaggerations committed by successive enthusiasts.

A simplified but revealing history of criticism since the thirties could thus be written just by tracing her corrections, whispered, as it were, from the wings.

First Moment. Troubled by the excesses of dry historicism in the early years of the century, she joined many others who found a sense of liberation in the return to close reading celebrated by "new" critics like I. A. Richards in *Practical Criticism* (1929). But unlike too many of us Chicago neo-Aristotelians and most of the New Critics, she saw the folly of ignoring diversity of response. Too many of us too much of the time, in the late forties and through the fifties, pictured ourselves as expert prospectors delving endlessly for the gold: the one right reading. Instead of seeing varieties in readers' responses as invitations to rhetorical "exploration," we too often understood them—as indeed many teachers still do—as invitations to battles that allow for only one true victor. Put more politely, we saw our task as the quite honorable one of correcting the misreadings of the misguided students sitting before us.

Although she insisted, like all serious teachers, on close attention to texts, fully respecting their unique powers, she shifted the emphasis dramatically toward a close reading of the responses of close readers. What she later called the "transactional" theory allowed her to preserve a respect for the author's intentions and the text's powers, while moving beyond the arid explication de texte that filled too many journals in the fifties.

Practicing in a pragmatic philosophical tradition that is only now receiving the revived attention it deserves (Dewey, for example, was one of her heroes), she cared more about turning all students into better readers than about turning a few students into disciples of the one right reading or kind of reading.

Second Moment. Thus it is now easy to see just how far in advance she was of those who in the sixties were hailed as the founders of "reader-response criticism." Some few reader-response critics did acknowledge her as a founder, but I've not seen any full recognition of just how far ahead of the pack she was. Perhaps that relative neglect resulted from her absolute resistance to the excesses of reader-response theory: the notion that all readings are equally valid. She never lets her reader forget that though all serious responses are worth exploration, we have no reason to think that "every evocation from a text is as good as every other" (267). Thus while she helped spawn a generation of reader-response critics who saw "literature as a source of insight and emotional liberation" (224, 4th ed.), she never lost hold of the difference between genuine liberation and intellectual chaos.

Third Moment. Then came the canon wars. Current defenders of this or that canon could easily quote her selectively as favoring their side. Her book is full of advice on how to lead students to the discovery of just why this or that classic is indeed a classic. She reminds us steadily, however, of what too many ardent canonists forget, that "too often . . . the classics are introduced to children at an age [or to adults at a stage] when it is impossible for them to feel in any personal way the problems or conflicts treated" (206). "When one thinks of all that great literary works can yield, one is horrified to see them so often reduced to the level of language exercise books. . . . Those who cram the classics down students' throats long before they are ready are careless of the fate of the great works of the past" (206–07).

Fourth Moment. Implicit in this attitude toward the classics are the good reasons that underlie another pendulum swing— toward "multiculturalism." Though she might well be shocked by some recent excesses in discarding great works of the past, throughout this book we meet pleas to forget those lists of "essential" works, throw away those Hirsch-ite lists of essential knowledge bits, and think instead about what literary works and what approaches to them will work for the students in front of you. Genuine responses to literature always entail a meeting of the "cultural environment" of the reader with that of the text. "That the play is 'great literature' may have determined its selection in the first place, but that means nothing unless the play has human significance today" (224–25)—significance for *this* reader coming to it with *these* cultural presuppositions (see especially chapter 6, "Some Basic Social Concepts").

Fifth Moment. Here we come more directly to the ways in which the book, having incorporated and transformed close reading, respect for the canon, and multiculturalism, implicitly addresses the issues raised by postmodernist theories. To argue this point would require a full essay, one that would underline three current fashions yet avoid their excesses.

First, as I've already implied, her work is radically interdisciplinary, shattering all sharp borderlines dividing philosophy, the social sciences, and literary criticism and pedagogy. Though she never bought into the more extreme political dogmas of the thirties, her thinking, like that of the most influential theorists today, was infused with the best thought of anthropologists, psychologists, sociologists, and economists (see "For Further Reading," p. 299).

Second, this breadth of influences helps account for the way in which so much of this book accords with what prophets of "cultural critique" now teach. Though respecting the unique achievements of "genius," Rosenblatt is steadily aware of how the cultural moment of both authors and readers affects both what is created and what the reader makes of it. In fact, it is this awareness of the deep cultural embeddedness of every writing and reading act that produced her emphasis on attending to each reader's stance as a crucial part of every literary "exploration."

Third, many postmodernists talk as if they had invented liberated reading—"resistant" reading, "reading against the grain," reading that invigorates and transforms readers by freeing them from critical constraints. What I've been saying all along should make it clear that Rosenblatt has long been far ahead of that game. Though her emphasis on the word *values* may seem old-fashioned to some, she is as radically insistent on building "free" readers as any postmodernist. But again she provides a corrective for the excesses: in respecting the reader's fate as the true center of all teaching of literature, it is a great mistake to assume that where any reader is *now* is where that reader *ought* to be after careful reading. And with that word *ought* we keep alive the notion that some ethical directions are better than others, that some ways of reading are better than others, that some ways of teaching are better than others. As Derrida and other deconstructionists are now finally emphasizing, pursuits like "liberation" and "empowerment" do not render meaningless but rather re-emphasize the importance of ethical concepts like "responsibility," "justice," and "respect."

In short, what Louise Rosenblatt offered us in 1938 and offers us still is a cogent defense of the essential reasons for teaching literature in the first place. To talk of this book in those terms, however, may have the unfortunate effect of perpetuating the biggest mistake we have made about Rosenblatt's work—that is, thinking of it as relevant only or mainly to primary and secondary teaching. Though the pedagogical emphasis is dominant throughout, what she says is as relevant to an advanced graduate seminar on *Middlemarch* or *Pedro Páramo* as to a high school class reading *Macbeth* or *Beloved*. Consequently we can be sure that her work will continue to speak its polite corrections through whatever pendulum swings come next.

It will also require of us new kinds of thinking because of the cultural changes since she wrote. Can we hope that some young reader of her work will take it in, fully, and then be tempted to address its diverse and complex implications for our TV and video generation? Some have done this already, but far too few. Can we hope that Rosenblatt's plea that we treat reading as a transaction between two great kinds of stuff— literary works and living persons—will be extended more aggressively to the treatment of *viewing* as transactional in the same sense: not just providing for the new superficial kinds of technological feedback but for the creation of truly critical viewers? Can we hope for a generation of viewers who engage fully in thinking through their emotional responses, moving toward deeper self-knowledge? Can we hope for teachers who will educate students to resist passive absorption and develop active *transaction*?

In other words, the students we meet in classrooms today need something more than education in conducting transactions with books. To survive as the kind of people Rosenblatt would have us become, they need what seems to be the much more difficult art (though new technologies are making it possible): slowing down the image, recognizing that living with the flow of images and talking back to them is, as Rosenblatt says of reading literature, a "mode of living" (264), a training for the life that occurs after the images are turned off.

Wayne Booth
January 1995

PREFACE TO THE
FIFTH EDITION

Democracy and literature, the intertwined themes of this book, take on a special relevance to education for the contemporary world. When I was writing the book, democracy was threatened from without. The fading of those external forces has made it very clear that democracy is not simply a structure of political institutions but, as Dewey said, "a way of life." Democracy implies a society of people who, no matter how much they differ from one another, recognize their common interests, their common goals, and their dependence on mutually honored freedoms and responsibilities. For this they need the ability to imagine the human consequences of political and economic alternatives and to think rationally about emotionally charged issues. Such strengths should be fostered by all the agencies that shape the individual, but the educational system, through all its disciplines, has a crucial role. The belief that the teaching of literature could especially contribute to such democratic education generated this book.

These democratic potentialities were being frustrated, in my view, by the traditional teaching and criticism of literature, based on faulty assumptions about the nature of reading and the aesthetics of literature. Hence it was necessary to present the theory of literature on which my philosophy of teaching rested. Aspects of the theory are often conveyed in terms of their implications for teaching. At the heart of it is the idea of the poem as an event in the life of a reader, as a doing, a making, a combustion fed by the coming together of a particular personality and a particular text at a particular time.

No major textual changes have been made in this edition of *Literature as Exploration*, though for some of my basic concepts I substitute terms I developed in *The Reader, the Text, the Poem* and other later writings. Since the second edition, I have used the terms *transaction* and *transactional* to emphasize the essentiality of both reader and text, in contrast to other theories that make one or the other determinate. *Interaction*, the term generally used, suggests two distinct entities acting on each other, like two billiard balls. *Transaction* lacks such mechanistic overtones and permits emphasis on the to-and-fro, spiraling, nonlinear, continuously reciprocal influence of reader and text in the making of meaning. The meaning—the poem— "happens" during the transaction between the reader and the signs on the page.

But a poem will not actually result unless the reader performs in a certain way. When "reader response" took on the dimensions of a movement, I found it necessary to underline the distinctive view of the reading process on which this book rests. The reader is recognized not only as active but also as carrying on certain different processes in nonliterary and literary transactions with the text. Both cognitive and affective elements are present in all reading. The differing amounts of attention accorded these aspects constitute a continuum ranging from predominatly nonliterary to predominantly literary.

To abstract the information or the directions for action needed after reading a sociological essay or a medical report, for example, the reader must focus attention primarily on the impersonal, publicly verifiable aspects of what the words evoke and must subordinate or push into the fringes of consciousness the affective aspects. I term this *efferent* reading, from the Latin *efferre* 'to carry away.'

To produce a poem or play, the reader must broaden the scope of attention to include the personal, affective aura and associations surrounding the words evoked and must focus on—experience, live through—the moods, scenes, situations being created during the transaction. I term this *aesthetic* reading. (This shift of attention is so essential, so much taken for granted and ignored, that usually only its effects are noted. Imagine a physiologist explaining the workings of the human body but failing to mention the essential breathing in and out of air.)

These stances are not opposites but form a continuum of possible transactions with a text. According to different purposes, readings of the same text may fall at different points on the efferent-aesthetic continuum, on different "mixes" of attention to public and private aspects. Much of our reading falls in the middle of the continuum, hence the need to adopt an appropriate selective stance. Traditional teaching—and testing—methods often confuse the student by implicitly fostering a nonliterary, efferent approach when the actual purpose is presumably an aesthetic reading.

My insistence that there is no poem, no literary work, unless there has been an aesthetic reading has sometimes been seen as making the personal reading an end in itself. I view it, rather, as essential to the beginning of a process of organic growth, in which the capacity for thinking rationally about emotional responses can be expanded. Such reading can nourish both aesthetic and social sensitivities and can foster the development of critical and self-critical judgment. Hence chapter 3, on the setting for spontaneity, is followed by chapters stressing reflection on the initial experience, interchange with others, and rereading in the light of broadened intellectual frameworks. Chapter 6 is devoted to a discussion of assumptions derived from various disciplines.

Actually, the process of reflection on our linguistic transactions that I have described could serve all the arts. That, incidentally, is my reply to those who dismiss the printed word as soon to be obsolete. Even if this debatable prediction were to come true, the efferent-aesthetic continuum simply describes the two main ways we look at the world, and the transactional process would still apply to transactions with whatever media prevail. Whether they will yield as rewarding an experience is a separate question.

The idea of the transactional continuum is also in keeping with the current post-Einsteinian view of science as an interpretive endeavor, in which the observer must be taken into account in the observation and absolute objectivity is unattainable. It may seem paradoxical that in a book dedicated to redressing the neglect of the aesthetic approach, I call for an awareness of the scientists' ways of thinking about human affairs. My purpose is to counteract the tendency toward polarization of art and science and to stress their complementary contributions.

Recognition that there can be no absolute, single "correct" reading of a text has sometimes been seen as accepting any reading of a text. Without positing a single, absolutely correct reading, we can still agree on criteria by which to evaluate the validity of alternative interpretations of a text. The development of such judgment becomes a part of literary education. In later writings on literary theory, I have cited the justification of this idea of a warrantable interpretation to be found in Dewey's *Logic*.

For various reasons, the format of this book remains essentially the same as in earlier editions. A reminder of when the book first appeared is the generic *he*, then taken for granted, no matter how feminist, as in this case, the writer might be. To remedy this would have required a total rewriting. I must simply assume that my readers are sufficiently free of old patriarchal attitudes to keep in mind my statement at the beginning of chapter 2, in which I point out that "the reader" is a fiction, that there is no generic reader, that each reader is unique, bringing to the transaction an individual ethnic, social, and psychological history. Gender, of course, is a part of that uniqueness.

Although other "postmodern" critics share certain relativist assumptions with me, they have often derived from them extreme conclusions entirely alien to mine. I have added part 4, which may serve to situate the book in its past and present intellectual contexts. I have chosen the title "Reaffirmations" precisely because I am aware of how many problems face our society, how many reactionary tendencies affect our educational system. Since the first publication of this book, there have been various other such cyclic movements forward and backward. Despite this, there have been major democratic advances that must be preserved. Always there have been those who kept alive an understanding of our democratic ethos. I hope that transactions with this book may strengthen their defense of past achievements and their efforts to enhance the education of people for a democratic way of life.

LMR
Princeton, New Jersey
23 April 1995

PART ONE

THE PROVINCE OF LITERATURE

CHAPTER 1

THE CHALLENGE OF LITERATURE

In a turbulent age, our schools and colleges must prepare the student to meet unprecedented and unpredictable problems. He needs to understand himself; he needs to work out harmonious relationships with other people. He must achieve a philosophy, an inner center from which to view in perspective the shifting society about him; he will influence for good or ill its future development. Any knowledge about humankind and society that schools can give him should be assimilated into the stream of his actual life.

It is not only for some future way of life that he needs to be prepared. During his school years, he is already part of the larger world, meeting the impact of its domestic and international tensions, adjusting to adults who bear the marks of its successes and failures, discovering the possibilities it holds open to him. As he plays his youthful role, he is creating the personality and ideals that will shape his role as an adult. Young people everywhere are asking, "What do the things that we are offered in school and college mean for the life that we are now living or are going to live?"

Teachers of literature have been too modest about their possible contribution to these demands. Their task, they have felt, is to make their students more sensitive to the art of words, to induct them into our literary heritage. Leaving to others more mundane preoccupations, they had enough to do, it seemed, in busying themselves with purely literary matters.

The demand that the teaching of literature have some relation to the pupil's immediate human concerns has usually been countered by pointing to the horrors of the didactic, moralistic approach to literature. Wise teachers have opposed any tendency to make of literature a mere handmaiden of the social studies or a body of documents illustrating moral points. The Victorians, the argument runs, demonstrated the sterility of seeking in literature only social or moral lessons; those who see literature in such terms reveal their blindness to the special nature and primary value of literature.

Yet when the literary experience is fully understood, it becomes apparent that teachers of literature have indeed been somewhat shortsighted. They have not always realized that, willy-nilly, they affect the student's sense of human personality and human society. More directly than most teachers, they foster general ideas or theories about human nature and conduct, definite moral attitudes, and habitual responses to people and situations. Preoccupied with the special aims of their field, they are often not conscious of dealing, in the liveliest terms, with subjects and problems usually thought of as the province of the sociologist, psychologist, philosopher, or historian. Moreover, these attitudes and theories are proffered in their most easily assimilable form, as they emerge from personal and intimate experience of specific human situations, presented with all the sharpness and intensity of art.

The teacher of literature will be the first to admit that he inevitably deals with the experiences of human beings in their diverse personal and social relations. The very nature of literature, he will point out, enforces this. Is not the substance of literature everything that human beings have thought or felt or created? The lyric poet utters all that the human heart can feel, from joy in "the cherry hung with snow" to the poignant sense of this world "where youth grows pale, and spectre-thin, and dies." The novelist displays the intricate web of human relationships with their hidden patterns of motive and emotion. He may paint the vast panorama of a society in a *War and Peace* or a *Human Comedy*. He may follow the fate of an entire family in a *Buddenbrooks*. He may show us a young man coming to understand himself and life, grappling with his own nature and the society about him, as in *A Portrait of the Artist as a Young Man* and *Invisible Man,* or he may lead us to share in the subtle moods and insights of men and women, as in *The Ambassadors* and *Remembrance of Things Past.* The writer of stories catches some significant moment, some mood, some clarifying clash of wills in the life of an individual or a group. An author may give us the humorous tale "Rip Van Winkle" or the revelation of character in Chekhov's "The Darling" or the harsh image of frustration in *Ethan Frome.* The dramatist builds a dynamic structure out of the tensions and conflicts of intermingled human lives. He may use the comic incongruities of social conventions and human affectation, as in *The Rivals,* or he may create a somber symphony out of man's inhumanity to man and the inscrutable whims of fate, as in *King Lear.* The joys of adventure, the delight in the beauty of the world, the intensities of triumph and defeat, the self-questionings and self-realizations, the pangs of love and hate—indeed, as Henry James has said, "all life, all feeling, all observation, all vision"—these are the province of literature.

Whatever the form—poem, novel, drama, biography, essay—literature makes comprehensible the myriad ways in which human beings meet the infinite possibilities that life offers. And always we seek some close contact with a mind uttering its sense of life. Always too, in greater or lesser degree, the author has written out of a scheme of values, a sense of a social framework or even, perhaps, of a cosmic pattern.

No matter how much else art may offer, no matter how much the writer may be absorbed in solving the technical problems of his craft, in creating with words new forms of aesthetic experience, the human element cannot be banished. Thus, a writer such as Gertrude Stein, who was preoccupied with technical innovation, will have lasting value only as her work suggests to other writers new means of conveying emotions and a sense of the flow of life. The most sophisticated reader, extremely sensitive to the subtly articulated qualities of the poem or play or novel, cannot judge its technical worth except as he also assimilates the substance that embodies these qualities. Even the literary work that seems most remote, an imagist poem or a fantasy, reveals new notes in the gamut of human experience or derives its quality of escape from its implicit contrast to real life.

George Santayana has summed up this basic appeal of literature:

The wonder of an artist's performance grows with the range of his penetration, with the instinctive sympathy that makes him, in his mortal isolation, considerate of other men's fate and a great diviner of their secret, so that his work speaks to them kindly, with a deeper assurance than they could have spoken with to themselves. And the joy of his great sanity, the power of his adequate vision, is not the less intense because he can lend it to others and has borrowed it from a faithful study of the world. (228–29)

Certainly to the great majority of readers, the human experience that literature presents is primary. For them the formal elements of the work—style and structure, rhythmic flow—function only as a part of the total literary experience. The reader seeks to participate in another's vision—to reap knowledge of the world, to fathom the resources of the human spirit, to gain insights that will make his own life more comprehensible. The teacher of adolescents, in high school or in college, knows to what a heightened degree they share this personal approach to literature.

In contrast to the analytic approach of the social sciences, the literary experience has immediacy and emotional persuasiveness. Will President Madison or Rip Van Winkle live more vividly for the student? Will the history of the Great Depression impress him as much as will Steinbeck's *The Grapes of Wrath*? Will the theoretical definitions of the psychology textbook be as illuminating as *Oedipus* or *Sons and Lovers*? Obviously, the analytic approach needs no defense. But may not literary materials contribute powerfully to the student's images of the world, himself, and the human condition?

The English teacher will urge that his aims are to help students understand what they read, to acquaint them with the history of literature, to give them some insight into literary forms, and to lead them toward a measure of critical discrimination; this seems to have nothing to do with teaching them psychological or sociological theories. The answer is that when he most sincerely seeks to fulfill these aims, he inevitably finds himself dealing with materials that at least imply specific psychological theories and social attitudes. Since literature involves the whole range of human concerns, it is impossible to avoid assuming some attitude toward them. Moreover, because the implied moral attitudes and unvoiced systems of social values are reinforced by the persuasiveness of art, the teacher should bring them out into the open for careful scrutiny.

English teachers are trained to be scrupulous concerning the scholarly accuracy of their statements about literary history. But how often do they stop to scrutinize the scientific bases of the views concerning human personality and society that insinuate themselves into their work? How often have they critically considered the ethical criteria implicit in their judgments on literature—and, incidentally, on life? How often is there even an awareness of the ever-present implied generalizations concerning human beings and society? While attention has been lavished on the historical and technical aspects of literature, these assumptions have been accepted as a by-product requiring no preparation.

What, then, are some of the ways in which the teaching of literature does impinge on problems usually associated with the concerns of, for example, the psychologist or sociologist? A review of the accepted practice in literature classes—indeed, of much literary criticism as well—would reveal an amazing amount of attention given to topics that could be classified under the heading of psychological theorizing. The creation of vivid characters constitutes a large part of the novelist's, the dramatist's, the biographer's art. How can we read *Hamlet* or *Crime and Punishment* or *The Great Gatsby* without preoccupation with the psychology of the characters?

The student, therefore, is often asked to define the nature of the particular characters in the work he has been reading. He is also encouraged to see some relation between motive and action: To what influences did Macbeth respond? What can explain Lady Macbeth's early determination and later breakdown? What was the influence of the characters on one another in *A Separate Peace*? We do not need the abundant evidence of textbook and teacher's manual to know that such questions will arise. After reading *Hamlet*, the high school student, like the Shakespearean authority, often turns to theorizing about the rational and irrational elements in human behavior. Joseph Conrad's *Lord Jim* imposes reflection on the effect of a sense of guilt and failure on personality. Moreover, the teacher is usually careful to develop the student's sensitivity to the evidence of changes in character set forth in such works as *Ethan Frome, Great Expectations, Huckleberry Finn*, or the plays of Shakespeare.[1]

Once we embark on anything approaching a discussion of characters, it is impossible for us to avoid committing ourselves

---

[1] Since the discussion applies to the whole literature program, illustrations will be drawn from both high school and college levels. Chapters 4 and 7 consider the adequacy of the usual reading lists.

to some definite assumptions. Many different views of human motivation may lend themselves to the attempt to understand Othello's rapidly aroused jealousy, to square that with his nature as it is displayed at the opening of the drama, and to see why his jealousy should have led so unswervingly to murder. Of course, these problems may be evaded by maintaining that the psychological consistency of Othello's character is merely a theatrical illusion. E. E. Stoll contended that any psychological interpretation is merely superimposed on a series of incidents, actions, and speeches that were dictated by dramatic conventions and theatrical needs for the sole purpose of creating a convincing and exciting play, without concern for subtle psychological consistency (5–9). However, it would still be necessary to explain why Othello seems a living, integrated personality and not a mere series of theatrical effects. In thinking back over our experience of the tragedy, we find that we have fitted what the dramatist offers us into some preconceived notions about human behavior, about the extent of human credulousness or the effects of jealousy. We judge whether Othello is a credible character in the light of our own assumptions about human nature.

For instance, when high school students make the relationship between Hamlet and his mother the core of their interpretation of his actions, whether or not they even know the name Freud, they have absorbed, somehow, somewhere, certain of the psychoanalytic concepts. Similarly, in interpreting *Othello* students may reveal an extraordinary diversity of theoretical frameworks. One student may emphasize the details offered by the dramatist concerning Desdemona's and Othello's sense of racial difference and may base on that an explanation of Othello's readiness to believe in his wife's infidelity.

Another student may see Othello as a man fundamentally insecure, unsure of his ability to hold Desdemona, and thus ready to believe himself betrayed. Still another student may phrase Othello's problem in moral terms as the struggle between the nobler and the baser elements in his nature. There will also be the student who accepts the characters' statements about their acts, assumes that everything they do is consciously willed, and passes judgment accordingly. Each student has found the play intelligible in terms of his own understanding of human motivation.

Students (and teachers) often assume that they are merely making explicit the author's particular view of human psychology. The process of interpretation is more complex than that, however. The reader must remain faithful to the author's text and must be alert to the potential clues concerning character and motive. But he must do more than that: he must seek to organize or interpret such clues. His own assumptions will provide the tentative framework for such an interpretation. He may discover that this causes him to ignore elements in the work, or he may realize that he is imputing to the author views unjustified by the text. He will then be led to revise or broaden his initial tentative assumptions.

Such a process surely would have been generated by an interchange among students holding the opinions about Othello sketched above. The challenge would be twofold: to determine whether their interpretations were supported by the text and at the same time to test the adequacy of the psychological assumptions guiding their interpretations of the text. As the body of critical writings on *Othello* demonstrates, the text permits a wide range of interpretations that bring to bear a variety of psychological hypotheses. The student reader will be less likely to impose irrelevant or unjustified interpretations if he has been led to scrutinize his psychological assumptions and to become aware of alternative possibilities.

When the text provides an unambiguous view of characters and reflects a particular psychological theory, as in the plays of Ben Jonson or in many recent works based on Freudianism, the task of the classroom might seem to be restricted to simple explication. If it were possible not to intrude any direct or indirect comment, the effect would still be implicit approval of each author's view of human motivation. This could result only in the student's being subjected to a series of discrete, inconsistent notions. But such complete neutrality would be impossible. Something of approval or disapproval would be conveyed through tone of voice, kinds of questions raised, length of time devoted to the work, or emphasis on one or another aspect. Hence the necessity remains for the teacher to recognize his responsibility toward the handling of psychological concepts. The students need to be helped both to understand the author's presentation of his characters and to acquire some means of critically relating it to other views of human nature and conduct.

Works of the past—the *Odyssey*, the Arthurian legends, *Beowulf*, Elizabethan drama, Victorian novels—engender a major psychological question: What are the basic human traits that persist despite social and cultural changes? To what extent are the resemblances of one age to another, as well as the differences, due to environmental influences? Indeed, this question of persisting or "universal" human traits is one that arises constantly in discussions of literature. The phrase *human nature* recurs again and again in the discussion of books, and the manner of its use conveys a great many unformulated implications.

Questions such as the following about *David Copperfield* are often encountered:

> One passage in this chapter shows David beginning to read human nature correctly. Where is it?
>
> What baseness of human nature is revealed by different persons in this chapter? What goodness of human nature?

Or consider a very recent instance, a third-grade unit on the fable that suggests to the teacher such psychologically oriented questions as these:

> Why did each of the animals leave home?
>
> Was the story the bandit told his friends really what he thought he saw?
>
> Did he make it up to shield his cowardice?
>
> How would each of these animals act if they were people?

Or in a sixth-grade unit on Chaucer's *Chantecleer and the Fox*:

> How do these animals form particularly appropriate pictures of the human follies, evils, or incongruities which they exhibit?

The term *human nature* is itself a controversial one. Nevertheless, some set of notions dominates our sense of human behavior, and discussion of particular characters or works builds up in the student's mind a predisposition toward such a set of ideas. "These are the significant elements in human personality; these are the kinds of forces that dominate people's lives and lead them to act in certain ways" are the generalizations constantly implied in discussion of specific characters. Even if the teacher desired to, he could not evade transmitting certain generalized concepts concerning character and the ways in which it is molded and motivated.

In recent years, great strides have been made in the fields of psychology, sociology, and anthropology toward a clarification of the fundamental problems of human behavior. The layman's tendency to speak of human nature as though it were constant and unchanging has been searchingly questioned; the plasticity of the human creature has been discovered to be almost endless. Anthropologists have revealed to us societies in which human beings have suppressed or rigidly regulated some of the drives, such as sex or the desire for self-preservation, that we tend to consider most fundamental and ineradicable. Our primary impulse is to equate human nature with the particular motivations, modes of behavior, and types of choice that we have from childhood observed in the society about us. The inescapable molding influence of the culture into which we are born is an extremely important concept. The teacher should have this clearly in mind before discussing questions concerning character and motivation or even before introducing the student to the images of human behavior presented in our own and other literatures.

The danger is in the unquestioning adoption of the general attitudes toward human nature and conduct that permeate the very atmosphere we live in. Unfortunately, the ideas that are taken most for granted are often the ones that merit the most skeptical scrutiny. For instance, the notion that the conscious motives of the individual determine action is implied in most casual discussions of behavior: If a person transgresses, it is because he has willed it. The problem of praise and blame is thus a simple one. Yet present-day psychology stresses the importance of unconscious factors that motivate behavior. A classroom discussion of essays, letters, journals, autobiographies, or any of the other literary forms that deal with individual conduct automatically creates the necessity for advancing one or another view. Whether he wishes to or not, the teacher will either reinforce or counteract these assumptions. He will increase the hold of the voluntaristic view of human motivation or replace it with a keener sense of the complexities in the many environmental, physiological, and involuntary psychological factors that influence behavior. Even writers, like Shakespeare, who may not have consciously held this broader view have nevertheless often indicated significant environmental and physiological factors that may explain their characters' personalities and actions. The teacher may or may not make the student aware of the possible relationships between such things. In either case he is helping to determine the student's sense of these questions.

Despite the desire to leave these issues to the specialists in psychology, teachers of literature must resign themselves to the fact that they cannot avoid encroaching on these extremely important and interesting questions concerning human behavior. The problem is that the average teacher or college instructor in literature is not necessarily equipped to handle these topics in a scientific spirit. Hence the discussion of characters and motivation tends to follow the superficial lines of ordinary everyday conversations about people. The students may thus very easily conclude that merely on the basis of one's own meager experience and casually acquired assumptions one may make valid judgments on human motives and conduct.

To provide a critical framework, the instructor needs some knowledge of the dominant conceptions in psychology.

The teaching of literature inevitably involves the conscious or unconscious reinforcement of ethical attitudes. It is practically impossible to treat any novel or drama, or indeed any literary work of art, in a vital manner without confronting some problem of ethics and without speaking out of the context of some social philosophy. A framework of values is essential to any discussion of human life. In most cases the concern with specific episodes or characters may veil the fact that these generalized attitudes are being conveyed. Yet any specific discussion implies the existence of these underlying attitudes.

When the student has been moved by a work of literature, he will be led to ponder on questions of right or wrong, of admirable or antisocial qualities, of justifiable or unjustifiable actions. The average student spontaneously tends to pass judgment on the actions of characters encountered in fiction. Sometimes this tendency is furthered by the type of analysis and discussion of literature carried on in the classroom. Although the practice of many teachers is superior to the level represented by the suggested questions in textbooks and prepared unit materials and although there has been a reaction—too extreme in some quarters—against "moral" interpretations, questions that ask the student to pass judgment still tend to be common teaching practice. For example, in the third-grade unit on the animal fable mentioned earlier, the children are asked to build a "repertory of words and phrases" suggested by the antithesis of the "wise" beast and the "foolish" beast. This would elicit and perhaps crystallize attitudes toward different types of behavior. Or consider the implications of questions such as these concerning *The Scarlet Letter:*

> Which in your opinion is the guiltiest of the three: Hester Prynne, Arthur Dimmesdale, or Roger Chillingworth? Which suffered most?
>
> What characters do you consider admirable? Why?

There is little in the first question to suggest to the student that perhaps he should seek not to pass judgment but to understand how the whole tragic complication grew out of the way of life in that Puritan community. The question also rules out an interpretation of this novel as a study in how a sense of sin affects character.

The teacher will do neither literature nor students a service if he tries to evade ethical issues. He will be exerting some kind of influence, positive or negative, through his success or failure in helping the student develop habits of thoughtful ethical judgment. The teacher should scrutinize his own ethical criteria, which must color anything that he says or does in the classroom. He should not foist his own bias on students, but objectivity should not create the impression that value judgments are unimportant. The literature classroom can stimulate the students themselves to develop a thoughtful approach to human behavior.

Thus far, only those ethical and psychological assumptions have been mentioned that seem to deal with the more personal elements in the field of human relations. Literature also embraces matters that are special to the historian, the economist, and the sociologist. Such concerns are implied even by the traditional phrasing of the aims and content of the literature program. For example, the object might be to acquaint the student with tales of adventure in exotic settings. Suggested readings might be *The Count of Monte Cristo, Kon-Tiki, The Time Machine, Mutiny on the Bounty*, or the *Odyssey*. In these books, the student's attention will be focused on the vigorous action and the foreign scenes. Yet various considerations that might be classified as historical or sociological will creep in. Some novels, for instance, will involve an understanding of the historical periods treated. Such works as the *Iliad* or Elizabethan dramas invite reflection on the idea that in different ages and in different parts of the world societies have created extraordinarily dissimilar social, economic, and political structures that pattern the life of the individual in ways very different from our own. Perhaps in some genres, such as science fiction, this is even a too glibly presented cliché.

Social and historical considerations enter even more obviously into the study of any period of literature or the chronological treatment of any form such as poetry or drama. In presenting these materials, the teacher consciously, and probably even to a greater extent unconsciously, will be stressing various notions concerning historical problems; he will be transmitting various positive or negative assumptions concerning the influence of social and political circumstances on other phases of people's lives. The process of social change (of which literary change is but one aspect), the influence of technological conditions on the social and intellectual life of a society, the factors that lead people in one age to be obsessed by aspirations very different from those of another age—such problems are necessarily implied by any survey of the history of literature. Even by ignoring them the teacher is affecting, though in a negative way, the student's ability to understand these problems.

And what about attitudes toward personal relationships? Here the role of the teacher of literature is most clear. Think, for instance, of such works as *Ah, Wilderness!*, *Romeo and Juliet*, *All My Sons*, or *The Scarlet Letter*: they evoke attitudes toward the relationship between husband and wife, patterns of family life, and the concept of romantic love. Or consider the attitudes toward the child and questions of relationships between parents and children implied in the reading of *Tom Sawyer*, *David Copperfield*, *The Ordeal of Richard Feverel*, *Sons and Lovers*, and many of Wordsworth's poems.

The young people who encounter such works of literature are building up their sense of the socially favored types of adjustment in our culture. In books they are meeting extremely compelling images of life that will undoubtedly influence the crystallization of their ultimate attitudes, either of acceptance or of rejection. Here again the teacher will exert an influence through the whole framework of ideas and attitudes that he builds up around the experience of the particular sense of social relationships presented by any particular work.

Literature treats the whole range of choices and aspirations and values out of which the individual must weave his own personal philosophy. The literary works that students are urged to read offer not only "literary" values, to use a currently favored abstraction, but also some approach to life, some image of people working out a common fate or some assertion that certain kinds of experiences, certain modes of feeling, are valuable. The teacher who is aware of the potential absorption or rejection of social attitudes will be led to investigate his own role in this process.

How quick teachers of literature would be to con-demn the teacher of history or zoology who interlarded his discussions with dogmatic statements about literature. How unscholarly they would think the biology instructor who felt that what he had absorbed about literature from newspapers, magazines, and perhaps a random course at college justified his passing on the merits of Milton's poetry, his insinuating that free verse was a ridiculous innovation, or his making casual judgments about the authorship of the disputed passages in *Sir Thomas More*. Yet too often literature teachers feel that the social concepts and attitudes absorbed from everyday life, plus a scattered reading on a subject here and there or a rapid survey of the field in a college course, are ample preparation for using literature as the springboard for discussions of human nature and society. They are forced to the rejoinder that the very nature of literature necessitates such discussions; these matters cannot be evaded by judicious selection. But this should bring recognition of their responsibility to equip them-selves to handle a vital and inevitable phase of their teaching.

Probably the comparative youth and lack of unanimity of the social sciences partly explain this casual encroachment on their territory. A more respectful attitude developed long ago toward the natural sciences. The English teacher would be considered grievously lacking who propagated in his class-room the idea that the sun moves around the earth (see *Paradise Lost*, bk. 8) or that incantation was the approved method of curing the sick. From a "purely aesthetic" point of view, which ignores the fact that the person experiencing the work of literature comes to it out of a particular world and will return to it, this may not matter. One could appreciate many literary works just as well aesthetically though holding these exploded beliefs. The fact is, nevertheless, that the student will return to the world of today. His literary experience will have been confusing rather than helpful if he brings from it ideas that are relics of an outgrown past.

A parallel scrupulousness is needed concerning psychological, social, and ethical concepts that the student may absorb from his reading. Just as the student will be able to enjoy Milton's *Paradise Lost* without necessarily accepting Milton's cosmology, so he must be able to absorb from the literature of the past and of the present what is sound and relevant to his own needs in this age. A zestful reading of, let us say, Walter Scott is compatible with a sense of the anachronism, particularly for an American, of an acceptance of Scott's feudalistic philosophy. The literature teacher may not be primarily concerned with giving scientific information; yet it is his responsibility to further the assimilation of habits of thought conducive to social understanding. He shares with all other teachers the task of providing the student with the proper equipment for making sound social and ethical judgments. Indeed, the English teacher can play an important part in this process, since the student's social adjustments may be more deeply influenced by what he absorbs through literature than by what he learns through the theoretical materials of the usual social science course.[2]

---

[2] This argument cuts both ways, of course, and leads to the conclusion that literary materials have their place also in the social science curriculum. See chapter 7.

The already overburdened literary scholar, aware of the great mass of materials and information that he must absorb, will probably protest that he is now being called on to assimilate the great body of knowledge accumulated by the social sciences, too. This obviously is impossible. The prospective teacher of English cannot be given the training demanded of the social scientist. It is imperative, however, that undergraduate and graduate programs provide time for building up a sound acquaintance with at least the general aspects of current scientific thought on psychological and social problems. Many undergraduate programs now include some introductory work of this kind, but rather haphazardly. The practicing teacher must feel the necessity for constantly increasing such knowledge. Teachers of literature cannot neglect to establish a rational basis for this inevitable and highly important phase of their work.

This chapter has sought to suggest how intimately the concepts of the social sciences enter into the study of literature. Many problems remain to be clarified concerning the relation between this much neglected aspect and the more widely recognized concerns of English teaching. The emphasis thus far may seem to resemble "the social approach" to literature. Unfortunately, the champions of this view, in a pendulum-swing reaction against extreme aestheticism, have sometimes been led to neglect the fact that literature is a form of art. The defenders of aesthetic or literary values, on the contrary, have often felt it necessary to reject all social concerns. The thesis of this book is that no contradiction should exist between these two phases of art—that, in fact, they are inextricably interrelated. Those who see in literature only social documents and those who admit only so-called pure aesthetic values offer equally limited insights. The increase of literary sensitivity, no less than the fostering of social awareness, requires a concern for the issues raised in this chapter. A philosophy of teaching based on a balanced recognition of the many complex elements that make up the literary experience can foster the development of more fruitful understanding and appreciation of literature.

To view literature in its living context is to reject any limiting approach, social or aesthetic. Although the social and aesthetic elements in literature may be theoretically *distinguishable*, they are actually *inseparable*. Much of the confused thinking about the aesthetic and the social aspects of art would be eliminated if the debaters realized that an object can have more than one value: it can yield the kind of fulfillment that we call *aesthetic*—it can be enjoyed in itself—and at the same time have a social origin and social effects. The task of the coming chapters will be to make this point clear and to elaborate its implications for the reader and the teacher.

CHAPTER 2

THE LITERARY EXPERIENCE

Terms such as *the reader, the student, the literary work* have appeared in the preceding pages. Actually, these terms are somewhat misleading, though convenient, fictions. There is no such thing as a generic reader or a generic literary work; there are only the potential millions of individual readers of the potential millions of individual literary works. A novel or poem or play remains merely inkspots on paper until a reader transforms them into a set of meaningful symbols. The literary work exists in the live circuit set up between reader and text: the reader infuses intellectual and emotional meanings into the pattern of verbal symbols, and those symbols channel his thoughts and feelings. Out of this complex process emerges a more or less organized imaginative experience. When the reader refers to a poem, say, "Byzantium," he is designating such an experience in relation to a text.

Teachers at all levels should have the opportunity to observe the child's entrance into the world of the printed page. The child must have attained the physical and intellectual capacity to perform this highly complex operation, the act of reading. He should be emotionally ready to meet this challenge. Essential, too, is a sufficiently rich experience, so that words are signs for things and ideas. A set of marks on a page— CAT—becomes linked to a certain crisp sound in the ear. Eventually, the connection will become automatic, but it will be read as a word only when for the child that sign and that set of sounds are joined to the idea of a certain class of furry, four-footed animals.

Those who think of language as simply a self-contained set of signs linked to sounds ignore the essential third element, the human being who must make the linkage between them if there is indeed to be a meaningful word. Language is socially evolved, but it is always constituted by individuals, with their particular histories.

It is easy to observe how the beginning reader draws on past experience of life and language to elicit meaning from the printed words, and it is possible to see how through these words he reorganizes past experience to attain new understanding. Teachers who work with older students in school and college do not always recognize that those students are faced with a similar situation. Like the beginning reader, the adolescent needs to encounter literature for which he possesses the intellectual, emotional, and experiential equipment. He, too, must draw on his past experience with life and language as the raw materials out of which to shape the new experience symbolized on the page.

The teacher of literature, then, seeks to help specific human beings discover the satisfactions of literature. Teaching becomes a matter of improving the individual's capacity to evoke meaning from the text by leading him to reflect self-critically on this process. The starting point for growth must be each individual's efforts to marshal his resources in relation to the printed page. The teacher's task is to foster fruitful interactions—or, more precisely, transactions—between individual readers and individual literary texts.

Interaction has customarily been associated with the notion of separate, predefined entities acting on one another. The underlying metaphor for this is the machine. In response to developments in the philosophy of science, *transaction* is being used to designate a process in which the elements are aspects or phases of a total situation. The underlying metaphor is organic, as in the ecological view of human beings in a reciprocal relation with the natural environment.

In the past, reading has too often been thought of as an interaction, the printed page impressing its meaning on the reader's mind or the reader extracting the meaning embedded in the text. Actually, reading is a constructive, selective process over time in a particular context. The relation between reader and signs on the page proceeds in a to-and-fro spiral, in which each is continually being affected by what the other has contributed.

The reader approaches the text with a certain purpose, certain expectations or hypotheses that guide his choices from the residue of past experience. Meaning emerges as the reader carries on a give-and-take with the signs on the page. As the text unrolls before the reader's eyes, the meaning made of the early words influences what comes to mind and is selected for the succeeding signs. But if these do not fit in with the meaning developed thus far, the reader may revise it to assimilate the new words or may start all over again with different expectations. For the experienced reader, much of this may go on subconsciously, but the two-way, reciprocal relation explains why meaning is not "in" the text or "in" the reader. Both reader and text are essential to the transactional process of making meaning.

The usual terminology—for example, "the reaction of the reader to the literary work," "the interaction between the reader and the work," or references to "the poem itself" as a determinate entity—tends to obscure the view of the literary experience presented here. Hence the need to differentiate between the text (the sequence of printed or voiced signs) and the meaning, the literary work. The poem or the novel or the play exists in the transaction that goes on between reader and text. (See below, p. 30; see also Dewey and Bentley; Rosenblatt, *Reader*.)

Literature lends little comfort to the teacher who seeks the security of a clearly defined body of information. He does have "knowledge," of course. There are even those reassuring things called facts—facts about the social, economic, and intellectual history of the age in which literary works were written; facts about the responses of contemporary readers; facts about the author and his life; facts about the literary traditions he inherited; facts, even, about the form, structure, and method of the work. Yet all such facts are expendable unless they demonstrably help to clarify or enrich individual experiences of specific novels, poems, or plays. The notion of "background information" often masks much that is irrelevant and distracting.

The uniqueness of the transaction between reader and text is not inconsistent with the fact that both elements in this relation have social origins and social effects. If each author were completely different from every other human being and if each reader were unique in all respects, there could, of course, be no communication. There are many experiences that we all have in common—birth, growth, love, death. We can communicate because of a common core of experience, even though there may be infinite personal variations. Human beings participate in particular social systems and fall into groups by age, sex, occupation, nation. These, too, offer general patterns on which individual variations can be played. The forces of social conditioning are also pervasive in the formation of specific emotional drives and intellectual concepts.

Just as the personality and concerns of the reader are largely socially patterned, so the literary work, like language itself, is a social product. The genesis of literary techniques occurs in a social matrix. Both the creation and reception of literary works are influenced by literary tradition. Yet ultimately any literary work gains its significance from the way in which the minds and emotions of particular readers respond to the linguistic stimuli offered by the text.

In the past the danger has been that one aspect or the other of the literary experience has been emphasized. On the one hand, literature deals with and ministers to human life and human needs. On the other hand, this is accomplished by means of artistic form, through the exercise of literary craftsmanship creating works of high aesthetic appeal. To treat literature merely as a collection of moralistic pamphlets, a series of disquisitions on humankind and society, is to ignore that the artist is concerned not with indirect commentary on life but with the addition of a new experience in life, namely, the work of art.

When concern with the human elements in literature has become confused with the purely practical approach to those elements in life itself, distortion and critical confusion have followed. Literary works have then been judged solely in terms of their conformity to conventional aims and standards. Such an approach made possible the elevation of the novels of the now unread Miss Yonge over those of George Eliot or Charlotte Brontë. This approach is possible only when the nature of literature as an art is forgotten.

When, usually in reaction against the practical point of view, only the formal and technical elements of the work have been considered important, an equally disastrous distortion has resulted. An excessive preoccupation with the externals of form and technical brilliance, such as Oscar Wilde exemplifies, has led to a breakdown of sound critical standards. The very remoteness of a work from the living core of human preoccupations comes to be considered a merit. The literary craftsman is elevated above the true artist.

In recent decades the influence of both the New Criticism and postmodern critical approaches has also tended to diminish the concern with the human meaningfulness of the literary work. The stress on close reading was unfortunately associated with the notion of the impersonality of the poet and the parallel impersonality of the critic. The work itself was said to be the critic's prime concern, as though it existed apart from any reader. (See Rosenblatt, "Poem" 123–28.) Analysis of the technique of the work, concern with tone, metaphor, symbol, and myth, has therefore tended to crowd out the ultimate questions concerning relevance or value to the reader in his ongoing life.[1]

Since to lead the student to ignore either the aesthetic or the social elements of his experience is to cripple him for a fruitful understanding of what literature offers, the teacher of literature needs much insight into the complex nature of the literary experience.

What, then, happens in the reading of a literary work? The reader, drawing on past linguistic and life experience, links the signs on the page with certain words, certain concepts, certain sensuous experiences, certain images of things, people, actions, scenes. The special meanings and, more particularly, the submerged associations that these words and images have for the individual reader will largely determine what the work communicates to *him*. The reader brings to the work personality traits, memories of past events, present needs and preoccupations, a particular mood of the moment, and a particular physical condition. These and many other elements in a never-to-be-duplicated combination determine his interfusion with the peculiar contribution of the text. For the ado-

---

[1] "The pernicious practice of converting every literary work into a moral homily is perhaps the abuse most frequently committed. But the Commission believes that no discussion, no study, no reading of any work is complete without some consideration of possible extrinsic meaning, meaning that brings that work directly against the reader's own philosophical convictions and experience. It may be ironic that, after so many years of complaint about teachers who taught the moral instead of the work, warning should now be given against the incompleteness of any study of literature that avoids this consideration. But the Commission believes that 'close reading' may as readily sterilize the study of literature as moralizing once stultified it" (*Freedom* 72-73).

lescent reader, the experience of the work is further specialized by the fact that he has probably not yet arrived at a consistent view of life or achieved a fully integrated personality.

Another factor that adds to the variability of the teaching situation is the great diversity in the literary works themselves. There is a decided difference between the emotional satisfactions to be derived from a lyric by Sir Philip Sidney and a lyric by Robert Browning; an even greater diversity of appeal is made by works of different literary types and moods, such as *The Brothers Karamazov* and *As You Like It*. Obviously, very different kinds of sensitivity and knowledge are required for the fullest appreciation of each of these works. The infinite diversity of literature plus the complexity of human personality and background justify insistence on the special nature of the literary experience and on the need to prepare the student to engage in the highly personal process of evoking the literary work from the text.

Those who associate psychological or social interests with a narrow didacticism or instrumentalism tend to misinterpret the thesis of chapter 1—hence the need to reiterate that we are concerned with social and psychological insights as they flower from the actual aesthetic experience. Grammar and syntax are involved in any literary work, yet no one would mistake a novel for a treatise on grammar. One should be just as careful to avoid the confusion of seeming to discuss literary works as though they were treatises on sociology or psychology. The crux of the matter is that the text embodies verbal stimuli toward a special kind of intense and ordered experience—sensuous, intellectual, emotional—out of which social insights may arise. The following discussion seeks to dispel the confusion that so often results from a fixation either on something called pure art or on the social implications of literature cut off from their roots in personal aesthetic experience.

Philosophers, to be sure, have defined the aesthetic experience in a great many ways. Often they have been concerned with fitting art into previously developed metaphysical systems, or they have emphasized one out of the many springs of aesthetic enjoyment. The play impulse, the instinct for imitation, the urge for self-expression, the desire to communicate, the religious or the mythic impulse are some of the many suggested sources of the human drive to create and enjoy art. This is merely further documentation that art satisfies a great many different human needs and impinges on the broad range of people's personal and social concerns.

In our everyday lives, preoccupied as we are with accomplishing some task or attaining some goal, we must often ignore the quality of the moment as it passes. Life presents a confused mass of details from which we select for attention only those related to our practical concerns. Even then our attention is focused not on the details themselves but on their practical bearing. We usually cannot stop to savor their quality. Yet it is being increasingly recognized that subconsciously we are often responding qualitatively to our surroundings. In our approach to a work of art, interest is centered precisely on the nature and quality of what is offered us.

This illuminates the difference between reading a literary work of art and reading for some practical purpose. Our attention is primarily focused on selecting out and analytically abstracting the information or ideas or directions for action that will remain when the reading is over. (I term such reading *efferent*, from the Latin *efferre* 'to carry away.') A paraphrase or a summary of a biology text or a rephrasing of the technical language of a law may be quite as useful as the original.

Someone else can read the newspaper or a scientific work for us and summarize it acceptably.

No one, however, can read a poem for us. If there is indeed to be a poem and not simply a literal statement, the reader must have the experience, must "live through" what is being created during the reading. The transaction with any text stirs up both referential and affective aspects of consciousness, and the proportion of attention given to these will determine where the reading will fall on a continuum from predominantly efferent to predominantly aesthetic. An aesthetic purpose will require the reader to direct more attention to the affective aspects. From this mixture of sensations, feelings, images, and ideas is structured the experience that constitutes the story or poem or play. This is the object of response during and after the reading event. (See pp. xvii, 292).

Definitions of the aesthetic experience often postulate that art provides a more complete fulfillment of human impulses and needs than does ordinary life with its frustrations and irrelevancies. Undoubtedly, such a sense of fulfillment and emotional equilibrium is largely due to the intense, structured, and coherent nature of what is apprehended under the guidance of the text. Yet those engaged in the task of developing sensitivity to a particular art form will not need to be reminded that any such complete experience depends not only on the work itself but also on the reader's capacities and readiness. Sound literary insight and aesthetic judgment will never be taught by imposing from above notions of what works should ideally mean. Awareness of some of the things that actually affect the student's reactions will allow the teacher to help the student in handling his responses and achieving increasingly balanced literary experiences.

When in the course of our daily affairs we exclaim, "How funny!" or "How tragic!" we have engaged in an embryonic artistic process. We have seen a pattern in human life; we have juxtaposed certain events in our minds, have perceived their relationships, and have thus disengaged their humor or tragedy. The author does this in a more completely creative form, since he enables us to share his vision. No one would question that in the creation of the literary work the writer does more than passively reflect experiences as through a photographic lens. There has been a selective force at work. From the welter of impressions with which life bombards us, the writer chooses those particular elements that have significant relevance to his insight. He inscribes verbal signs that he hopes will enable readers to perceive selected images, personalities, and events in special relation to one another. Thus, out of the matrix of elements with common meaning for him and his readers, he builds up a new sequence, a new structure, that enables him to evoke in the reader's mind a special emotion, a new or deeper understanding—that enables him, in short, to communicate with his reader.

The reader, too, is creative. The text may produce that moment of balanced perception, a complete aesthetic experience. But it will not be the result of passivity on the reader's part; the literary experience has been phrased as a *transaction* between the reader and the author's text. Moreover, as in the creative activity of the artist, there will be selective factors molding the reader's response. He comes to the book from life. He turns for a moment from his direct concern with the various problems and satisfactions of his own life. He will resume his concern with them when the book is closed. Even while he is reading, these things are present as probably the most important guiding factors in his experience.

The same text will have a very different meaning and value to us at different times or under different circumstances. Some state of mind, a worry, a temperamental bias, or a contemporary social crisis may make us either especially receptive or especially impervious to what the work offers. Without an understanding of the reader, one cannot predict what particular text may be significant to him or what may be the special quality of his experience. Hence it is important to consider some of the selective factors that may mold the reader's response to literature.

The reader seeks in literature a great variety of satisfactions. These sometimes quite conscious demands are in themselves important factors affecting the interrelation between book and reader. A freshman class at a New England women's college was unexpectedly asked, "Why do you read novels, anyway?" Here are some of the spontaneous answers:

I like to read a novel for relaxation after I have been studying hard all day.

I like to read anything that is well written, in which the author gives you interesting descriptions and exciting adventures.

I like to find out about the things that happen to people and how they solve their problems.

I had an interesting experience with a novel a few weeks ago. I discovered that one of the characters was in the same fix that I was in. I got a great deal from seeing how the character in the book managed.

I like to read about as many different kinds of situations as possible—just in case I myself might be in such a situation some day.

These students summarized, in simplified form perhaps, a number of the personal satisfactions that adolescent and adult alike seek from literature. Their remarks are akin to Guy de Maupassant's comment:

> The public as a whole is composed of various groups, whose cry to us writers is:
> "Comfort me."
> "Amuse me."
> "Touch me."
> "Make me dream."
> "Make me laugh."
> "Make me shudder."
> "Make me weep."
> "Make me think."
> And only a few chosen spirits say to the artist:
> "Give me something fine in any form which may suit you best, according to your own temperament."   (ix)

In its simplest terms, literature may offer us an emotional outlet. It may enable us to exercise our senses more intensely and more fully than we otherwise have time or opportunity to. Through literature we may enjoy the beauty or the grandeur of nature and the exotic splendor of scenes in far distant lands. Furthermore, it may provide experiences that would not otherwise be either possible or wise to introduce into our own lives. The love of action and adventure, the interest in kinds of people and ways of life alien to our own, the delight in scenes of strong emotion, in pictures of physical violence, even in images of hatred and evil, may be due to the release they provide for drives repressed by our culture. And literature affords an outlet for other than antisocial emotions. A great work of art may provide us the opportunity to feel more profoundly and more generously, to perceive more fully the implications of experience, than the constricted and fragmentary conditions of life permit.

The college students, bearing out the contention of the preceding chapter, placed greatest emphasis on literature as a means of broadening one's knowledge of people and society. This reflected their curiosity about life, a curiosity shared with younger adolescent and preadolescent students. For the average adult reader as well, literature contributes to the enlargement of experience. Through the medium of literature we participate in imaginary situations, we look on at characters living through crises, we explore ourselves and the world about us.

The capacity to sympathize or to identify with the experiences of others is a most precious human attribute. Scientific studies of reactions to works of art have revealed how pervasive is our tendency to identify with something outside ourselves. This has been found to be true even of nonhuman subjects. We tend to "feel ourselves into," to empathize with, the painting of the tree that is swaying in the wind, until the successful artist will have somehow made us that very tree itself. Even the delicate poise of an architectural column or the symmetry of a Greek vase will be felt in the pull and balance of our own muscles, though we may not be conscious of the source of our pleasure. How much more directly and completely is this tendency to project ourselves into the object of our contemplation fulfilled when we are concerned with the personalities and joys and sorrows, with the failures and the achievements, of characters in literature!

This tendency toward identification will certainly be guided by our preoccupations at the time we read. Our own problems and needs may lead us to focus on those characters and situations through which we may achieve the satisfactions, the balanced vision, or perhaps merely the unequivocal motives unattained in our own lives.

The students valued literature as a means of enlarging their knowledge of the world, because through literature they acquire not so much additional *information* as additional *experience*. New understanding is conveyed to them dynamically and personally. Literature provides a *living through*, not simply *knowledge about*: not the fact that lovers have died young and fair, but a living through of *Romeo and Juliet*; not theories about Rome, but a living through of the conflicts in *Julius Caesar* or the paradoxes of *Caesar and Cleopatra*. In contrast to reading the historian's generalized and impersonal account of the hardships of the pioneer's life, they share these hardships with the heroine and her family in Willa Cather's *My Ántonia*. The sociologist analyzes for them the problems of the African American in our society; in Richard Wright's *Native Son*, James Baldwin's *The Fire Next Time*, Ralph Ellison's *Invisible Man*, they themselves suffer these problems in their human dimensions. The anthropologist can teach them the ethnology of the Eskimo and the social patterns in the Philippines or India; in Peter Freuchen's novel *Eskimo*, in Carlos Bulosan's *The Laughter of My Father*, and in Kamala Markandaya's *Nectar in a Sieve*, students themselves become part of these cultures. They may read encomiums on the devotion and disinterestedness of the scientist; in *Madame Curie* or *Arrowsmith* they share the scientist's single-minded zeal, frustrations, and intellectual and emotional rewards of success.

The college students were equally frank about the escape value of literature. They were especially ready to speak of release from the circumstances and pressures of their everyday lives. This term *escape* has perhaps been used too often in an indiscriminately derogatory sense; there are useful and harmful forms of escape. Anything that offers refreshment and a lessening of tension may have its value in helping us to resume our practical lives with renewed vigor. The unfavorable overtones of the term are due to the failure of much of the so-called literature of escape to accomplish this. (See pp. 200–04.) The greatest literary works may have for a particular reader the value of an escape. Our lives may be so monotonous, so limited in scope, so concentrated on practical survival that the experience of profound and varied emotions, the contact with warm, subtle personalities, the understanding of the wide range of human capacities and human problems may be denied us except through the medium of literature. Or a great work may give even to the person living a full and happy life a moment of change, of escape from practical demands. The capacity of a particular book to offer such values will be directly related to the emotional needs of the reader and his particular situation and preoccupations.

Another important potential satisfaction from literature, which the students only implied, is the possibility of compensating for lacks or failures through identification with a character who possesses qualities other than our own or who makes fuller use of capacities similar to our own. The young girl may in this way identify with Juliet or with Elizabeth

Bennet; the boy, chafing at his childish status, may identify with an epic hero. This compensatory mechanism may in part explain our vivid identification with characters very different from ourselves. Here again, the force of the reader's emotional reactions will be channeled in ways dictated by his sense of his own shortcomings. This process is usually considered in terms far too crude, since literature may provide subtle kinds of compensation. The human being has latent capacities for many modes of life and action that he would not elect but whose exercise through literature will nevertheless give him satisfaction.

The ability to understand and sympathize with others reflects the multiple nature of the human being, his potentialities for many more selves and kinds of experience than any one being could express. This may be one of the things that enables us to seek through literature an enlargement of our experience. Although we may see some characters as outside ourselves—that is, we may not identify with them as completely as we do with more congenial temperaments—we are nevertheless able to enter into their behavior and their emotions. Thus it is that the youth may identify with the aged, one sex with the other, a reader of a particular limited social background with members of a different class or a different period.

One student made rather surprisingly articulate another personal value of literature: its objective presentation of our own problems. It places them outside us, enables us to see them with a certain detachment and to understand our own situation and motivation more objectively. The young girl irked by the limitations of the small-town environment may derive such objectivity from Sherwood Anderson's *Winesburg, Ohio*. The boy unconsciously rejecting an overpossessive mother may gain insight from Sidney Howard's *The Silver Cord* or D. H. Lawrence's *Sons and Lovers*. This process of objectification may also go on in a disguised form. Without conscious admission of the relevance of the literary experience to our own practical situation, our attitudes may be clarified either by a violent reaction against what we have read or by assimilation of it.

To have impact, a work need not treat circumstances overtly similar to the reader's situation. The power of the work may reside in its underlying emotional structure, its configuration of human drives. Thus, an adolescent boy may resent restraints imposed by accepted authority—family, school, or employer. At this moment of his life, he might find in *Mutiny on the Bounty* satisfying expression of his rebellion; he might react with extraordinary intensity to *The Devil's Disciple* or *The Loneliness of the Long Distance Runner*. College freshmen have been known, very disconcertingly, to sympathize inordinately with Lear's unfilial daughters. Similarly, the youth who has just experienced disillusionment with friends might find the relationship between Othello and Iago the most significant part of the entire play. When *Hamlet* is a moving experience for the adolescent today, may it not be because the play gives form to a prevalent mood of uncertainty and disillusionment, of reluctance to undertake aggressive action in a world gone awry?

An intense response to a work will have its roots in capacities and experiences already present in the personality and mind of the reader. This principle is an important one to remember in the selection of literary materials to be presented to students. It is not enough merely to think of what the student *ought* to read. Choices must reflect a sense of the possible links between these materials and the student's past experience and present level of emotional maturity.

There is an even broader need that literature fulfills, particularly for the adolescent reader. Much that in life itself might seem disorganized and meaningless takes on order and significance when it comes under the organizing and vitalizing influence of the artist. The youth senses in himself new and unsuspected emotional impulsions. He sees the adults about him acting in inexplicable ways. In literature he meets emotions, situations, people, presented in significant patterns. He is shown a causal relationship between actions, he finds approval given to certain kinds of personalities and behavior rather than to others, he finds molds into which to pour his own nebulous emotions. In short, he often finds meaning attached to what otherwise would be for him merely brute facts.

Substantiating Maupassant's complaint, none of the students made articulate a sense of that emotional equilibrium which is a mark of a complete aesthetic experience. This omission is undoubtedly explained in part by the difficulty of describing such moments of mental and emotional poise or illumination. It is probably even more largely explained by the fact that the adolescent's attention is to an extraordinary degree focused on the personal import of what he reads. We have glanced at several of the factors that produce this preoccupation with the human contribution of literature.

Yet for the adolescent, too, these human concerns are embodied in the aesthetic experience. The student who has lived through the experience of *Othello* will have been carried along on the wave of feeling and insight to the moment of ultimate resolution. His sense of the gamut of human experience and emotion will have been broadened. He will have entered, for the time, into a world of strange moral values and responsibilities. But this participation in human affairs will have been possible only because *Othello* is above all a work of art. The resonant blank verse, the opulent imagery, the swiftly paced structure of the play are an integral part of this reliving of Othello's and Desdemona's tragedy. The entire experience has a structure and an inner logic, a completeness that only the great work of art can offer. The student would tend not to speak of this phase of the matter, precisely because these formal and stylistic elements of the drama were an aspect of his apprehension of its human import.

It is possible to do justice to this problem of form and style without being false to the psychological process involved in the relationship between book and reader. Note that we have been discussing those social insights and the human understandings that may arise specifically from the experience of literature. *The enhancement of these human values will therefore depend on the intensification and enrichment of the individual's aesthetic experience.*

Any theory about art that tends to break up the response to literature into distinct segments, whether under the headings "social" versus "aesthetic" or "form" versus "content," is misleading. Of course, teachers must themselves have a zestful appreciation of the sensuous and formal aspects of literature if they are to be of any help to their students. Yet if they do not in addition see these aspects of literature in their organic relation to those broader human aspects that we have been discussing, they will merely tend to impoverish their students' sense of both literature and life.

More than merely the intellectual content of literature was involved in the discussion in chapter 1 and in the preceding consideration of factors molding the reader's response. Those factors influence the reader's sensitivities to all aspects of the work of art as an integral whole. Indeed, although one may talk about qualities of form and style or about content, this theoretic division has little to do with the actual psychological situation when we are responding to a given literary work. Each of these aspects of the work exists by virtue of the other aspects.

We may, for example, talk about something called the sonnet form, but such a form can be apprehended only as it is embodied in a particular sonnet made up of particular words. We cannot dissociate from the total effect of the poem the meaning of the words—the images, concepts, and emotions that they denote, the nuances of feeling and the associations that cluster about them. It is equally impossible to distill from the total effect the sound of the words or the beat of the verse. We can tap out the rhythmic pattern of a poem, but will anyone contend that our sense of that tapping is the same as our experience of the rhythmic pattern when it is embodied in a sequence of sonorous and meaningful words? Obviously, the effect of a sonnet on a person who does not know the language can offer few clues to the impression that would be produced by the sound and rhythm on a person who understood the meaning of the words as well. The complete effect of a particular sonnet results from the fact that different elements act on us simultaneously, reinforce and, one might almost say, create one another. Similarly, in music we may define a particular form such as the fugue, but we can never experience the form abstracted from the complex texture of some specific musical work.

It is equally impossible to experience content apart from some kind of form. It is a cliché to say that a paraphrase of a poem does not represent the actual content of the poem. Certain of its concepts and implications have merely been abstracted and rephrased. One might, for example, state the various ideas and name the various emotions encountered in *The Rime of the Ancient Mariner*, but this would, in a sense, be offering not only a different form but also a different content. The various concepts and images take on significance and emotional and intellectual overtones from precisely the form in which they are experienced in the poem. Even a transposition of the different stanzas would have given them a different significance. To encounter an idea after our emotions have been aroused through various images and rhythms gives that idea a very different significance from what it would have if presented in another rhythmic pattern or in another sequence. Hence the term *content of the literary work* is confusing when used to indicate abstract intellectual import.

If we think about the total experience of the reader, we shall not be thus misled. We shall see that the formal relations in the literary work—the verse form, rhyme scheme, sentence structure, plot structure—or the other sensuous elements, such as the imagery, do not have a separable or even a clearly distinguishable effect. How can we legitimately dissociate anything called the content of a poem from the interplay of sensations and concepts and emotional overtones produced by the particular words in the particular relations to one another in which they are found in the text itself? Only as we become sensitive to the influence of subtle variations in rhythm and in the sound and emotional overtones of words, only as we become more refined instruments on which the poet can play, will we be able to experience the full import of the poem.

Similarly, it is essential to hold firmly to the totality of the reader's experience of the literary work whenever we are tempted to speak as though the structure of a play or novel were distinct from the specific sensations, emotions, personalities, and events presented in the work. The sense of the form or structure of the play or novel results from the fact that these particular elements and no others are *experienced* in particular relations to one another. Just as in a melody a particular note takes on color and character from its context, so in a play or novel the significance of any particular scene or personality is the result of the context in which it is encountered.

To return to *Othello*: recall the scene in which Desdemona sings the "Willow Song." This has great poignancy; we have lived through the mounting tension of the intrigue, and now the innocent Desdemona sings as Emilia prepares her for the night. This episode would have little pathos or even interest for anyone who knew only that scene of the play or if that scene were placed at some different point in the play. It would be hard to say whether the transposition would be a change in form or in content. The actual result would be to make the reader or the audience see and feel fewer human implications in the scene. Similarly, although we may speak of the structure of the play and even make diagrams that purport to represent the rising tension and the climax, we must remember that the rising tension results from the reader's identification with certain personalities presented to him and from his vicarious experience of emotions and ideas.

46

Thus we find ourselves involved in a circular argument. If we start with form or structure, we find that we are merely talking about the particular relationships of certain human sensations, concepts, and emotions. If we talk about so-called content, we find that we are merely dealing with the significance that arises from a particular series of relations among certain sensations, concepts, and emotions. Teaching practices and assignments should be scrutinized to make sure that students are not given the idea that the formal relations in a literary work exist apart from, and are merely superimposed on, something called the *content*. Much truer to the reality of both literary creation and literary experience is the sense of how organically interfused are these two phases of the work of art.

Of course, students need to understand the nature of the diverse literary forms—the lyric, the epic, the novel, the essay, the drama—forms that our literary ancestors and contemporaries have developed through the cyclic process of "convention and revolt." We want to share with our students the pleasure to be derived from a discriminating response to the means that the author has employed and the variations or reversals he has based on the traditional pattern. Knowledge of the problems of artistry, a recognition of the author's aims and of the technical difficulties involved in achieving these aims often tend to increase enjoyment. Pleasure arises from discovering the kind of structure that the artist is creating, from seeing things fall into a pattern. Awareness of the function of various characters or episodes or images illuminates what the work as a whole "means." However, that perception of order or pattern is important to the average reader only in relation to the impact of the work as a whole. And these sensitivities to the author's technique are not necessarily best fostered or manifested through a labeling of devices or an analysis of forms.

One of the best ways of helping students gain this appreciation of literary form and artistry is to encourage them to engage in such imaginative writing. In this way they will themselves be involved in wrestling with the materials offered them by life or by their reaction to it; they will discover that problems of form and artistry are not separable from the problems of clarifying the particular sense of life or the particular human mood that the work of art is destined to embody.

The reader's role, we recall, is an active, not a passive, one. The artist using the medium of words must, like other artists, make his appeal primarily to the senses if his desire is "to reach the secret spring of responsive emotions." Unable to tangibly represent objects, the writer must select significant images that will stimulate his reader to undertake the process of sensuous and intellectual re-creation. The greater the reader's ability to respond to the stimulus of the word and the greater his capacity to savor all that words can signify of rhythm, sound, and image, the more fully will he be emotionally and intellectually able to participate in the literary work as a whole. In return, literature will help the reader sharpen further his alertness to the sensuous quality of experience. Such training is extremely necessary in our society, geared as it is toward a neglect of the quality of the means in an obsession with practical ends.

Here again, even a discussion of the writer's artistic medium necessarily leads to emphasis on the kinds of human experience toward which words point. Words themselves, it is true, not only refer to something else but also possess a sensuous quality of their own. The child, long before he understands

48

the meaning of the words, will derive pleasure from the sound, the rhythmic movement, and subtle inflection of a lyric by Blake. But this represents only the thinnest and most fragmentary response to words. Those pleasant sounds can evoke for him extraordinarily rich experiences as his mental and emotional capacities are enlarged and he comes to know what the words symbolize. We must foster the child's delight in the music of words, but we must also help him link up definite experiences and concepts with those sounds as they occur in different contexts; he must come to understand more and more what a word implies in the external world. These aims apply, of course, throughout the whole process of the individual's acquisition of language. Perhaps adolescent students are often impervious to the appeal of literature because for them words do not represent keen sensuous, emotional, and intellectual perceptions. This indicates that throughout the entire course of their education, the element of personal insight and experience has been neglected for verbal abstractions.

Teachers who themselves possess a lively awareness of the world about them will seek to develop the student's sensuous endowment so that he may gain from life and literature the greatest measure of enjoyment of sound, color, and rhythm. As the student looks more closely at the world of sight and sound, he will also come to distinguish their effect on his own moods. He will come to notice dominant impressions, to see certain patterns in events, to sense the clues to the states of mind of other people. Sensuous details will acquire significance as they lead him to glimpse the emotional undercurrents that flow so swiftly beneath the surface of everyday life. In the same way, greater receptivity to the sensuous stimuli offered by literature must be paralleled by enriched emotional associations with them.

On the one hand, emphasis on abstract verbalization, on intellectual concepts cut off from their roots in concrete sensuous experience, is destructive of responsiveness to literature. On the other hand, image, form, structure, the whole sensuous appeal of literature can be fully apprehended only within the framework of a complex sense of life. Sensitivity to literary technique should be linked up with sensitivity to the array of human joys and sorrows, aspirations and defeats, fraternizings and conflicts.

The teacher realistically concerned with helping his students develop a vital sense of literature cannot, then, keep his eyes focused only on the literary materials he is seeking to make available. He must also understand the personalities who are to experience this literature. He must be ready to face the fact that the students' reactions will inevitably be in terms of their own temperaments and backgrounds. Undoubtedly these may often lead the student to do injustice to the text. Nevertheless, the student's primary experience of the work will have had meaning for him in these personal terms and no others. No matter how imperfect or mistaken, this will constitute the present meaning of the work for him, rather than anything he docilely repeats about it. Only on the basis of such direct emotional elements, immature though they may sometimes be, can he be helped to build any sounder understanding of the work. The nature of the student's rudimentary response is, perforce, part of our teaching materials.

The individual reader brings the pressure of his personality and needs to bear on the inextricably interwoven "human" and "formal" elements of the work. If his own experience of life has been limited, if his moral code is rigid and narrow or slack and undiscriminating, the quality of his response to literature will necessarily suffer. Conversely, any sensitivity to literature, any warm and enjoyable participation in the literary work will necessarily involve the sensuous and emotional responsiveness, the human sympathies, of the reader. We shall not further the growth of literary discrimination by a training that concentrates on the so-called purely literary aspect. We go through empty motions if our primary concern is to enable the student to recognize various literary forms, to identify various verse patterns, to note the earmarks of the style of a particular author, to detect recurrent symbols, or to discriminate the kinds of irony or satire. Acquaintance with the formal aspects of literature will not in itself ensure aesthetic sensitivity. One can demonstrate familiarity with a wide range of literary works, be a judge of craftsmanship, and still remain, from the point of view of a rounded understanding of art, aesthetically immature. The history of criticism is peopled with writers who possess refined taste but who remain minor critics precisely because they are minor personalities, limited in their understanding of life. Knowledge of literary forms is empty without an accompanying humanity.

When literary training is viewed as primarily the refinement of the student's power to enter into literary experiences and to interpret them, there will be little danger of excessive emphasis on one or another approach. We shall be aware of the need to sharpen the student's responses to the sensuous, technical, and formal aspects of the literary work. But we shall see these as merged with—reinforced by and reinforcing—responses to those elements in the work that meet the reader's need for psychological satisfactions and social insights. Particularly for the adolescent reader, the desire for self-understanding and for knowledge about people provides an important avenue into literature. The young reader's personal involvement in a work will generate greater sensitivity to its imagery, style, and structure; this in turn will enhance his understanding of its human implications. A reciprocal process emerges, in which growth in human understanding and literary sophistication sustain and nourish each other. Both kinds of growth are essential if the student is to develop the insight and the skill needed for participation in increasingly complex and significant literary works.

This view of the literary experience raises a number of questions. What does it signify for actual teaching aims and methods? How can students develop sensitivity to all the organically related facets of the literary work? What adolescent needs and interests should the teacher be aware of? How can the study of literature enable students to understand themselves better and to see human beings and society in a broader context of emotions and ideas? In short, how can students be helped to achieve literary experiences of higher and higher quality? Parts 2 and 3 will consider such questions.

PART TWO

THE HUMAN BASIS OF LITERARY SENSITIVITY

CHAPTER 3

THE SETTING FOR SPONTANEITY

During a reorganization of education on the Indian reservations some years ago, it was discovered that in some classes the Indian boys and girls were being required to read Restoration comedies. It seems ridiculous that these children, whose past experience had been only the conditions of the reservation village and the vestiges of their native culture, should be plunged into reading the sophisticated products of a highly complex foreign country remote in space and time. Can it be doubted that the children could make nothing of it? Any show of "understanding" a Restoration play would undoubtedly be only a parroting of empty words and phrases to satisfy a teacher's demand.

The plight of these Indian children probably differs only in degree from the average American child's relation to much of the literature he reads in his classroom. The relevance of literary materials has too often been measured in terms of purely verbal operations. To demonstrate "understanding" of a work has been primarily a matter of paraphrasing, defining, applying the proper rubrics. This can be accomplished even when the work presents nothing that awakens an intimate personal response. Too often, the average student might utter Coleridge's lament in "Dejection" when the poet gazed at the sky and the stars and could only "see, not feel, how beautiful they are!" The teacher is concerned with making the student "see" what in the work of literature has made *others* deem it significant. Whether the student himself "feels" this is an entirely different question and one that is rarely considered.

Undoubtedly in many English classes today the student functions on two separate and distinct planes. On one plane, he learns the ideas about literature that his teacher or the literary critic presents to him as traditional and accepted by educated people. On the other plane, he reads the literature and reacts to it personally, perhaps never expressing that reaction or even paying much attention to it. Only occasionally will there be a correlation of these two planes of activity. Teachers frequently approach a book or a poem as though it were a neatly labeled bundle of literary values to be pointed out to the student. If the consensus of critical opinion recognizes certain virtues in a given work, the critics' direct experience of it has led them to perceive those values. The student's repetition of that critical opinion would have validity only when he himself had lived through an experience similar to the critics'. When the images and ideas presented by the work have no relevance to the past experiences or emotional needs of the reader, only a vague, feeble, or negative response will occur.

It is not at all surprising that so few of even our college graduates have formed the habit of turning to literature for pleasure and insight. The novel or play or poem has been made for them too much something to know *about*, something to summarize or analyze or define, something to identify as one might identify the different constellations on a star map or define the qualities of a particular chemical element. For is there a great difference, after all, between the process of memorizing the properties of hydrogen or its peculiar reactions to changes in temperature and the process of memorizing that the Romantic movement was a reaction against eighteenth-century classicism, was concerned with the individual, and produced a great deal of "nature poetry"? How many students have reeled this off for an examination and yet never have felt the full impact of a Romantic poem! Literary history has many values as have the various approaches developed by literary critics and scholars. But all the student's knowledge about literary history, about authors and periods and literary types, will be so much useless baggage if he has not been led primarily to seek in literature a vital personal experience.

Far from helping the student in this direction, much literature teaching has the effect of turning him away from it. He is to a certain degree insulated from the direct impact of the work. He comes to it with the idea that he should see in it first of all those generalized values or kinds of information that the literature class stresses—summaries of plot and theme, identification of certain characteristics that mark its period or genre, certain traits of style and structure. Much of even the best literature teaching is analogous to typical American spectator sports. The students sit on the sidelines watching the instructor or professor react to works of art. Though the student may develop a certain discrimination in the appreciation of professorial taste, this often tends to obscure the need for the student himself to develop a personal sense of literature.

The great value of the various scholarly and critical approaches to literature *in their proper place* will be considered in chapters 5, 7, and 8. But they can be very easily transformed from useful aids into preoccupations that claim the center of attention and crowd the student's personal experience with literature into the dim outer fringe of vision. One could, for instance, become quite proficient in the history of Italian literature without knowing the language and without having read any Italian work even in translation. One would be able to sketch the sweeping lines of literary change, to discourse glibly on the special characteristics of the different periods, to name the contributions of its great writers, and to recount their biographies. It would be possible to learn summaries of the so-called content of their works, as for example the story and the philosophy of *The Divine Comedy*. One might even hold forth on its relations to the dying medieval culture and the dawning Renaissance. Without acquaintance with the works themselves, all this information would lack essential substance. Much of the activity concerning literature with which the average student busies himself in school and college has something of this character. The frame is elaborately worked out, but there is a blank where the picture should be. Missing are the personal experience and understanding of the literary works that historical and biographical information should enhance.

The problem that the teacher faces first of all, then, is the creation of a situation favorable to a vital experience of literature. Unfortunately, many of the practices and much of the tone of literature teaching have precisely the opposite effect.

They place a screen between the student and the book. The solution of this primary problem is therefore complicated by habitual attitudes and academic practices. The majority of English teachers still need to concentrate on this problem, for in many English classes today the instructor never even glimpses the student's personal sense of the work discussed. The teacher may be interested in, let us say, *Pride and Prejudice* from the point of view of the history of the novel form in England, or he may be eager to discuss the relation of style and theme. The student, however, may be impressed by the revelation that then, even as now, the business of finding a mate was no simple matter and that then, even as now, personality clashes and the gap between generations were important. In many cases there is an unbridged gulf between anything the student might actually feel about the book and what the teacher, from the point of view of accepted critical attitudes and his adult sense of life, thinks the pupil should notice.

This often leads the student to consider literature something academic, remote from his own present concerns and needs. He recognizes a traditional aura about literature but discards it when his school days are past. (We all know the student who says, "But I have *had* Shakespeare," as though it were something to suffer through and forget, like the measles.) Thus he does not learn to turn spontaneously to the literature of the past or to the comparably good literature of the present; such works, he feels, must be approached only in full dress and with all the decorum of critical method handed down by the teacher. He is cut off from the personal value they might have for him. Instead he turns to the pulp magazines, comic books, or lurid drugstore paperbacks.

For many students, the only thing approaching a personal literary experience is provided by such trashy writings. This is certainly not because there is no good literature that could arouse their interest and fulfill their needs. Obviously, one reason for this situation must be the frequently defensive attitude toward "good" books built up in the mind of the student in school and in college. He has been given to understand that there are proper ways to react, there are certain things to look for—that he must be ready to discuss the characterization or to analyze plot and subplot or to talk about the author's choice of words. To some extent this is a reflection of that blight on our educational system, its emphasis on the attainment of good marks rather than on the value of the work or the knowledge for its own sake. Instead of plunging into the work and permitting its full impact, he is aware that he must prepare for certain questions, that his remarks on the work must satisfy the teacher's already crystallized ideas about it.

The teacher of college freshman literature courses is often perturbed to find this attitude affecting the work of even the most verbally proficient students. They read literary histories and biographies, criticism, introductions to editions, so-called study guides, and then, if there is time, they read the works. Their interest in the author's life is often on a par with that of the Hollywood gossip column; or they have learned at best to view the work as a document in the author's biography. Their quest is for the sophisticated interpretation and the accepted judgment. If they have learned techniques of close analysis, they tend to look on the work as a means of displaying their analytic virtuosity. They seem shut off from the personal nourishment that literature can give. Hence they are often insecure and confused when given the opportunity and responsibility to express their own honest responses to the work.

I. A. Richards published the classic documentation of this point in 1929. Giving no clues to title, authorship, period, school, or literary value, he asked his class at Cambridge University to write comments on unidentified poems. As he reports in *Practical Criticism*, the students found it extremely difficult to make up their minds about the poems or even to work out possible opinions from which to choose. They set forth an extraordinary variety of views, and the "reckless, desperate" tone of many of their comments revealed their bewilderment. Instead of being able to apply to the poems neatly ticketed interpretations and judgments appropriate to their authorship and their literary period, the students were forced to base their comments on their own intimate reactions. In most cases, their training in literary history and their fund of critical dicta on good poetry were of very little use in helping them handle their unvarnished primary personal responses. They were thus at the mercy of personal obsessions, chance associations, and irrelevant conventional opinions about poetry. Hence they often failed to understand the poems or to discriminate differences in literary quality.

Evidently, in most cases an unprecedented demand was being made on these students. Yet during the whole course of their literary training they should have again and again been given the opportunity to handle their primary responses to the text. A secure approach to poetry would have utilized the "background" they possessed; but it would have been a tool, not a crutch.

Surely the majority of American students, subjected to similar experiments, would not yield a different picture even today, after several decades in which close reading has been increasingly stressed in colleges and secondary schools. The average American student probably would not reveal as much literary background, let alone the ability to utilize it. We insist that students should not consult histories of literature or works of criticism to find out what to think about an author, but we have usually not sought to discover why they are so lacking in self-reliance.

Few teachers of English today would deny that the individual's ability to read and enjoy literature is the primary aim of literary study. In practice, however, this tends to be overshadowed by preoccupation with whatever can be systematically taught and tested. Or the English program becomes what can be easily justified to parents and administrators, whose own past English training has produced skepticism about the value of the study of literature. The professional preparation of the English teacher, moreover, often has little relation to actual conditions in the classroom.

How then can students be enabled to have such vital experiences with literature that they will indeed come intimately and lastingly into their literary heritage? This has always been the concern of the teacher who is also a lover of literature. He has known that without this all his conscientious lecturing and questionings, all his techniques are valueless. To attempt a comprehensive solution to this problem would, of course, be fatuous. The following discussion will naturally tend to emphasize those aspects that seem to have been most generally neglected. The purpose is not to set a pattern or formula for any one teacher or class to follow but to underline general considerations that should influence practice.

Unless the teacher himself values literary experience, revision of his aims or his methods will be futile. By implication, any definition of the ideal relation between the student and the literary work applies also to the teacher. As long as an artificial and pedantic notion of literary culture persists, students will continue in their indifference to the great works of the past and present.

The teacher's personal love of literature, however, has not always been proof against the influence of routine, pedantic notions concerning teaching methods. He is dismayed at the results indicated by the low level of taste about him; he undergoes constant frustration, or he consoles himself by focusing on the rare student who seems to possess the divine spark. To develop many such students, the teacher must liberate himself as well as his pupils from self-defeating practices. He should not relinquish his own zestful sense of literature as a living art.

The persistence of many of the routine procedures in literature teaching makes it necessary to phrase some primary duties in negative terms. First is the necessity not to impose a set of preconceived notions about the proper way to react to any work. The student must be free to grapple with his own reaction. This primary negative condition does not mean that the teacher abdicates his duty to attempt to instill sound habits of reading or sound critical attitudes. Nor does this imply that historical and biographical background material will be neglected. The difference is that instead of trying to superimpose routine patterns, the teacher will help students develop these understandings in the context of their own emotions and their own curiosity about life and literature.

The youth needs to be given the opportunity and the courage to approach literature personally, to let it mean something to him directly. The classroom situation and the relationship with the teacher should create a feeling of security. He should be made to feel that his own response to books, even though it may not resemble the standard critical comments, is worth expressing. Such a liberating atmosphere will make it possible for him to have an unself-conscious, spontaneous, and honest reaction.

When the student feels the validity of his own experience, he will cease to think of literature as something that only a few gifted spirits can enjoy and understand in an original way. How often, when urged to speak out for himself, a student will respond, "But I'm not literary, the way Jane or John is!" Nothing is more conducive to this than the attitude of the instructor that he is one initiated into the esoteric mysteries of art, suffering with amused tolerance the Philistine reactions of the class. The instructor's function is, rather, to help students realize that the most important thing is what literature means to them and does for them.

Another negative means of furthering a spontaneous response is to avoid placing undue importance on the particular form in which the expression of the student's reaction should be couched. He should be able to express himself freely. Nor should there be constant insistence on summaries or rehashes of the work. That may become as artificial and inhibiting as any of the other routine methods. The young reader should feel free to let his comment take the form dictated by what he has lived through in reading the book. To set up some stereotyped form will probably focus the student's attention on what is to be required of him after he has read the book rather than on the work itself as he evokes it from the text.

The effect of such assignments is illustrated by a father's report of his twelve-year-old daughter's experience with *Great Expectations*, which she had selected for individual reading. Her reaction was intense. She said to him, "This is a very, very deep book. You're thinking about the story, the strange things that happen to Pip—and all of a sudden you see another meaning back of it." She groped toward a phrasing of those "deeper" symbolic meanings and offered an unusually mature interpretation of the book. Later, her father found her at her desk, in despair before a blank sheet of paper with only the title of the book written on it. To his remark that surely she had much to say, she replied that none of those ideas would serve; she had to write a book report—summarize the plot, sketch the setting, describe any two characters, write a brief opinion or blurb. The little formula provided by the teacher as a guide had instead divorced the youngster from her actual experience of the novel. The book report she finally ground out revealed none of this response. Fortunately, her involvement in this powerful work had made her temporarily forget the assignment. The next time, she would be on her guard, less likely to pay attention to much beyond what would be useful for the book report. Conscientious teachers often thus unwittingly defeat their long-term aims by classroom methods, day-to-day assignments, and devices for evaluation.

An experience reported by a teacher documents this point: "As I was leafing through a tenth-grade poetry text, I found myself drawn into rereading the old Scottish ballad 'Edward, Edward' with its step-by-step revelations of a crime and its fearful aftermath. In the dialogue with his mother, you recall, he reveals that the blood on his sword is that of his 'fadir deir.' He utters his desperate decision to do penance wandering over the seas, leaving his halls to fall into ruin, his wife and children to wander the world as beggars. And then there is that final stanza:

> 'And what wul ye leive to your ain mither deir,
>   Edward, Edward?
> And what wul ye leive to your ain mither deir?
>   My deir son, now tell me O.'
> 'The curse of hell frae me sall ye beir,
>   Mither, mither,
> The curse of hell frae me sall ye beir,
>   Sic counseils ye gave to me O.'

"As I finished the poem, it was as though I had been participating in a Greek tragedy in capsule. Associations with Oedipus and Orestes were a measure of my involvement. And then I turned the page—'What is the name of this kind of poem? What characteristics does it share with other poems of this type? What is the effect of the refrain?'

"The shock of these questions drew me away from all that I had undergone in reading the text—the structure of feeling called forth by the pattern of events, my darkening mood as I saw the destruction of the family by the son's desperate crime and desperate penance, the horror of the final interchange. For the moment, I was the student, rudely torn from all this by the textbook editor's questions."

Is this not typical of what often happens in the classroom? Out of misguided zeal, the student is hurried into thinking or writing that removes him abruptly and often definitively from what he himself has lived through in reading the work. It therefore becomes essential to scrutinize all practices to make sure that they provide the opportunity for an initial crystal-lization of a personal sense of the work.

Although all students should not be required to give the same sort of expression to their reaction, in most cases a personal experience will elicit a definite response; it will lead to some kind of reflection. It may also lead to the desire to communicate this to others whom the boy or girl trusts. An atmosphere of informal, friendly exchange should be created. The student should feel free to reveal emotions and to make judgments. The primary criterion should be not whether his reactions or his judgments measure up to critical traditions but, rather, whether the ideas and reactions he expresses are genuine. The variety and unpredictability of life need not be alien to the classroom. Teachers and pupils should be relaxed enough to face what indeed happened as they interpreted the printed page. Frank expression of boredom or even vigorous rejection is a more valid starting point for learning than are docile attempts to feel "what the teacher wants." When the young reader considers why he has responded in a certain way, he is learning both to read more adequately and to seek personal meaning in literature.

There is no formula for giving students the assurance to speak out. One experienced teacher has found that his students are encouraged by mention of comments made by other students in past discussions. Another finds that classes that are accustomed to the traditional recitation pattern may be reluctant to engage in spontaneous discussion but will welcome the chance to write brief anonymous comments on a work at the beginning of a meeting. Some of these comments selected at random will serve to elicit further frank reactions and interchange. This teacher sometimes analyzes the written comments and later reports on trends and contrasts as a way of focusing on problems of importance to the group. Sometimes a general "unstructured" question, to borrow a term from the psychologist, will be enough to open the discussion. The teacher needs to maintain the conviction that it is important to place the discussion of the text in this matrix of personal response. He also needs to develop the security to permit a rather free-flowing discussion to begin with, before the group can be helped to focus on problems and skills of interpretation relevant to them.

A situation conducive to free exchange of ideas by no means represents a passive or negative attitude on the part of the teacher. To create an atmosphere of self-confident interchange he must be ready to draw out the more timid students and to keep the more aggressive from monopolizing the conversation. He must be on the alert to show pleased interest in comments that have possibilities and to help the students clarify or elaborate their ideas. He must keep the discussion moving along consistent lines by eliciting the points of contact between different students' opinions. His own flexible command of the text and understanding of the reading skills it requires will be called into play throughout.

One of the most valuable things the students will acquire from this is the ability to listen with understanding to what others have to say and to respond in relevant terms. If they have thus far been subjected to the typical school routine, the tendency is at first for them to address themselves only to the teacher; the conversational ball is constantly thrown to the teacher, who then throws it to another student, who again returns it to the teacher, and so on. In a more wholesome situation, the ball is passed from student to student, with the teacher participating as one of the group. This interchange among students must be actively promoted.

But should not the teacher or instructor enter more positively into the picture? Should his function be only to select a sufficiently wide range of good books, place them on the shelves of a library, turn the students loose to seek their own mental and emotional nourishment, and then listen to their spontaneous comments? Even the decision about what should be placed on the shelves of this library would make the teacher's task an influential one. Ideally, general considerations such as have been suggested thus far would guide his choices: an understanding of adolescent needs and conflicts and a recognition of any circumstances in their personal and social backgrounds that would make certain books of the past or present particularly interesting and illuminating.

This need to select from the body of literature those works to which particular students will be most receptive implies a knowledge not only of literature but also of the students. If the language, the setting, the theme, the central situation are all too alien, even a great work will fail. All doors to it are shut. Books must be provided that hold out some link with the young reader's past and present preoccupations, anxieties, ambitions. Hence, a standard literary diet prescribed for all has negated the reality of the school situation. In our heterogeneous society, variations from group to group and from individual to individual require a wide range of literary materials that will serve as the bridge from the individual's experience to the broad realms of literature. Such factors as the students' general background, level of maturity, linguistic history, and major difficulties and aspirations would guide the teacher's selection of works to bring to their attention.[1]

There is much to be said for Newman's vision of a university as a place where young people have access to books. Until quite recently, after all, English literature was not a subject for organized study and teaching. Yet it was a vital and absorbing interest to many, perhaps because there was no superstructure of traditional teaching practice connected with it. If the student turned to English literature, it was because he felt its personal value. He read with a free spirit, not because the academic powers decreed a knowledge of it necessary, but perhaps precisely because it was outside the stultifying routines of the curriculum. Unfortunately, it sometimes seems that it would be much better if students were turned loose in a library to work out a personal approach to literature for themselves.

Nevertheless, the teacher of literature may have a powerful and beneficial influence. The basic postulate is that such influence will be the elaboration of the vital influence inherent in literature itself. Important as it is, the selection of a humanly significant book list is only the first of the teacher's important functions. To reject the routine treatment of literature as a body of knowledge and to conceive of it rather as a series of

---

[1] Much in the following chapters will relate to this matter of selection. Ultimately, of course, students should learn to select their own books. An account of how high school students developed increasing maturity and breadth of choice when permitted to choose the books to be added to the school library is to be found in Lou L. La Brant's *An Evaluation of the Free Reading in Grades Ten, Eleven, and Twelve*. See also *Were We Guinea Pigs?* (Ohio State Univ.) and the report on these students as adults, *The Guinea Pigs after Twenty Years*, by Margaret Willis. Under the restricted conditions of most public school systems, however, the pressing need is that teachers should be aware of what books students require and should exert pressure for their introduction into the school library.

possible experiences only clears the ground. Once the unob-structed impact between reader and text has been made possi-ble, extraordinary opportunities for a real educational process are open to the teacher.

A situation in which students did nothing but give free rein to their reactions, their likes and dislikes, would undoubtedly have psychiatric value. The psychologists warn us about the neurotic effects of the stressful nature of our whole culture. In the compulsive atmosphere of the average school and college today, there is a tremendous pressure on students to fulfill requirements and to meet standards. A literature class where the student could feel that everything that he thought or said was equally valuable might possibly have a therapeutic effect. But the development of literary understanding is a more posi-tive goal. The study of literature should give the student the form of emotional release that all art offers and, at the same time, without strain or pressure, should help him gain ever more complex satisfactions from literature. A spontaneous response should be the first step toward increasingly mature primary reactions.

Certainly, lively, untrammeled discussion bespeaks an admirable educational setting. The fact that the student is articulate and eager to express himself is a wholesome sign. The teacher has given the student a feeling of adequacy, of having experiences and ideas worthy of consideration. Yet all of this, as great an achievement as it represents, only means that the obstacles to real education have been eliminated. The student still needs to acquire mental habits that will lead to lit-erary insight, critical judgment, and ethical and social under-standing. There still remains the necessity for positive aids to intellectual development. Though a free, uninhibited emotional reaction to a work of art or literature is an absolutely *necessary* condition of sound literary judgment, it is not, to use the logician's term, a *sufficient* condition. Without a real impact between the book and the mind of the reader, there can be no process of judgment at all, but honest recognition of one's own reaction is not in itself sufficient to ensure sound critical opinion. Given this free response, all things shall be added unto us. The implication is that there are other things to be added. Teachers who have been pioneers in freeing themselves from the old routines will be especially aware of the importance of envisaging this constructive phase of the problem.

One occasionally meets a student who has been given unlimited scope and is refreshingly honest in expressing his reactions to literature. Often, nevertheless, although his attitude toward books may be unspoiled by false reverence for what is "correct," his is not an emotionally organized or reasoned approach to literature. He is still at the mercy of his raw reactions, still uncritically ready to proffer every judgment dictated by the chance circumstances of his own personal life. Undoubtedly he is much better off than students who have been deadened to any direct sense of literature, but he is still functioning at the lowest critical level. He needs to retain his spontaneity and yet to develop further, to make each literary experience the source of enhanced capacities for his next experience. For he can begin to achieve a sound approach to literature only when he reflects on his response to it, when he attempts to understand what in the work and in himself produced that reaction, and when he thoughtfully goes on to modify, reject, or accept it.

This chapter has underlined the importance of a relationship between teacher and students that will permit the student to respond intimately and spontaneously to literature. This aim, it was seen, has sweeping implications for classroom procedure and for the choice of works to be read and discussed. Yet enabling the student to approach the text without artificial restrictions and to respond in his own terms is only one aspect of the teacher's role. This has simply established the conditions for carrying out another equally important aspect: to initiate a process through which the student can clarify and enlarge his response to the work. This entails complementary objectives: on the one hand, a critical awareness of his own reactions and, on the other hand, a keener and more adequate perception of the potentialities of the text. Both kinds of advance will go on simultaneously, each making the other possible. The complementary character of these two phases of the development of critical powers has hitherto been insufficiently recognized. They will be the concern of the next two chapters.

CHAPTER 4

WHAT THE STUDENT BRINGS
TO LITERATURE

O<small>nly</small> certain aspects of the teaching process have thus far been considered; in any actual class the different phases will not be so sharply separate. The creation of a setting for personal response is basic, as is a situation in which students stimulate one another to organize their diffuse responses and formulate their views. But as the discussion proceeds, the teacher will become involved in the further task of leading the students toward a fuller participation in what the text offers. This requires that the student critically revaluate his own assumptions and preoccupations. The teacher can help in this process only if he understands some of the possible forces molding the student's response and can anticipate some of the major needs and concerns of adolescents in our society.

In the interchange of ideas the student will be led to compare his reactions with those of other students and of the teacher (later, if necessary, of established critics). He will see that a particular work may give rise to attitudes and judgments different from his own. Some interpretations, he will discover, are more defensible than others in terms of the text as a whole. Yet he will also become aware of the fact that sometimes more than one reasonable interpretation is possible—a point to be considered more fully in chapter 5. From this interplay of ideas questions will arise: Why was his reaction different from those of the other students'? Why did he choose one particular slant rather than another? Why did certain phases of the book or poem strike him more forcibly than others? Why did he misinterpret or ignore certain elements? The attainment of a sound vision of the work will require the disengagement of the passing or irrelevant from the fundamental and appropriate elements in his response to the text. What was there in his state of mind that led to a distorted or partial view of the work? What in his temperament and past experience helped him understand it more adequately? What questions and obscurities remain?

The reading of a particular work at a particular moment by a particular reader will be a highly complex process. Personal factors will inevitably affect the equation represented by book plus reader. His past experience and present preoccupations may actively condition his primary spontaneous response. In some cases, these things will conduce to a full and balanced reaction to the work. In other cases, they will limit or distort.

The experienced teacher will undoubtedly be able to recall many illustrations of responses to literature colored by some personal factor. A personal preoccupation or an automatic association with a minor phrase or an attitude toward the general theme will lead to a strong reaction that has very little to do with the work. A word such as *home* or *mother* or a phrase such as *my country*, with its many conventional, sentimental associations, may set off a reaction that tends to blind the reader to the context of these words. The same thing happens on perhaps an even larger scale in connection with fiction and drama. A young college graduate, for example, expressed herself most forcibly concerning *Anna Karenina*. She had no sympathy, she said, for Anna, who was so preoccupied with her own affairs and who did not appreciate her husband; he was undoubtedly the kind of man who loves deeply but is unable to communicate his feeling to others. When asked to point out in the text itself the basis for her interpretation, she replied, "But there are people like that, with very warm hearts and intense affections, who are unable to let others know it. Why, my own father is like that!"

The personal sources of this reader's response were revealed here more clearly than is usually possible in a classroom or a school situation. Something accidental to the book had caused her to identify Karenin with her father. This is typical, however, of the less obvious ways in which we tend to project something out of our own experience that probably has been only vaguely suggested by the text. Some such projection of the student's own experience or preoccupation may also cause the reader to have a much more intense emotional experience than is appropriate. Rosamond Lehmann might have been astonished at hearing a seventeen-year-old girl pronounce *Invitation to the Waltz* "the greatest tragedy I ever read." It is not difficult to deduce that this girl's personal history and present preoccupations would explain her reaction to this wistful story of a young girl's first formal dance.[1]

---

[1] A college teacher who read this chapter in manuscript was reminded of an example of such "overweighting" that occurred in one of his classes. "A young man of lax views, and, I fear, lax practice, suddenly discovered to his immense delight

It is easy to detect the influence of the reader's preoccupations and past experiences when, as in the preceding instances, they lead to an interpretation unsupported by the text. Richards labeled this kind of misreading "mnemonic irrelevance." Sometimes emphasis on the negative influence of the reader's personal concerns obscures their positive contribution. The reader's fund of relevant memories makes possible any reading at all. Without linkage with the past experiences and present interests of the reader, the work will not come alive for him, or, rather, he will not be prepared to bring it to life. Past literary experiences make up an important part of this equipment that the reader brings to literature, but they have usually been emphasized to the exclusion of other elements derived from general life experience. To share the author's insight, the reader need not have had identical experiences, but he must have experienced some needs, emotions, concepts, some circumstances and relationships, from which he can construct the new situations, emotions, and understandings set forth in the literary work.

Moreover, that work will have been a vital experience to the extent that these new elements can be assimilated into, and perhaps even modify, the original background of personality. The reader must possess not only the intellectual potentialities but also the emotional readiness to participate in just this vicarious experience. In a motion picture theater a ten-year-old boy was heard to exclaim, just as the hero and heroine fell into the traditional closing embrace, "This is the part I always hate!" That feeling is evidently not shared by the millions of

that he had Shakespeare's authority for what he was saying and doing. Quoting Sir Toby's 'Dost thou think, because thou art virtuous, there shall be no more cakes and ale?' he solemnly announced, 'That is the greatest sentence ever written!'"

adults who view such pictures weekly. Another instance: The vocabulary of Hemingway's "The Killers" is probably within the range of fourth-graders, but they would be unable to organize the words into a meaningful story. They would not possess the awareness required to re-create it with all its implications. This quite obvious point concerning emotional readiness is often forgotten. In the molding of any specific literary experience, what the student brings to literature is as important as the literary text itself.

Under usual teaching conditions the opportunities for coming to know the individual student are unfortunately rare. All the more reason, therefore, for the teacher to acquire some general understanding of the possible experiences and preoccupations typical of the particular group of students with which he is dealing. This will aid him in his choice of appropriate literary works and in his handling of the students' spontaneous responses to literature. What, then, does the adolescent bring to literature?

One approach to this question would be to consider in detail the segment of the present adolescent generation self-consciously in revolt against the older generation and the establishment. Inheriting a world globally intertwined yet unable to restrain ethnic and religious enmities, rejecting the practical values of the society, distressed at the slow advance of civil and social rights for African Americans and other minorities, eager to enter into adult sex life, seeking intensity of experience through music and drugs—surely, these young people reveal the seriousness of the problems of their whole generation. Yet basically they are manifesting in extreme form processes that have been inherent in the situation of the adolescent in our society for decades. The following pages will not attempt a detailed picture of the (by no means homogeneous) present adolescent generation but will instead suggest some persistent underlying factors affecting the adolescent in our culture.

The adolescent reader comes to the experience of literature out of a mass of absorbing and conflicting influences. It has become a cliché to describe as a time of storm and stress this stage when children are coming into possession of the physical and temperamental endowments with which they will function as adults. The marked physical changes that occur at this time have probably been excessively blamed for the difficulties that beset the adolescent years. Anthropologists have pointed out societies such as Samoa where these physical changes occur without emotional upheaval. In other cultures the period of personal turmoil may fall at an entirely different age and without reference to physiological changes. Nevertheless, although not the sole reason for the problems of adolescence in our society, these changes do have certain emotional repercussions. The girl or boy recognizes transformations in emotional drives and personality traits. A heightened self-consciousness and curiosity about the self usually follow. Obviously this will color attitudes toward the essentially human art of literature.

The self-consciousness of the adolescent often centers on a concern with normality. His size, his height, his weight, his speed in movement, his strength are constantly measured against what is considered appropriate for his age and social group. Philip Carey's sensitivity about his deformed foot in *Of Human Bondage* or Piggy's self-consciousness in *Lord of the Flies* can symbolize the agonies of embarrassment that many boys and girls suffer because of much slighter and perhaps almost undetectable deviations from what they have come to consider normal. Temperamental traits are subjected to equally searching scrutiny: aggressiveness or shyness, physical courage or timidity, the capacity to make friends will be measured against some kind of norm.

Even the subtler emotional traits, feelings of anger and envy, of loyalty and affection toward others, may trouble him if he is not sure that others have similar feelings. He seeks some standards against which to measure himself and derives his sense of them from a great many different sources, among which may be literature, a point discussed more fully in chapter 7. This preoccupation is at least a possible factor in students' responses to particular works.

The distress, insecurity, and bewilderment that often accompany these physical and social changes are probably in large part due to the lack of mental preparation for them. Particularly is this true of attitudes toward sex. In some societies, sexual maturation brings with it no insecurity because from early childhood the youth has been prepared for it. The adolescent in our culture often must seek knowledge about sex from surreptitious and unwholesome sources. Even when he has been adequately informed, the nervousness, prudery, and even prurience about sex in the society about him will undoubtedly cause complications. These difficulties have been intensified in recent years by a paradoxically rapid change in legal and social attitudes toward frankness about sexual behavior in, for example, the mass media. Another complicating factor is that youth are seeking to adopt adult behavior at progressively younger levels. Many of the interests and problems formerly characteristic of the high school years are now encountered in the junior high school. In this context of fluctuating attitudes toward sex, the boy and girl must make an adjustment to this newly recognized phase of their nature.

Even teachers who are aware of this preoccupation of youth too often tend to evade or gloss over anything in literature that might have a direct bearing on this vital concern. They thus rule out one of the most unfailingly powerful factors in the student's experience with literature. There is, of course, the opposing danger: the adult excessively zealous to prove his emancipation may initiate a crude pendulum swing that will reinforce a self-conscious sexuality, already sufficiently exploited by advertisements, mass media, and recent fiction. The adult's responsibility is to free himself and the youth from the distortions of both prudery and exaggerated reactions against it. Then understanding of the potential beauty and dignity of this aspect of human life can be honestly fostered.

The youth, like Maugham's Philip Carey, wishes to find out "man's relation to the world he lives in, man's relation with the men among whom he lives, and, finally, man's relation to himself." The adolescent becomes more conscious of himself as a member of a family and a community. He becomes eager to impress others, to gain their friendship, and to be admitted into special groups, particularly of his peers. This often leads to intense self-consciousness about his own personality and to a great interest in the ways in which people influence one another. Adolescents experiment with various ways of approaching people; they seem to try on different social personalities as one might try on new clothes. And, indeed, clothing is an important aspect of the adolescent culture.

The initiated adult tends to forget the awakening curiosity of the adolescent eager to see behind the façade of appearances. During childhood he has accepted the bare framework of relationships as they have presented themselves to him, in his family, in his neighborhood, and in the larger world. Now as he nears adult years, he finds these relationships acquiring new and unsuspected meanings. Parents who had been taken for granted, their relation to each other summed up in their common parental role, are suddenly seen to have hitherto-unsuspected intense emotional ties. In many biographical novels the adolescent hero or heroine is shown suddenly discovering the complex, hidden emotional life of the parents.

Thus it is with much of the adult world. The boy and girl question: What are the emotional realities behind the world of appearances? What indeed does it mean to the individual—and potentially to me, the adolescent, about to "live"—to be a leader or a follower, to be a member of a community, to earn one's living, to create a family and a circle of friends, to meet the ups and downs of fate, to know love and birth and death? What does it feel like, from within, to be this kind of person or that? to be angelic, cruel, dominating, passive? What are the satisfactions, what are the elements, of the many roles that may be played? No longer satisfied with a childlike acceptance of the mere external gestures and trappings, he wishes to experience these things from within. It is often to fiction—in one or another medium—that he turns. Here he seeks emotional release for the impulses already strong within him but denied satisfaction in his life as a minor; he seeks also the insight he craves into the possibilities that life offers, the roles perhaps open to him, the situations in which he might find himself.

Still in the dependent childhood relation to the family yet feeling himself practically an adult, the youth often begins to question familial authority. Even in a fairly stable society the period of adolescence brings with it a heightened tension within the family group. The youth strives to assert his existence as an individual apart from it. He sets up the goal of psychological as well as economic independence. These attitudes frequently come into conflict with the desire of the family to continue its dominance and with the psychic need of the parents to feel themselves still an essential force in the life of their offspring. In the present period of great social transformations such strains and stresses have been tremendously intensified, and emancipation from the family becomes of even greater concern to the adolescent. Moreover, many who are members of minority groups, in effect, subcultures, will have grown up in families structured differently from the dominant pattern. The adolescent needs to understand that different cultures or ethnic groups assign different functions to the family. He will profit also from comprehension of the role of both dependence and independence in the development of the individual.

In recent years increasing attention has been given to study of the individual in relation to the cultural environment. The theories of personality development represented by the various schools of psychology have also become quite generally known. They are often incorporated into the training of teachers and are discussed in books and newspaper columns for parents. Yet in the education given the adolescent in America there is still little to enlighten him along these lines. He will sense needs and curiosities, and here again it will often be only from the reflection of life offered by literature that he will acquire such insights.

The difficulties of the present-day adolescent are tremendously complicated by the fact that he is living at a moment when our society is singularly lacking in consistency, when economic and social changes are going on with unprecedented speed, and when few of the traditional ideas remain unquestioned. The boy and girl are suddenly catapulted from the relatively stable environment of the family into a world of innumerable alternative patterns; the burden of many choices is placed on them. They often find the ways of life, the ideas, and the activities valued within the family to be ill adapted to the conditions of a changing world.

More probably than any other generation, the adolescents of today have the opportunity—sometimes felt as an awesome task—to formulate their own ideal life patterns. It is no longer assumed that the families they establish will be organized on one pattern; an extraordinary range of possible relationships with their mates and with their children can be envisaged. Similarly, in their choice of work the settled values need no longer hold. The prestige of the successful business executive is questioned; the social value of the scientist, the artist, or the technician is increasingly recognized. Similar breadth of choice and challenge to personal creativity meet the adolescent as he seeks to develop a social philosophy and a set of values. Formerly, political questions or possible alternative organizations of society often seemed remote and academic to the adolescent involved in plans for his own personal life. Today, even the least socially conscious individual is forced into some recognition of the influence of the surrounding society. As he turns to literature, he cannot ignore this welter of shifting and uncertain social conditions.

This jolt to habitual attitudes has probably increased awareness of the indirect ways in which these attitudes are usually
assimilated. In a stable society, the image of the rights and the
responsibilities appropriate to, for example, the various family
roles would be absorbed from childhood experience in the
family and the community. Although more of these aspects of
behavior have been forced into consciousness in our changing
age, the processes of social patterning must be recognized.
Ready-made standards and attitudes are derived from the family background, from the actions of neighbors, from repeat-
edly encountered images of accepted behavior. The very
emotions with which a situation is spontaneously met have,
after all, been learned through the force of cultural suggestion. A woman is indignant at the thought of her husband
taking a second mate because from childhood on she has constantly observed that situation coupled with that reaction. For
the same reason, a woman in certain African tribes will automatically acquiesce when her husband proposes to take a second wife. Notions of right and wrong, of approved behavior
and appropriate responses, are in largest measure the result of
such unconscious assimilation.

The present-day youth must often mediate between conventional ideas of life roles and the unprecedented circumstances of contemporary life. Innumerable influences in his
environment will have given him a definite image, for instance,
of the ways of behavior and feeling, even of the kind of temperament, appropriate or possible for a man or a woman. His
parents and his family, through their own example and through
explicit statement of the accepted attitudes, will have done
much at an early point to set this mold. These will have been
reinforced not only by the men and women about him but

also by the distinctions between the things proper for men and for women repeated endlessly in the newspapers and popular magazines, by the types presented with monotonous similarity on the screen. Literature, it should be recalled, is another of these image-forming media. The human complications that are recognized as important and valid enough to be given explicit attention in fiction, in the newspapers or other mass media reflect overwhelmingly the stereotyped notions of masculine and feminine nature and behavior. The man, dominant, masterful, superior; the woman, emotional, dependent, clinging—these are the images most often and most forcibly presented even in this supposed age of woman's emancipation. These stereotypes will affect in some way the actions, feelings, and choices of the individual.

The post–World War II generations that seem in such large measure to have broken away from these conceptions still feel the pressure of these older, more deeply rooted images. The redefinition of possible roles for man and woman has gone on constantly in terms of revolt or readjustment to the older attitudes that still permeate our environment. On the one hand, the traditional notions of the behavior of man and woman are being constantly reiterated; on the other hand, the adolescent meets with increasing frequency images of men and women behaving in ways alien to the traditional ideas. Women enter into activities thought appropriate only for men; children are given freedom that would formerly have been considered dangerous; grandmothers behave in ways formerly thought scandalous.

The adolescent's own assumption of adult roles cannot therefore be as automatic as in the case of the youth in a more stable society. Indeed, the adolescent group is increasingly self-conscious in its relation to the older generation, and many are seeking much earlier entrance into adult roles. The adolescent's choices, nevertheless, will probably in large part be made on an emotional basis. Against the weight and pressure of the traditionally accepted image, there will be exerted the dramatic appeal of the new and perhaps more practical image. Many today seem to have retreated into a teenage culture as a way of evading the effort to sort out what is sound in the adult world. The assumption of the new type of role will often be made under the compulsion of new economic and social conditions. The old attitudes and habits of response will be constantly intruding themselves, complicating the individual's life, creating insecurity and confusion.

Out of such preoccupations the adolescent comes to his experience of literature today. Anything that his reading may contribute must take its place in the complex web of influences acting on him. His attention will be diverted to those phases of any work that apply most clearly to his own emotional tensions and perplexities. He may often conceal the reactions dictated by his particular obsessions, yet a teaching situation such as was outlined in the preceding chapter would encourage him to articulate his response.

Still another conditioning factor affects the student's sensitivity to literature. The individualistic emphasis of our society builds up a frequent reluctance to see the implications for others of our own actions or to understand the validity of the needs that motivate other people's actions. That the success of the individual must so often be at the expense of others places a premium on this kind of blindness. Teachers of literature need to take this cultural pressure into account, since it is so directly opposed to the attitude of mind they are attempting to foster. For literature by its very nature invokes participation in the experiences of others and comprehension of their goals and aspirations.

Furthermore, much of what the student reads and sees will tend to coarsen his sensibilities and to make him less able to respond fully to the complex and subtle nature of good literature. It would be fatuous to ignore the crude, oversimplified, and false pictures of human behavior and motivation presented by the mass media and the drugstore paperbacks. Not even the school as a whole, let alone the teacher of literature with his much more limited scope, can hope fully to counterbalance the great weight of the influences met in the surrounding society and in such institutions as the newspaper or television. The mere reading of a play by Shakespeare or a novel by George Eliot or Henry James cannot in itself be expected to wipe out the effect of all the desensitizing influences met outside the school or college.

Yet this does not justify a defeatism that would despair of influencing any but the gifted or those with unusually favorable backgrounds. On the contrary, understanding of the function of the literature teacher must be revised and broadened. He must do more than merely expose the student to great art. Although the reading of a novel will not in itself counteract all the unfavorable pressures, it can be a means for helping the student to develop conscious resistance to those influences. And this requires constant alertness to the nature of the social forces acting on the student.

When a student reads a particular work, one of innumerable possible variations on this general picture of adolescent concerns will come into play. The particular community background of the student, whether he comes from the North or the South, from city or country, from a middle-class or underprivileged home, will affect the nature of the understanding and the prejudices that he brings to the book. Toni Morrison's *The Bluest Eye* or Nadine Gordimer's *July's People* will elicit a very different response from students of northern and southern (or Westchester and Harlem) backgrounds. Sinclair Lewis's *Main Street* and John Dos Passos's *Manhattan Transfer* will not mean the same thing to the city boy and the country boy. The daughters of a mill owner and of a factory worker will probably react differently to Frank Norris's *The Octopus* or Sherwood Anderson's *Poor White*. And similar differences appear in responses to the literature of the past and of England. That the American people are becoming increasingly urban may explain the growing difficulty of keeping alive the love of English poetry, so permeated by country imagery.

The student will bring to his reading the moral and religious code and social philosophy assimilated primarily from his family and community background. His parents may stem from a Main Street setting, or they may have turned from a life such as John Cheever pictured to assume the duties of parenthood. Or like James Baldwin, he may have survived a ghetto childhood. Adolescents at the end of the century especially reflect such economic and ethnic diversity. The religious background of the student might also play an important part. In a class studying Milton's *Paradise Lost*, a devout Catholic responded very differently from the student who had been brought up in an agnostic milieu. Similarly, a discussion of *Romeo and Juliet* was given a rather unusual turn by one student's insistence that there was no tragedy since the lovers would be reunited after death. Such diversity of response arises also from varying social and economic views. The child of well-to-do middle-class parents who, after reading Henry Roth's *Call It Sleep*, insists that "some people like to be dirty and ragged and just won't work" will have rather a special approach to Dickens's *Hard Times* or Hugo's *Les Misérables*. Students will necessarily differ in the sensitivities they bring to many aspects of literary works.

Other differences of equipment, not as broad or as easily detected, also affect reading. The adolescent preoccupation with family relations may take a wide variety of forms. For example, the degree of adjustment or maladjustment between the student's parents may be reflected in the student's receptivities or rejections. An extreme instance is the woman who confessed that she had hated almost every story or play she had read in high school because they ended on the note "they lived happily ever after," so contradictory to her own parents' unhappy disagreements. Authors, she felt, must be in some vast conspiracy of untruth. Here, certainly, is an instance in which acquaintance with some of the novels dealing with marital maladjustments might have led her to realize that writers attempt to illuminate the whole range of human experience and that, therefore, their images of possible happiness might also be given some credence. As for this woman's daughter, growing up in the present era of explicitness about sexual relations, perhaps her literary fare is equally narrow but her need is to encounter some portrayals of fulfillment in marriage!

Anything, of course, that has entered into and shaped the development of the student's personality may be significant for his literary development. The teacher cannot hope to glimpse many of these factors, of whose import the student most of all will be unaware. Yet such general social attitudes will ultimately condition the whole texture of the student's experience of life as well as of literature. In the interplay between the book and the personality, failures in sensitivity, misinterpretations, and distorted reactions often have their roots in such influences. The effort to help the student arrive at a more balanced and lucid sense of the work thus involves the parallel effort to help him understand and evaluate his personal emphases.

There is very little systematic information available concerning the specific ways in which the individual personality colors the responses to literature. The book by I. A. Richards cited on page 61 offers some valuable illustrations of individual reactions to poetry.[2] His elaborate and subtle analyses of his students' comments on poetry reveal some of the typical patterns of response, and his discussion "Irrelevant Associations and Stock Responses" is especially pertinent here. Illustrations from his book as well as from the experience of other teachers will serve to place these findings in a social and psychological context.

---

[2] This is a work that every teacher of literature should read. It has been a seminal book for generations of critics and teachers. See also James R. Squire, *The Responses of Adolescents While Reading Four Short Stories*; James R. Wilson, *Responses of College Freshmen to Three Novels*; and Walter D. Loban, *Literature and Social Sensitivity*. Bibliographies of research on response to literature can be found in Alan C. Purves and Richard Beach, *Literature and the Reader: Research in Response to Literature, Reading Interests, and the Teaching of Literature*, and Richard Beach and Susan Hynds, "Research on Response to Literature," in E. J. Farrell and J. R. Squire, *Transactions with Literature*.

The impact of the literary work is dulled when the reader brings to the text a fund of ready-made, sharply crystallized ideas and habits of response. These responses are so easily touched off that they sometimes interfere with interpretation. Richards gives an illustration of this in several students' comments on Edna St. Vincent Millay's sonnet "What's this of death, from you who never will die?" The mention of death at once elicited ready-made responses concerning the question of immortality. These prevented the students from understanding either the idea or the effect that the poem was aiming at. The students made a number of irrelevant comments on death or responded to only those phrases in the poem that had some connection with their own preconceived ideas on the subject.

A similar instance occurred in a high school discussion of "The Eve of St. Agnes." One of the students announced that she thought the poem silly and sentimental. She defended this by adding that the poem was all about "romantic love twaddle." In her early adolescent rebellion against the seeming adult obsession with this subject, she had not been willing to respond and had completely misunderstood the tone of the poem.

Subjects such as home, mother, childhood, birth, death, and my country possess whole constellations of fixed attitudes and automatic emotional reflexes. The popularity of such authors as Edgar Guest, Ella Wheeler Wilcox, and James Metcalfe depends in large part on the emotion-arousing efficacy of such subjects, regardless of what the poet may phrase about them. The discussion of D. H. Lawrence's "Piano" by Richards's students offers further examples of how ready-made responses and irrelevant associations may interfere with the reading of any work that deals with a familiar subject (in this case childhood recollections of a mother playing the piano). The Cambridge students were sufficiently sophisticated to be on their guard against the automatic appeal of such elements in Lawrence's poem. For some of them, however, this fear of sentimentality became a barrier to understanding the poem. They recognized the stereotyped nature of the sentiments aroused by elements in the text and blamed the poem for a conventionality inherent in their own feelings. They were so busy resisting the possible automatic response to the idea of home and mother that they failed to perceive how the text might offer safeguards against sentimentality.

When in wartime mediocre poetry on patriotic themes elicits an intense response, the whole environment is creating the emotions that the text seems to arouse. An antipathy to war may similarly vitiate critical judgment. An intelligent young man of pacifist beliefs picked up *A Shropshire Lad* and glanced at "1887," written on the occasion of Queen Victoria's jubilee. Shocked and indignant, he did not wish even to finish this poem that, by the very swing of its verse and the use of such traditional phrases as "God has saved the Queen," "saviors," "the land they perished for," seemed designed to arouse patriotic and warlike sentiments. Others have read the poem, especially its last stanza, as an ironic warning against blind patriotism. Whatever may have been the author's intention, the text permits either interpretation. At any rate, the reader's problem is to be aware of how much his own preconceptions enter into his interpretation of its tone and to dissociate his attitude toward war from his judgment on the effectiveness of the poem.

Students will undoubtedly come to literature with increasingly strong attitudes toward political and social themes. Such subjects are being discussed frequently and heatedly in their homes, in the newspapers, over the radio and on television. This suggests a whole complex of definite attitudes and automatic responses that may cause difficulties.

Richards reports such a stock response from students whose antipathy to the glorification of royalty led them to object to a poem on George Meredith's eightieth birthday that referred to him as "king of our hearts today." (It must be recalled that the students did not have the benefit of the clue provided by the title.) At a performance of *King Richard II* in New York, one of the spectators revealed a similar blindness owing to antiroyalist sentiments. He was annoyed at the appeal that the play patently had for him. "Why should I care about whether Richard or Bolingbroke wins out? The whole idea of kingship is an anachronism for us today." This antipathy blinded him to the play's more universal interest, its subtly nuanced portrait of a man unable to wield the power thrust on him yet histrionically delighting in going through the motions of command and as histrionically savoring the drama of his own downfall. If the protagonist had been a present-day dictator or the president of a great corporation or university, this irate spectator would have been able to grasp the revelation of human character that his automatic reaction to the idea "king" had obscured. We may sympathize with his political views and yet regret that he was not able to handle his primary response in such a way as to appreciate the basic values of the work before him. The controversial nature of much of the literature being written today often creates such obstacles to sound literary judgment. Students should be helped to handle their responses to the political and social tendencies of a work. These should not block attention to its sensuous, emotional, and intellectual elements. An attitude toward the work's social implication is by no means irrelevant, but it should be brought to bear on the text itself, its specific verbal signs, and should not be a screen between the reader and his evocation of the work.

This type of predetermined response elicited by the general subject of the work is rather easily detected. The same kind of excessive reaction may be produced by a word or a phrase or an episode in a work whose general theme has nothing to do with this particular prejudice or emotional fixation of the reader. An instance of this is the Cambridge students' misreading of the poem on George Meredith merely because the word king set off an irrelevant automatic response. The young girl's reaction to the love element in "The Eve of St. Agnes" is another illustration.

The earlier discussion of some of the conditions affecting the adolescent today suggested various other factors that would encourage narrow or stereotyped preconceptions. For example, a rural or urban background or regional loyalty would tend to build up stock responses. The southern girl who praised as good books all those that offered a romanticized picture of the South and condemned such works as To Kill a Mockingbird obviously was not functioning on a literary level.

The fixed ideas and emotional associations that cluster about family and sex relations also may lead to irrelevant responses. An example is a Cambridge student's condemnation of D. H. Lawrence's poem "Piano" on the ground that no sensible person would want to give up his adult independence and return to the limitations of childhood. Resentment at restraints placed on him in childhood may explain this reader's misunderstanding of the poem. His response was to something in his own mind and background, not in the text. A group of college girls arguing about *Tom Jones* revealed the extent to which each girl's reactions were affected by her image of the ideal young man, an image, in some instances, sufficiently crystallized to hinder understanding of the various phases of Tom's character that Fielding presents.

In addition to preventing an understanding of what is read, rigid attitudes may seriously impair the reader's judgment even of what he has understood. Richards reports instances in which the reader had understood the fresh interpretation that the poem presented but condemned it because he was still dominated by stereotyped ideas and conventional feelings. Here the difficulties arise from the fact that a student will have absorbed from his environment cruder standards than are worthy of the literary experiences made available to him.

This was forcibly brought home to a teacher who in his course on short story writing was perplexed by the superficial nature of the students' work. In his discussion of the problems presented by the short story form, he had selected from such writers as Poe, Hawthorne, Maupassant, Flaubert, and Mansfield those stories that seemed to handle in more subtle ways problems dimly suggested in the students' writings. However, he discovered that the usual literary diet of the students was not the work of writers of this caliber but the stereotyped products of third-rate magazines.

The students' justification of their reading was in psychological terms. These stories were easy to read, offered no difficulties to the understanding. They ended happily and gave one a sense that success was not too difficult of attainment. In some cases the explanation was merely that these cheap stories were more easily available. Obviously, the instructor's expression of disapproval would have accomplished little. He wisely started from the level at which he found his students. By getting them to discuss some of the stories they liked, he helped them become aware of the stereotyped formulas and trick effects. The class then turned to other kinds of escape writing, such as Poe's stories, that require a more complex response and a more subtle perception of the writer's technique. The instructor's aim was gradually to lead the students to approach without resistance those stories he considered most significant.

At once the human element entered, for obviously the students were seeking in the cheap success stories a release from the sense of pressure and competitiveness that permeated the world in which they lived. They had to be willing to relinquish the easy relaxing drug that made up their reading diet and to welcome the challenge of those stories that attempted to present an honest and searching image of life.

The instructor had to dissipate any feeling that the stories he suggested were to be studied principally from the formal point of view. The concern with technique had to be subordinated to a concern with the state of mind, the attitude toward people and life situations revealed by great writers of the short story. Fundamentally, this also proved to be the sounder approach to the problems of technique. The subtle qualities of mood, the ironic contrasts between personality and situation, the kinds of conflicts between characters as well as the solutions of the conflicts—all these things were involved in an understanding of the technical means the writers had employed.

The students had been unable to assimilate the examples of technical success in the short story because they had been unable or reluctant to understand and assimilate the insights that the writers of those stories had sought to give.

The teacher of literature should be on the alert for such possible stock responses. In large part they represent the dogmatic, platitudinous ideas about people and life that one meets on all sides: in the newspapers and the mass media or in everyday conversation. Similarly, they show themselves in ways of feeling that have become so conventional that they have lost all individual quality or fine shades. Popular songs are repositories of such sentiments. Such responses are aroused with great ease in the commercialized appeal to stock sentiments represented by Mother's Day and Father's Day and by much of the advertising in the mass media.

Yet the very essence of literature is a rejection of such stereotyped, superficial, and unshaded reactions to the mere outlines of situations or to the appeal of vague and generalized concepts. A poem or a novel should provide fresh insight. Readers, therefore, must be helped to develop flexibility of mind, a freedom from rigid emotional habits, if they are to enter into the aesthetic experiences the artist has made possible.

Obviously, the aim should not be to create in the student such a state of flexibility and such a passivity to new kinds of experience that he will lose all the advantages of an integrated personality or a settled structure of ideas of his own. In one of his letters Keats describes the poet as possessing no character of his own because he could identify himself so completely with other forms of being and could adopt so readily new and untried forms of response. Precious as that capacity may be for a poet, in such an extreme form it is not a practical asset for the conduct of everyday affairs! A stock response, as Richards says, may often be a convenience. Just as it would be disastrous if at every occasion for walking we had to reason out the best way of putting one foot before the other, so in our intellectual and social life crystallized attitudes and ideas are useful. By automatically taking care of the major part of our lives, they leave us energy for meeting the new and unprepared-for situations.

Sufficient flexibility is needed to free oneself from the stock response when it prevents a response more appropriate to the situation. This is as true of the problems encountered in our daily lives as it is of our encounters with literature. Much of the mismanagement of personal relationships results from following a stereotyped and automatic reaction to the general outlines of a situation instead of responding to the special characteristics and changing qualities of that situation. The mother, accustomed to her children's dependence on her for the management of their lives, continues to expect the same kind of dependence long after the children have grown beyond the need for it. The young man who has been accustomed to his mother's housewifely attention to his physical well-being becomes irritated when his wife, employed in business, overlooks these things. Years of economic expansion promote the idea that a person without a job is shiftless and unenterprising; when a recession or depression makes it impossible for many of even the most enterprising to have jobs, the same attitude toward the unemployed persists in some quarters.

In the experience of literature, free of the demands that practical life makes for speedy, economical response and action, this capacity for flexibility should surely be exercised and enlarged. Fundamentally, the goal is the development of individuals who will function less as automatic bundles of habits and more as flexible, discriminating personalities. Our great heritage of literary experiences can be fully enjoyed and understood only by such personalities.

These remarks concerning stock responses can be translated into terms of the breadth or adequacy of the individual life experience. Something in the reader's own background or personality prevents him from understanding fully all that the work offers. His notions about possibilities of human character may be too limited, or his moral code too rigid, to encompass the complex human situations and emotions presented in literature. In its simplest terms, as we have seen, this inadequacy of experience may take the form of the city child's inability to respond fully to country imagery; or a more extreme example is the Indian children's difficulties with Restoration comedy. How much of the adolescent's indifference to great literature is the result of inadequate experience? How much of the shallowness or captiousness of his opinions on books is a by-product of a similar approach to situations in life?

Just as in medicine much of the knowledge about normal physiological processes is derived from the study of pathological conditions, so in literature understanding of what goes on when an individual reads a poem or a novel or a play is illuminated by study of the causes for inadequate responses. They document the basic fact that any sound response to literature is dependent on the quality of the reader's personal contribution. He does violence to a poem or a story when some obsession or blindness clouds his vision of what the author has presented. He does justice to it when his own temperament, his own experience, and a flexibly receptive attitude permit him to see clearly what the text itself offers and to perceive its significance. Precisely because it appeals to certain elements in his nature as his past experience has molded it, is the literary effect intense.

If the student's structure of attitudes and ideas is built on too narrow a base of experience, he should be helped to gain broader and deeper insight through literature itself. That is why throughout this discussion the emphasis has been on the transaction between the reader and the text. When the reader becomes aware of the dynamic nature of that transaction, he may gain some critical consciousness of the strengths or weaknesses of the emotional and intellectual equipment with which he approaches literature (and life). Since he interprets the book or poem in terms of his fund of past experiences, it is equally possible and necessary that he come to reinterpret his old sense of things in the light of this new literary experience, in the light of the new ways of thinking and feeling offered by the work of art. Only when this happens has there been a full interplay between book and reader and hence a complete and rewarding literary experience.

Evoking a work of art can have this effect because it does more than merely recall to us elements out of our own past insights and emotions. It will present them in new patterns and new contexts. It will give them new resonance and make of them the basis for new awarenesses and enriched understanding. It will tend to supplement and correct our own necessarily limited personal experience. Our habitual responses, our preoccupations and desires may be given added significance. They will be related to the emotional and sensuous structure created by the author, and they will be brought into organic connection with broader and deeper streams of thought and feelings. Out of this will arise a wider perspective and a re-adjustment of the framework of values with which to meet further experiences in literature and life.

These considerations reinforce the belief concerning the teacher's opportunities set forth at the end of chapter 3. That the personal contribution of the reader is an essential element in any vital reading of literature justifies the demand that the teacher create a setting that makes it possible for the student to have a spontaneous response to literature. But the preceding discussion makes more apparent the basis for the view that this represents only the first step, absolutely essential though that first step is. Once the student has responded freely, a process of growth can be initiated. He needs to learn to handle with intelligence and discrimination the personal factors that enter into his reaction to books. Through a critical scrutiny of his response to literary works, he can come to understand his personal attitudes and gain the perspective needed for a fuller and sounder response to literature.

This chapter has been concerned with the preoccupations and needs that the adolescent may bring to literature. To help the student critically to understand his own contribution to the literary experience becomes an aspect of helping him do justice to the text. The thesis of chapter 1—that the teaching of literature necessarily involves helping the student handle social, psychological, and ethical concepts—now falls into place. The next chapter will approach the problem of the clarification of the student's response more specifically in terms of the kinds of knowledge that will contribute to his understanding of the literary work.

CHAPTER 5

BROADENING THE FRAMEWORK

A free exchange of ideas will lead each student to scrutinize his own sense of the literary work in the light of others' opinions. The very fact that other students stress aspects that he may have ignored or report a different impression will suggest that perhaps he has not done justice to the text. He will turn to it again to point out the elements that evoked his response and to see what can justify the other students' responses.

The preceding discussion of adolescent concerns has dealt with some of the factors that lead the individual to be especially receptive to some of the stimuli offered by the text, to ignore others, or even to read into it unfounded implications. All this has assumed that a personal response can be either more or less relevant to the text itself. Therefore, in any teaching situation an awareness of the student's preoccupations and emotional needs should constantly be brought to bear on the problem of ensuring that the student has responded to what is actually offered by the text. The teacher aims to help the student evoke its sensuous, emotional, and intellectual import as fully as possible.

Those least in sympathy with the point of view of the preceding chapters will probably maintain that the only task of the teacher is to help the student understand what he has read and that therefore the teacher need not be concerned with the personal preoccupations or reactions of the students. The crux of the whole problem lies in the word *understand*. The preceding chapters have shown that understanding is a much more complex personal process than many are willing to admit.

One oversimplified interpretation of understanding was rejected earlier when it was pointed out that the paraphrase is not the poem. A mere intellectualized definition of the meaning of a poem diminishes the work. The student will not be helped to understand if he is restricted to the plane of verbalization, of translation of the literary work into generalizations and abstractions. The ability to express the heart of an idea in clear terms that reveal its possible general application is indeed a rare and valuable one. But understanding does not begin on this level, certainly, nor does it necessarily culminate on this level.

Even if we take the word *understand* in a most limited sense, as it would apply to the definition of particular words, we ultimately become involved in elements of direct human experience that lead into all the complex considerations concerning the social significance of English teaching. For to understand a word is to see implications in a context significant for human beings. In our everyday lives we often use words as mere empty counters swishing over the surface of the mind with little or no direct sense of what they point to. Thus it is that much of our speech and writing has only the vaguest significance. Certainly this habit will not be counteracted by having students translate one set of words thus vaguely sensed into another set equally devoid of outline and content.

Understanding implies the full impact of the sensuous, emotional, as well as intellectual force of a word. Linking the signs on the page to the word is not enough. It requires linking the word with what it points to in the human or natural world. This involves awareness of the sensations it symbolizes, the systems or categories into which it fits, the complex of experiences out of which it springs, the modes of feeling or practical situations with which it is associated, the actions it may imply. Above all, the word cannot be understood in isolation; it must be seen in the variety of its possible contexts. Moreover, we must relate it to our own experience so that it may become part of our working equipment. Only then, as we place it in its relation to other sensations, ideas, attitudes, and patterns, all equally realized, shall we be in a position to say that we understand it.

The word *love*, for instance, cannot be defined without reference to some context. The varied experiences in life and literature that different individuals associate with the word will also affect the way in which they understand it. The words *virtue, justice,* or *democracy* would represent a similar necessity for encroaching on the whole framework of ethical and social implications. Thus, even so narrow an aim as the understanding of words leads back to the field of human experiences. And that process becomes involved at once in implied assertions concerning human nature and society. In this vital sense, understanding of even one word demands a framework of ideas about humankind, nature, and society.

With like inevitability, the task of helping a student understand a work of literature as a whole involves the context of the student's past experience as well as the historical, social, and ethical context into which he must fit the particular work. This will be true whether the work be "The Solitary Reaper" or *Paradise Lost, Hamlet* or *The Importance of Being Earnest, Anna Karenina* or *A Passage to India*.

Every time a reader experiences a work of art, it is in a sense created anew. Fundamentally, when we speak of understanding a work, we are actually reporting on what we have made of the signs on the page. Seeking to convey a particular sense of life, the author has set down that pattern of signs. Drawing on our own resources, we each have called forth and synthesized from that text a structure of concepts and sensations that for each of us is the work of art. Understanding requires an interpretation of this experience. We can agree on criteria for judging the relative validity of our interpretations. To what extent we have fulfilled the author's intentions is a separate question that again requires agreed-on criteria of evidence. But always we must return to the signs on the page, to see whether they support those intentions and interpretations.

Hence, even when limited to clarification of the student's understanding of the literary work, the teacher finds himself concerned with the student's personality and background and with the whole range of facts, problems, and theories implied by the work. The student will not experience it (or understand it) in a vacuum. The heightened sensuous observation, the keener and subtler perception of human emotions and actions will not etch themselves on a blank page. The interests, ideas, and feelings that the student brings enter into the transaction with the sequence of signs to create the structure of ideas and emotions that constitute the work. As the student is led to clarify his own sense of it, the teacher will be able to lead him to the various kinds of knowledge that will enable him to achieve the experiences offered by this particular text.

Thus, the clarification of the reader's personal understanding of the novel or poem or play carries with it a responsibility to the text itself. He seeks to recapture the particular approach to nature or society that dominates the evoked work. He notes the particular kind of awareness it embodies—whether it be the stark terror of "The Pit and the Pendulum" or the sense of time and slow change of *To the Lighthouse*. He becomes self-critical to see whether his own emphasis is supported by the text. He returns to it to make sure that he has done justice to the particular words in their particular order—sound and rhythm, image and metaphor, structure and point of view, indications of tone, clues to character. The discovery of what he overlooked will be as valuable in revealing his own blind spots and emotional fixations as it will be in giving him a sounder participation in the work itself.

The import of any work will remain thoroughly personal, since it is re-created by a specific personality with its own sense of values. Thus there is not necessarily only one "correct" interpretation of the significance of a given work. Not even an author's statement of his aims can be considered definitive. The text exists as a separate entity, a set of marks on a page, that may or may not fulfill his intentions and can possess for us more values than he foresaw. We must of necessity draw on our own reservoir of past experience to create what we understand to be the work.

Nevertheless, the student should be led to discover that some interpretations are more defensible than others. A complex work such as *Hamlet* offers the basis for various interpretations; yet their acceptability will depend, first, on whether they take into account as many as possible of the verbal signs present in the text and, second, on whether they do not imply signs that are not present in it.

An interpretation of *Hamlet*, no matter how subtle, that ignored the protagonist's soliloquies or his conversations with his mother would obviously be inadequate. Similarly, an interpretation that assumed ideas and attitudes for which no basis could be found in the text or ignored the fact that the language has changed since Elizabethan times would certainly be capricious. Thus, understanding of the work can be nourished through study of what is sometimes called background materials.

An undistorted vision of the work of art requires a consciousness of one's own preconceptions and prejudices concerning the situations presented in the work, in contrast to the basic attitudes toward life assumed in the re-created work. Often the reader integrates the work into a context of psychological or moral theories different from those that the author probably possessed. Always, therefore, a full understanding of literature requires both a consciousness of the reader's own angle of refraction and any information that can illuminate the author's implicit assumptions.

Students will benefit from their cooperative attempt to embrace all phases of the work in their formulation of its dominant effect. An example of this is a discussion of Keats's "The Eve of St. Agnes." A number of the students first spoke of the poem as a delightful story of romantic love. Others, accepting this characterization of the poem, condemned as irrelevant and jarring the introduction of the old Beadsman, the tombs, and the cold chapel in the opening of the poem and the death of old Angela and the Beadsman at the end. The group then found it necessary to decide what function these details might serve. They reread the text more carefully and decided that these elements provided an emotional background or undertone for the glowing colors and medieval atmosphere of the lovers' story. The contrast enhanced the warmth and sensuous vividness of the episode, threw over it an atmosphere of remoteness in time and space, and interwove the elegiac theme of death and the passing of all lovely things. The discussion stimulated the students to attend to all the components of the work, the minor chords as well as the major. Out of this came a fuller and more adequate response.

The effort to organize all the elements present in the text may also lead to considerations of human life and literary history. Thus the students' discussion of "The Eve of St. Agnes" helped make them aware of the presence in much of Keats's poetry of the sense that

> Ay, in the very temple of Delight
> Veiled Melancholy has her sovran shrine.[1]

They sought in Keats's letters and in the story of his brief life and literary enthusiasms the source of this feeling for the fleetingness of joy and beauty. They placed the work in the context of the life and personality of the author. Note, however, that the movement here was from interpretation of the text to author's life. This is diametrically opposed to the usual procedure in textbooks and many classrooms. To derive an

---

[1]Keats, "Ode on Melancholy."

interpretation of a text from the author's life or stated intentions is, of course, critically indefensible.

To see the writer as part of a literary tradition can also clarify personal response, especially for the more sophisticated students. Melodramatic or inconsistent elements in the form and plots of Shakespeare's plays may no longer trouble the reader when placed in the setting of Elizabethan theatrical traditions. Similarly, the attempt to differentiate between the special type of sensibility of different members of the same literary movement, such as Wordsworth and Coleridge or Conrad and James, will heighten perception of the special quality of the effects each sought to produce.

Thus students may find themselves embarked on a study of the biographical and literary background of the work. They will come to understand better the particular medium of expression that the author selected. They may see how reactions against the dead weight of literary tradition or the exhaustion of an earlier vein of literary sensibility, as in the case of Wordsworth or T. S. Eliot, will have led him to his particular emphasis. They will thus gain a profounder sense of the communal basis of even the most highly individualized insights and emotions.

The desire to understand a particular work will produce ever-widening circles of interest. Yet the focus of these concerns should continue to be the student's own sense of the work and his desire to clarify and refine his perception of it. Knowledge about the author's life and the literary influences acting on him will create the need for understanding the intellectual and philosophical, the social and economic conditions surrounding him. If the work is not a contemporary one, the contrasts and similarities between the conditions of that past age and the present will illuminate ways in which present-day reactions to the work may differ from those of the author's contemporaries.

Robinson Crusoe is for us the absorbing tale of a human being's ingenuity in wresting a livelihood from nature; the account of his religious meditations and conversion is much less stirring. The much pitied Pamela may seem to the young girl of today merely a shrewd and designing hussy. Hamlet's perplexities about whether the Ghost may be a benevolent visitant returned from purgatory or an evil spirit who has assumed his father's form seem unimportant to those who question the existence of ghosts at all. Similarly, there is much in the work today that has special and perhaps hitherto unexploited overtones. Hamlet's hesitations and melancholy questionings in a world out of joint have a compelling significance for the twentieth-century reader.

Here again, there will be profit in seeing that the reader's own reactions, like the work of art, are the organic expression not only of a particular individual but also of a particular cultural setting. Literary history will not seem like a clear stream flowing between banks that enclose but do not affect it. Rather it will be seen that the literary stream is fed by thousands of rivulets that have their sources in the surrounding intellectual and social environment.

These concentric circles of interest focused on the student's sense of a work will involve him in still deeper concern with human relations. He will see in the work a specific reflection of general ideas concerning good and evil. He will work out the scale of values that the writer applies to personalities and to relations among people. The student will apprehend Shakespeare's sense of the individual dominating even an adverse fate by the intensity and resonance of his nature. Or he will adjust to Jane Austen's human scale, her characters measured against only the society and the world they have created. Or he will share Hardy's sense of the individual human being as a helpless atom in the cosmic stream.

The young reader will be especially alert to the treatment of character. The writer does more than present human beings in action; he offers clues to the motives and the repercussions of those actions. He shows, too, many of the forces that shape human personality and conduct. Pamela's constant reference to the moral and social code differs greatly from Tom Jones's uncalculating behavior. George Eliot, William Makepeace Thackeray, Aldous Huxley, and D. H. Lawrence each provide a different view of the determining traits of human character. Often, too, the writer reveals the broader influences at work in the collective life of humanity. F. Scott Fitzgerald manifests the influence of social aspirations; Emile Zola and John Steinbeck show the force of economic pressures; Emily Brontë and D. H. Lawrence, each in a different way, evoke the power of human impulse and passion. An understanding of the individual sensibility or individual problems presented by the text may thus lead to an understanding of the implicit system of values and the sense of the relation of human beings to the world.

Such analysis of the work, such acquisition of new insights and information, will have value only as it is linked up with the student's own primary response to the work. His judgment on it will thus be thrown into sharper relief; for if he is indeed functioning freely and spontaneously, he will undoubtedly reflect not only on the work itself but also on the problems it presents and on the personalities and actions of the characters.

The attempt to work out the author's system of values and assumptions about individuals and society should enable the student to discover the unspoken assumptions behind his own judgment. His conclusions about this particular work imply the unarticulated theories of human conduct and ideas of the good that shape his thinking.

During group discussions the students, in a spirit of friendly challenge, can lead one another to work out the implications of the positions they have taken. They may discover that they are making assertions based on fundamentally contradictory concepts. A student who espoused with equal vigor the causes of Pamela and Tess and maintained that each of them was virtuous, found herself involved in arriving at some consistent understanding of that term. Becky Sharp and her humbler daughter Scarlett O'Hara led another student into similar difficulties. By bringing their generalizations into the open, students may be led to feel the need of putting their mental houses in order. They will see how often they have been dominated by ideas only because they have heard them repeated again and again. They will develop a more critical, questioning attitude and will see the need of a more reasoned foundation for their thoughts and judgments, a more consistent system of values.

The teacher's challenge, as well as the challenge of the other students, will stimulate each of them to search for knowledge that will clarify the problems he encounters and will supply the basis for valid judgments. Here the teacher of literature may legitimately see it as his function to point to the existence of helpful bodies of knowledge. He will have made a valuable contribution if the student leaves his experience of the literary work eager to learn what the psychologist, the sociologist, and the historian have to offer him. The core of direct emotional experience at the heart of the critical process outlined here should keep alive the sense of the human import of the more objective knowledge these experts provide. Thus, a teacher of tenth-graders in an affluent and divorce-ridden community was nonplussed by their rejection of *Ethan Frome*. They refused to take it seriously: the whole story was contrived, they said, because, to begin with, Ethan's meek acceptance of his lot was unthinkable. As the teacher led them to look more closely at the text and as they grappled with their own reactions, they discovered how little they knew about recent history and about economic, social, and cultural climates different from their own. They learned something about these matters, but they also learned something about entering into the structure of assumptions of a literary work. They gained both literary and social perspective.

Just such spontaneous recourse to the other disciplines was illustrated by a group of freshmen in a woman's college who had read Ibsen's *A Doll House*. One of the students attacked the play as profoundly insignificant since "Nora was a fool to have become so dependent on her husband." Others objected that she could do nothing else. You couldn't judge Nora, they pointed out, as you would a woman of today. Her relationship with her father and with Torvald reflected the position of women in the nineteenth century. Yet even those who recognized the historical background of the play could give very little accurate information about the status of women at that time. The students tried to find out what women's legal and political rights were in the nineteenth century as contrasted with the present. They discovered the differences among periods, countries, and even various states within the United

States. They emphasized the extent of woman's emancipation since the date of the play but admitted that some problems still persisted. They were also interested to discover the extent to which the greater emancipation had transformed women's relationships with husbands and children.

These insights deepened the students' sense of the play's significance. They no longer tended to regard Nora as an individual solving an individual problem. They considered her to a large extent the victim of a vast complex of conditions. They saw Torvald's attitude as the expression of a view of his rights sanctioned by the whole force of the society. To see the individual as shaped by a great many factors rooted in the society about him creates a broader perspective. The students also realized the value of suspending judgment until they had acquired a basis of scholarly information.

At certain points in the discussion the teacher had had pedantic twinges of conscience about the attention paid to subjects that could not be strictly defined as literary. He later realized that he need not have had qualms. Increased awareness of the complexities of human relationships led the students toward a fuller appreciation of the play itself. Some of the students became more aware of Ibsen's dramatic methods. Quite spontaneously, they discussed his extraordinary economy in conveying significant information about Nora's past relations with her father and her husband. They pointed out the clear structure of the play with its swift presentation of complex problems and its skillful creation of suspense. The final scene, although it presented no psychological or social solution, was judged theatrically effective because it involved overt action that clearly defined Nora's dilemma. Because they themselves raised the questions, there was nothing academically remote about these matters of form and technique; the students saw them as the author's choices, intimately related to what he was seeking to convey.

Background materials already receive much attention in school and college literature programs. The danger, however, is that such study tends to become an end in itself. This chapter has proposed a major criterion of the usefulness of background information: it will have value only when the student feels the need of it and when it is assimilated into the student's experience of particular literary works.

Challenged to establish the validity of his interpretation and judgment of the work, he will be stimulated both to examine the text more closely and to scrutinize the adequacy of his past experience and basic assumptions. He will test whether what he brings to the text has enabled him to do justice to its potentialities. This may lead him to probe further into literary techniques and forms. It may also impel him to acquire various types of knowledge—literary and social history, biography, philosophy, psychology, anthropology—that may deepen his understanding of the work. Such a process of clarification and enrichment of successive literary experiences will foster sound critical habits. From this kind of literary study there should flow, too, enhanced understanding of himself and the life about him. The coming chapters will consider in greater detail how literary sensitivity may contribute to such insight.

PART THREE

LITERARY SENSITIVITY AS THE SOURCE OF INSIGHT

CHAPTER 6

SOME BASIC SOCIAL CONCEPTS

Teachers of literature deal inevitably with its human implications. Must they then become experts in the social sciences? The answer obviously is no. But they are responsible for scrutinizing their assumptions about human nature and society in the light of contemporary thought. This chapter will turn away from literature itself to clarify some of the concepts about human relations that underlie the preceding discussion of the relation of social insight to literary sensitivity and judgment. This may elucidate a few of the key ideas with which the teacher should be familiar and which are more important than any of the specific findings of the various disciplines that study human behavior.

Some of these ideas have in recent years become generally current and are undoubtedly already known to the reader. They are formulated here to provide a coherent basis for considering their special relevance to the sphere of the teacher of literature. Chapters 7 and 8 will explore how basic social concepts may illuminate, and be illuminated by, the study of literature.

An axiom of contemporary educational thought is that, under the unprecedented and rapidly changing conditions of present-day life, to give youth a rigid set of dogmatic ideas and habits is a certain method of producing insecurity and bewilderment. Members of the older generations know that many of the habitual attitudes and ideas they took most for granted have with changed conditions become inappropriate and even antisocial. Habits of thrift were once much prized, only to have the economists decree that the socially valuable rule was to spend and invest, not hoard, until they again urged the need for saving. Women dutifully restricted the scope of their interests to the home, only to find that the functions of the home itself had changed and that as mothers, wives, and citizens they needed to develop broader interests and understanding. And the two-income family has created many practical and emotional problems. The traditional belief was that every American of any ability could rise unaided above the economic and social stratum into which he was born; now the ideal of equal opportunity is buttressed by a great network of laws. The doctrine that punitive measures prevent crime has been replaced by the view that the criminal is a symptom of weaknesses in our educational and social systems and should be cured, not simply punished. In politics, in the relations between men and women, in the adjustments between parents and children, in all phases of our personal and social life, similar discrepancies between habitual attitudes and changed circumstances have developed. And in some areas and some groups, the new attitudes have produced reactionary backlashes. Everything points toward a prodigious acceleration of changes demanding readjustments during the lifetime of those who are adolescents and children today.

Obviously, a rigid set of dogmatic ideas and fixed responses to specific conditions is the worst kind of equipment for the contemporary youth. As soon as actual conditions prove that his passively acquired code is useless or even harmful, he has nothing else to cling to. Having been made dependent on ready-made props, he will be precipitated into painful insecurity. This kind of insecurity, this craving for some easy, reassuring formula, makes the youth of other countries and sometimes of our own a ready prey to those enemies of democracy who hold out the delusive bait of ready-made solutions to all problems. Unprepared to think independently, the young man and woman seek to return to the infantile state in which there is no responsibility to make decisions; they are thus willing to blindly follow some "leader" whose tools they become.

The conditions of human life, the complexities of the interaction of personality on personality, the shifting images offered by human history, and the rapid flux of the life about us show how evasive of reality a dogmatic approach to human relations would be. Our literary heritage itself, with its reflections of the varied and contrasting forms of human life and personality, with its expression of so many different life goals and values, is eloquent rebuttal of any absolutistic approach to life. However satisfactory may be the system of values the teacher has worked out for himself, he is not justified in teaching it to his students, as one might teach a method of solving a problem in calculus. There is no proof that the conditions of life this generation of students will face or the highly diverse personal problems they will have to solve will be commensurable with any arbitrary measuring rod provided by the teacher.

The teacher, however, must do more than merely avoid explicit dogmatism. He must also avoid the insidious unconscious inculcation of dogma. Only a bundle of miscellaneous and unintegrated responses—in other words, not a functioning individual at all—could avoid conveying some attitudes toward experience. The teacher will inevitably possess some scheme of values, some particular way of approaching and judging people and situations. He should be critically aware of these attitudes instead of imposing them indirectly and unconsciously on his students.

The teacher should not, however, try to pose as a completely objective person. The assumption of a mask of unemotional objectivity or impartial omniscience is one reason why teachers and college professors sometimes seem not quite human to their students. A much more wholesome educational situation is created when the teacher is a really live person who has examined his own attitudes and assumptions and who, when appropriate, states them frankly and honestly. He does not have to seem to possess all the answers, which the students then need only passively absorb. Admitting his uncertainties and perplexities will stimulate the students to join him in the common task of seeking the knowledge that may clarify these problems.

But even this awareness of his own point of view and his frankness are not enough. The teacher needs to see his philosophy as only one of the possible approaches to life, from which his students should be given the opportunity to select for themselves. Tolerance of other points of view is extremely important for the teacher—an attitude those who are insecure and fearful of challenges to their authority find most difficult to maintain.

To rule out the conscious or unconscious transmission of an explicit set of ready-made answers to personal problems and ready-made judgments on people and society does not, however, mean an end to the teacher's responsibility, nor does it imply a nihilistic approach to life. Reluctance to impose a dogmatic philosophy may lead to an equally dangerous attitude of noncommittal relativism that refuses to admit any standards and tends to produce a paralysis of judgment on the part of the student. Such pseudoliberalism can lead to the feeling that there is nothing to believe, that there are no values to be sought in this confused world. Wholesale negativism will leave youth completely unprepared. In times of crisis when the inevitable choices must be made, they will tend to fall back on the old, stereotyped attitudes or to follow chance, irrational appeals.

Although no one code should be taught dogmatically, the need for the individual to work out his own principles and his own hierarchy of values is imperative. The task of education is to supply him with the knowledge, the mental habits, and the emotional impetus that will enable him to independently solve his problems—hence the teacher's need to clarify for himself the basic approaches to experience and the basic concepts concerning human nature and society that will be a useful preparation for the adolescent facing the uncertain future.

In order that the student may be prepared for the unpredictable demands that life will make on him, our schools and universities must be transformed, as C. S. Peirce said many years ago, from "institutions for teaching" into "institutions for learning." The student should go to school and college, not for the purpose of being taught ready-made formulas and fixed attitudes, but so that he may develop the will to learn. He must gain command of techniques that make possible a constantly closer approximation to the truth, and he must develop the flexibility of mind and temperament necessary for the translation of that critical sense of truth into actual behavior. Instead of accepting judgments in whole cloth, he must acquire a curiosity about the causes of human actions and social conditions; he must be ready to revise accepted hypotheses in the light of new information; he must learn where to turn for this information. He needs, in short, to develop a dynamic sense of life, a feeling that an understanding of causes makes for greater control of conditions. Instead of drifting with the stream of circumstance, he will be able to set up more rational personal and social goals and to understand better the conditions under which they can be achieved.

The implication here is that the social sciences have something positive to offer toward a solution of personal problems and toward a framework of ideas that will make possible constructive social action. To arouse in the student a desire for social understanding, the teacher of literature needs himself to be aware that such knowledge exists or at any rate that the foundation for it has been laid by the social sciences.

The literature teacher's responsibility toward the kind of information represented by the social sciences can be summed up in general terms: He should be aware of the existence of the various behavioral sciences and should possess a general understanding of what phases of human life they treat. Even though he may not have a detailed knowledge of these fields, he should at least understand their methods of approach and the basic concepts concerning human beings and society that they have developed. Without such knowledge he will probably be very effectively undoing in the English classroom whatever the teachers of social studies may have succeeded in accomplishing. Moreover, there is no reason why the English teacher's knowledge should stop at this minimum level. The training of English teachers should include carefully planned work in the behavioral sciences, and the practicing teacher should recognize his responsibility for constantly adding to his knowledge in these fields as well as in the field of literature.

Teachers of literature and the arts often think of themselves as saving the student from the stultifying effects of our present scientific age. The early Romantic opposition to the scientist as one who "murders to dissect" lingers on.[1] Teachers of English tend to consider themselves defenders of a lost cause, keepers of an imaginative or emotional oasis in the midst of our materialistic, science-ridden life.

This attitude toward science is to some extent due to a prevalent confusion between the effects of science and the effect of the practical, materialistic emphasis of our society. It is not science, but the way in which it has been misused, to which the English teacher should feel himself opposed. More and more evidence is accruing to demonstrate that science, properly exploited, may eventually so reduce time devoted to work that the entire population could have the leisure and the energy for the rich imaginative life that literature and the arts offer.

Even some of those who will admit this continue to assume that there is a fundamental and irreconcilable opposition

[1] Wordsworth, "The Tables Turned."

between science and literature.[2] It is still fashionable in some circles to stress the complexity of human personality and human affairs as an insuperable obstacle to the application of scientific method. The disagreements and conflicts among different schools of thought are pointed to as proof. Only lack of contact with the finest and soundest expressions of the scientific spirit, however, could enable opponents of the social sciences to make these unqualified claims.

An understanding of the spirit of scientific method and its application to human affairs is the most fundamental social concept that the teacher of literature should possess. A lively sense of the essential nature of scientific method will compensate for lack of detailed knowledge of the social sciences. In fact, without this basic understanding of the scientific attitude, any specific facts or theories drawn from the social sciences that he might introduce into discussions of literature would very likely be confusing to his students.

The artist, we are reminded, always conveys the special quality, the peculiar attributes, the unique flavor, of some personality or situation. The scientist, his artistic opponents assert, reduces life to its lowest common denominators and centers attention on whatever in a particular object makes it like every other one of its class. The layperson tends to think of the contribution of the scientist as being a body of laws or a system of classifications to be applied to nature and society.

[2] Another aspect of the literary person's antagonism to science is his reluctance to recognize that scientific works are often also literary works. See T. H. Huxley's *Man's Place in Nature*, Charles Darwin's *Origin of Species*, Adam Smith's *Wealth of Nations*, Arthur S. Eddington's *Stars and Atoms*, William James's *Principles of Psychology*, Loren Eiseley's *The Immense Journey*, Rachel Carson's *Silent Spring*.

This on the surface would seem to negate the artistic approach to life, which seeks to individualize rather than to generalize. But this view of science does it gross injustice.

Wholesale application of broad categories, lumping together many personalities or situations under broad labels, adoption of stereotyped attitudes or sweeping judgments are alien to the very spirit of science. Contemporary logic and theories of knowledge recognize the spontaneous quality of existence, the novel elements in nature, as much as do the arts. Part of the scientist's duty is to note in a given situation those factors that are unique or that are met here in new combinations that differentiate it from any other situations of the same type. Of course, the scientist recognizes that the human and physical world offers certain recurrent patterns on which can be built theories concerning the correlation of their various elements. These theories, he hopes, will enable us to understand the consequences that flow from particular combinations of qualities or events.

This desire of the scientist to work out fundamentally recurrent patterns evidently has given rise to the idea that the scientific approach is inimical to the artistic. Unfortunately, the social scientists themselves are largely responsible for the prevalent misconception. The tendency to take physics as the model science led to the mid-century dominance of behaviorism and the consequent narrowing of research problems and methods. Economists, sociologists, political theorists, and historians have too often developed a technical jargon that makes their findings seem remote from ordinary life. They must deal with mass movements, statistical data, the broad sweep of events; yet this should not entail neglect of the individual human behavior and personal motivations that give rise to these

social phenomena. With the decline of behaviorism, the cognitive and other schools of psychology have begun to reinstate
the study of consciousness and the use of introspective and
ethnological methods of research. The more creative thinkers
in all these fields are aware of the human import of their
work. And social scientists have begun to recognize that they
too are narrators and users of rhetorical devices. The view of
the social sciences presented here rests on such trends in the
hope that they will be more and more generally operative. It
is essential to see how the scientist uses his generalizations or
broad categories. His tentative generalizations are offered as a
framework of ideas and guiding principles to be applied to
specific situations. This framework will help to identify in a
given situation those elements that possess a particular characteristic pattern. But, equally important, they help him further discriminate wherein this situation differs from other
situations.

This process in no way violates the approach of the artist to
life; the artist is not concerned only with the unique. If every
author were entirely different from every other human being
and if each of us were unique in all respects, there could be
no art at all.

Fundamentally, comprehension of the author's theme must
be based on the general or typical emotions or situations that
are present in the work he is creating. At the same time, he
seeks to render its peculiar and special overtones, its subtle
departures from the typical. For example, there is much that is
unusual in the personalities and situations presented in Hardy's
Jude the Obscure; yet without the elements common to many
human beings, no matter how specially combined in the
character of Jude or Sue, we should not be able to understand

the work at all. Intent on the peculiar qualities or the strangeness of the situation created by the artist, we assume ideas concerning the general or the characteristic. The point of view of the artist requires a recognition of recurrent patterns, paralleled by the recognition that every personality and every situation has its own unique qualities.

The artist orders and classifies the data offered by life as much as does the scientist. The artist aims to make us experience imaginatively, to live through, these common patterns and special qualities; the scientist seeks to discover a framework of ideas concerning what is general and what is unique that we may apply to such experiences. This framework of knowledge, this set of guiding principles, offered by the scientist is never irrelevant to the experience derived from either life or art.

Science starts with the complexity of human nature and society but conquers the variety and intricacy of its subject matter by working out fruitful principles of explanation for limited phases of it. *Divide et impera*, the old Roman principle for success in conquering enemies, is the principle that science has used in overcoming the complexity of its materials. By approaching human affairs from different angles, anthropology, economics, psychology, and sociology have been able to discover a considerable body of information that furnishes the basis for a provisional understanding of human beings.

The social sciences share the tentativeness of any scientific finding. Since the 1970s, the development of Einsteinian and subatomic physics has led to a change in the scientific atmosphere. Without denying the effectiveness of the older Newtonian physics for some problems, the new paradigm assumes that humankind is not separate from nature but a part of it, transacting with the environment. This does not deny the value of the objective approach but affirms that there are no absolute scientific truths, that any observation presupposes an observer with particular assumptions or interests.

The social scientist recognizes that, like all other human beings, he is the product of a particular culture, a particular social environment, and that the assumptions assimilated from them must be taken into account as he works out a certain hypothesis concerning human personality and society and then attempts to discover all the facts that will tend to prove or disprove it. He admits that his results are always tentative, that he brings particular social and cultural assumptions to his observations, and that new information may lead to the adoption of new theories. He recognizes that, as we shall see later, comparison of different cultures provides perspective.

This very tentativeness of the scientific attitude has been said to make it extremely unsettling to the child or the adolescent. It is feared that great mental insecurity will result from the fact that there is nothing absolutely certain, that all ideas are subject to future revision. Such insecurity evidently arises when the scientific spirit is not thoroughly presented. Though prepared to relinquish belief in any particular findings or conclusions of science, we can still hold firmly to our faith in the scientific method itself.

Scientific knowledge is essentially a cooperative product. Only as a fact or theory is tested and verified by many competent minds, often widely scattered in time and space, does that fact or theory come to be accepted. The important thing is not that one generation rejects a particular theory of psychology worked out by the preceding (paralleling, say, the substitution of an Einsteinian for a Newtonian physics) but that there are innumerable minds all over the world working at these problems, building on what others have done before them, and contributing, each in his own way, to a greater approximation toward sound understanding. Bringing up young people to base their security on the idea of absolute certainty has led only to disillusionment and insecurity. They will be much better equipped if they place their faith in the cooperative striving toward greater and greater exactitude and universality that is the essence of the scientific spirit.[3]

The social sciences already offer much that can be assimilated into the fabric of our everyday life. If they do not provide rigid formulas for action, it is precisely because the scientific spirit stresses the need for understanding the special conditions that qualify any particular situation. Our society is seeking more and more to take advantage of what the social sciences can already explain about the various factors involved in its operations. Understanding of the typical as well as the special characteristics of any problem is the prelude to more intelligent and more successful solutions. The teacher of literature should

[3] "What is science? The dictionary will say that it is systematized knowledge. Dictionary definitions, however, are too apt to repose upon derivations; which is as much as to say that they neglect too much the later steps in the evolution of meanings. Mere knowledge, though it be systematized, may be a dead memory; while by science we all habitually mean a living and growing body of truth. . . . That which constitutes science, then, is not so much correct conclusions, as it is a correct method. But the method of science is itself a scientific result. It did not spring out of the brain of a beginner: it was a historic attainment and a scientific achievement. So that not even this method ought to be regarded as essential to the beginnings of science. That which is essential, however, is the scientific spirit, which is determined not to rest satisfied with existing opinions, but to press on to the real truth of nature. To science once enthroned in this sense, among any people, science in every other sense is heir apparent" (Peirce 6.302).

133

cling to this understanding of the flexible, questing nature of the scientific spirit—its readiness to utilize the insights that collective endeavors have thus far attained and its dynamic sense of truth.

These overarching considerations will protect the literary specialist from the danger of a dogmatic application of scientific theories or a substitution of scientific terminology for scientific insight. A bane of many discussions about human beings (and especially of much educational theory) is the use of a scientific jargon that masks from the speaker and the listener their lack of real understanding.

An illustration of this type of misuse of science is the employment of the jargon of psychological terminology. Recall, for instance, those people who swallow Freudian or Adlerian theory unquestioningly and who use their various categories loosely and lavishly. Accepting such labels as the *Oedipus fixation* or the *inferiority complex*, they evidently feel that they have clarified their understanding of a personality when they have applied one of these labels to it. Their facile use of such terms merely reveals their lack of understanding of the psychoanalytic approach itself. Any of the accounts of particular analyses recorded by Freud or his disciples reflects their sense of how special each case is. The operation of any such general emotional patterns as the Oedipus fixation or the inferiority complex differs in its particulars in each case. Even the recognition of these broad, typical patterns was arrived at only after prolonged study of the specific cases.[4] Having determined the

---

[4] In fact, this recognition of human variability and the need for an ever broader base for generalization explains psychiatrists' current revision of their theories in the light of a study of other cultures. See some early contributions: Karen Horney,

general pattern, the analyst tried to see how it had worked itself out in terms of the particular personality and the particular situation in which the person found himself. Only in this way, not by a mere process of labeling, could the psychiatrist offer any help. Equally valid illustrations of misuse of terminology might be drawn from other schools of psychology and other social sciences, for example, the nineteenth-century use of *the survival of the fittest* or the indiscriminate application of phrases such as *the law of supply and demand, the class struggle* (economics), *the relativity of morals* (anthropology), *evolution and progress* (sociology), *the inevitable decay of civilizations* (Spenglerian history), or *the decentering of the subject* (structuralism, poststructuralism).

That the teacher of literature inevitably deals with psychological problems does not argue that he should learn all the systems of classification of human types or all the theories of behavior. Nor should the discussion of literature necessarily be at all concerned with psychological classifications or terminology. Suppose a student docilely learned to classify literary characters according to whether they were extroverts or introverts or according to whether they showed signs of an inferiority complex or according to whether their actions could be phrased in Freudian or Jungian terms. Does it seem likely that such a student would be much better off than one who had passively learned to think in terms of the good people and the bad people or to classify them as types, such as the gossip, the bully, the old maid, or who might have been led to consider them only as Aryan and non-Aryan? Any rigid a priori classification used in this way merely becomes an obstacle to

The Neurotic Personality of Our Time; James S. Plant, *Personality and the Cultural Pattern*; John Dollard, *Criteria for the Life History*.

understanding people. As soon as he has labeled them, the student feels relieved of any further obligation to get at their inner qualities, to understand their special motivation, or to observe as many factors as possible that may enter into the external conditions influencing them.

Hence the teacher of literature should be conversant not so much with the details as with the spirit of psychological inquiry. If the teacher himself espouses any one school of psychology (and that might lend his teaching a consistency that the remarks about "human nature" uttered in most literature courses lack), he should be willing to recognize the existence of other schools and the student's right to know about them. For if the student is given a sense of the approach to human nature out of which psychological inquiry springs, he will be ready and eager to seek from the psychologists themselves the tentative answers they offer to his questions.

The same principle holds for the other behavioral sciences. The teacher of literature needs to convey the spirit of scrupulous inquiry and the flexible approach that is their characteristic. His contribution may be phrased largely in negative terms: he will not impose a dogmatic framework on the concept of human nature; he will not allow conventional assumptions to go unchallenged; he will not permit his students to fall back on pat, stereotyped formulas. In positive terms, he will awaken his students to an awareness of the complexity of human behavior and society and will stimulate them to seek the understanding that the social scientists are endeavoring to establish. He will share the psychologist's belief that knowledge concerning human nature must be the result of careful, controlled observation, that any hypothesis must be tested and retested, and that we must be particularly on our guard against imputing to human beings those traits or those psychological mechanisms that would justify or rationalize our own habitual methods of dealing with them.

What, then, are some of the basic concepts that should permeate the discussion when the reading of literature raises questions about human nature and experience? Perhaps an economical way of dealing with these questions within the limits of a chapter will be to start with certain ideas that often appear in the student's thinking and that the English teacher must therefore address. With these current conceptions as starting points, it will be possible to see what light the scientific approach can offer. This will have relevance to the problems that teachers constantly face in the classroom and may indicate how certain concepts can function in ordinary thinking about people and society. The object will be to further illustrate the value of a firm hold on certain fundamental concepts and the importance of bringing such concepts to bear on current attitudes.

One of the most glaring of the widespread assumptions encountered in students' reactions to literature is the traditional voluntaristic conception of human nature and conduct mentioned briefly in the first chapter. This view is based on the idea that any behavior can be interpreted as having been willed by the actor. The assumption is that in all situations the individual is free to accept or reject various modes of behavior. If a person is pleasant or unpleasant, social or antisocial, it is largely because he wishes to be so. One needs only to know the rules, the commandments of the society about one, in order to be provided with a guide to one's own conduct and a code for sitting in judgment on the conduct of others.

Although, stated thus baldly, these assumptions seem almost to condemn themselves and although this view has lost its hold in many areas of our political and social life, it still often dominates the average person's thinking. We see this reflected in his actual judgments on people or in the attitudes toward whole groups of people.

Scientific investigation and analysis, particularly in the fields of psychology, sociology, and anthropology, have during the past quarter century generally undermined this oversimplified theory of human nature and conduct. The plasticity of the human creature is being recognized. The human personality is thought of by the scientist as a complex of qualities and habits that are the end result of a great many different factors converging on and interacting with the individual organism. The innate physical and mental endowments of the individual are not ignored, but the individual, as we meet him functioning in society, is seen as the product of the particular ways in which these innate elements have been molded, stimulated, or repressed by external conditions.

The conception of the child as a little savage whose rebellious will must be broken and who must be coerced into civilized ways lost its currency at least a century ago. Equally mythical is the Romantic conception of the child as an unspoiled angel who is corrupted into the ways of the world as its "prison walls" close about him.[5] Instead, the human creature is seen to possess potentialities for an infinite variety of behavior. The circumstances into which he is born, the temperaments that act on him in his earlier years, the kinds of stimulation or repression to which he is subjected, and the

[5] Wordsworth, Immortality Ode 5.10.

satisfactions or frustrations he meets will have a powerful influence in patterning the mental and physical potentialities with which he is born.

Present-day psychology is devoting a great deal of attention to attempting to discover significant forces that contribute to molding the personality. To these forces are attributed differing degrees of importance by the various schools of psychology. Some focus their attention on basic biological factors. Others stress more the emotional relationships with the parents and with brothers and sisters as important factors in patterning the child's personality. Still others stress the social environment in which the child grows up; the economic conditions that surround him, whether an affluent environment permits unhampered activity or whether, as in the city slums, he is often forced to seek an outlet for his energy in destructive and underhand activities.

No matter which aspect of the forces acting on the child is stressed and no matter how much contemporary schools of psychology may differ concerning the methods, behavioristic or introspective, of studying the individual, they share this basic approach to human development. The behavior, the emotional patterns, the ideas and dominant drives that make up a personality are seen as the result of a process by which the particular mental and emotional habits are, so to speak, learned. Thus, a particular temperament or a particular action cannot be judged in itself. It has to be seen in relation to the whole stream of the individual's life, the various influences to which he has been subjected, the situations and events through which he has passed. This does not eliminate the concept of the will. But it does mean that we have to go beyond the particular action to see the context within which the "will" operates.

This view of the plasticity of human nature has been strengthened by the sociologists and the anthropologists, attacking the problem from other angles. From the immediate environment, particularly from the family group, the child acquires not only such things as physical mannerisms, habits of gesture and language but also emotional habits and major ideas concerning behavior. Similarly, the particular social group of which the child is a part contributes certain elements to his personality patterns and his mental and emotional habits. One illustration of how the ideas and attitudes of the surrounding society are incorporated into the individual personality is the acquisition from the environment of ideas of masculinity and femininity. These mold the individual's own behavior and his expectations concerning the behavior of others. In the same way are built up the patterns of feeling and behavior, the expectations and values that constitute the content of the individual's personality and sense of life.

In our own heterogeneous society this concept of the influence of the family and social environment on the individual is particularly important. The effort to fully carry out the democratic dream has brought the realization that in our highly complex civilization, people may be the products of practically different subcultures. In our cities, for instance, we find people who superficially seem to be conforming to the ways of life of the average city dweller and yet who, coming from different parts of the country and from different family, social, and ethnic backgrounds, may be motivated by entirely different conceptions of personal relationships. The young couple who have met and married in the city may represent the conjunction of two different patterns; the young husband coming from a small New England town with its leisurely tempo and thrifty, disciplined, undemonstrative way of life will have very different images of behavior from his wife, who may have grown up in the easygoing atmosphere of a western town where heartiness and vigorous action are valued more than discipline and decorum. Or they may have very different images of what constitutes the family, one perhaps used to a household in which several generations shared their activities and their pleasures and troubles and the other thinking of the family in terms of the biological unit of parents and children, seeing all others as outsiders toward whom no responsibility need be felt. Other patterns may reflect the high incidence of divorce or the home built around an unmarried mother.

Beyond such broad patterning factors exists an even more complex and perhaps even more powerful set of influences. The boy who has grown up as the subject of the excessive care and emotional attentions of a doting mother may seek in any other relationships as, for instance, in marriage, similar cherishing protection and emotional dependence. This may be so powerful that it prevents his assuming the emotional responsibilities usually associated with marriage and parenthood.

The anthropologists have contributed still another and broader framework within which to place this basic concept of psychological conditioning. By studying a great variety of societies or, to use the anthropological term, *cultures*, they have revealed the diversity of patterns into which humankind has poured its personal and group life. Around the universal activities of food getting, propagation, child rearing have been developed modes of behavior, types of personal relationships, ideas of good and evil, religious beliefs, social organizations, and economic and political mechanisms that result in cultures with seemingly nothing in common.

Some cultures may organize their economic life on the basis of the individualism of the Eskimo or on the basis of the economic communalism of the Zuni. Kinship may be reckoned according to matrilineal or patrilineal lines. The family may be organized on the basis of the biological unit of parents and children or on the system whereby a whole community constitutes the family group or in such a way that the child looks to his mother's brother as his guardian and protector rather than to his biological father. One folk may people the universe about them with malevolent spirits, another with benign spirits. Ethical codes may be set up that require the ruthless taking of human life or that deem it an unpardonable sin or, as in our own society, that make the taking of human life at times sinful murder and at other times (in war) a glorious social deed.

One culture may make the generous bestowal of property on others the means of social prestige, or, as in our own society, prestige may depend on the ability to accumulate and retain possessions. Some peoples may rear their children from the earliest age as a functioning part of the economic and social group, as among the Samoans; others may let them grow up almost completely outside the adult pattern, as among the Manus; or still others, like the Batciga, may let them create an organized child society of their own. For each item of social and personal relationships within any culture, other societies have erected not only contrasting and contradictory but almost incommensurable ideas and arrangements. Everything, from the structure of language or the ways of measuring time and indicating direction to social and economic organizations or ethical and religious codes, will reveal this extraordinary capacity of the human race to create diverse cultures on the basis of the biological needs of the individual and the group.

In terms of the individual, this implies, of course, that his personality, his needs and aims, will be molded by the particular cultural group in which he has been reared. Each culture tends to stimulate or nourish certain aspects of personality and to repress others. There would be a great difference in the resulting personality according to whether a particular human organism, whatever its innate tendencies, was born into a cultural pattern that values gentleness, moderation, and cooperativeness or into a culture that values aggressiveness, violence, and individualism. In one society the pugnacious, acquisitive man will be an admired leader; in another society he will be a misfit or an outcast. Everything from physical traits to the ability to dream dreams and see visions may receive different valuations in different cultures. An illustration of this from within our own cultural stream is the social value placed by medieval society on the seers of visions as opposed to our present-day skepticism. In other words, what is considered the approved or normal temperament or behavior in one culture, or even at one epoch in a civilization, may be disapproved of as abnormal in another.

The anthropological approach to the concept of normality is particularly useful to teachers of adolescents, since this is a problem that troubles many of them. Within the broad scale of temperaments and actions of which the human creature is potentially capable, different societies have placed the range of normality very differently. We especially need to recognize how powerful a hold the norms of our own group have on us. Whatever the concept of the normal, it is to a certain extent the result of historical causes, since ideas of normality have changed from country to country and from age to age. Therefore our own ideas of the normal have no particular divine sanction but must be judged rationally by their social effects.

Teachers sometimes fear that such a sense of the cultural relativity of norms will be unsettling to the adolescent. Will he not feel that there are no standards—that anything, any kind of behavior, is as good as any other? This, of course, is an attitude that could only lead to moral and intellectual chaos and should be carefully guarded against. Such a conclusion, however, can arise only out of a stress on one part of the anthropological facts. For if anthropology shows us the diversity of norms, it also shows us how closely personality and behavior are related to the whole framework of the culture.

The concept of the relativity of standards must be related to the anthropologists' emphasis on the need for seeing the culture as a whole. They warn against the tendency to think of different phases of society as distinct and unrelated. The ideas about physical beauty or attitudes toward property or the possession of intuitive powers in any one society will often tend to be colored by certain underlying drives, certain basic ways of envisioning human nature, certain values typical of the culture. Although it is unlikely that any culture is completely integrated—expecially such a complex culture as our own—the elements of culture influence one another:

> All the miscellaneous behavior directed toward getting a living, mating, warring, and worshipping the gods, is made over into consistent patterns in accordance with unconscious canons of choice that develop within the culture. Some cultures, like some periods of art, fail of such integration, and

about many others we know too little to understand the
motives that actuate them. But cultures at every level of complexity, even the simplest, have achieved it.   (48)

In the years since Ruth Benedict formulated this view of culture in her anthropological work *Patterns of Culture*, the concept has become basic, undergoing further definition and
elaboration. Parallel to the post-Einsteinian development in
the natural sciences, the importance of the observer in the
observation has been recognized. Anthropological study of
literate societies with a long history has led to emphasis on
the complexity of cultures, on the existence of multiple sub-
dominant strands. The flourishing of hermeneutics in recent
decades has been reflected in the description of culture as
underlying regularities of human experience implicit in the
formation of ordered clusters of significant symbols.

Hence, we must not view in isolation any detail of behavior in our own or any other society but must study it against
the background of the motives and emotions institutionalized
in that culture. The individual will be liberated from blind
subservience to the norms of his group, not by throwing over-
board all standards, but by seeing them in relation to the whole
complex of attitudes and values into which they fit.

Thus, it was not enough for women to resent the norms set
up by the Victorian image of the submissive, self-effacing
female. They had to learn in what ways this image was linked
with economic dependence and the habits of mind derived
from acceptance of political and intellectual authoritarianism.
It is not enough for the artist to chafe at the indifference or
scorn of the average American. When the artist sees that indifference as a corollary of the dominant emphasis on practical

action, he is ready to inquire into the historical sources and economic and social causes of these attitudes. How often is personality or achievement valued according to its translatability into terms of potential income? To what extent have these dominant attitudes been qualified during the past fifty years by recognition of contributions to general social welfare and by a growing emphasis on the value of every individual human being?

If we consider the norms concerning the relations between husband and wife or parents and children, for example, we must again see how pervasive are the fundamental drives of our culture. The institution of the family, which concentrates within itself so many economic and social functions, will necessarily be affected by the emphasis on material possessions or the extent to which cooperation or rugged individualism is socially approved. Thus it is futile to discuss recent changes in family relations or to forecast their future development without considering recent economic and social changes or what possible direction our whole society will take. If we are going in the direction of greater valuation of individual personality, family relations will be very different from what they would be if we moved toward approval of conformity and the suppression of the individual.

Far from furthering the rejection of all standards, an understanding of cultural conditioning illuminates the intimate relation between individual lives and the whole social fabric. The adolescent is thus provided with a broader perspective from which to view his own struggle to conform to or to modify the dominant norms. He must live within the framework of our own culture, of course. But he need no longer give unthinking adherence to its images of success. Unthinking total rejection should also be seen as conformity, a conformity in reverse, so to speak.

The youth can be liberated from submission to standards that may be peculiar to the particular environment in which he finds himself. If he is brought up in some limited geographic or social setting or if he is aware only of the most generally accepted standards, he may be equally in danger of too narrow a view. Our society is strikingly heterogeneous; a number of cultural subpatterns exist side by side. Ethnic, regional, and economic groups have developed very different images of the approved kinds of temperament, behavior, or social success. Often the individual born within one of these groups and measuring himself against its particular norms develops a feeling of inferiority that would disappear if he could become aware of the standards developed by other groups.

As our society demonstrates, the concept of cultural patterns and group norms does not rule out the possibility of individual differences within groups. Every society permits a certain degree of acceptable variation. Early childhood experiences and the particular society within which the individual finds himself set certain general patterns, but, after all, the experience of no two people, not even of two children within the same family, is identical. That in itself, even without the factor of congenital differences, would lead us to expect a diversity of personalities.

The study of the influences acting on the individual is therefore also concerned with the attempt to see at what points or in what ways emotional and mental habits are set up and the personality becomes crystallized. Despite the original plasticity of the human creature, once the personality pattern is formed, there is a certain resistance to change. Present-day psychology considers early childhood the most important period in the formation of basic tendencies and mechanisms. The psychoanalytic school especially emphasizes this phase of the individual's development and considers that if any remolding of the personality is attempted, it is necessary to penetrate the deep strata of feeling and habit shaped by early experiences in the family. Other schools of psychology postulate that under favorable conditions the structure of personality can be decisively affected in adolescence and adulthood, although such conditions are more likely to occur in childhood. This theoretical position leads to methods of inducing change in personality that are different from the prolonged analyses carried on by the depth psychologists.

The study of personality should prevent us from falling into the view directly opposed to the voluntaristic one, but equally erroneous: namely, that the individual is merely a kind of automaton entirely at the mercy of external pressures. Too often the youth is given only one side of the picture. He is encouraged to think of human beings either as entirely free agents or as the helpless pawns in a completely deterministic system.

The concept of cultural conditioning in no way implies a fatalistic notion that the human being is a puppet in the hands of some mythical, external power called the environment or the culture. Rather, the anthropologists view the human organism as transacting with the cultural environment. Every child is born into some kind of social environment, and this immediately exerts a patterning influence. But the individual in turn reacts selectively on the physical and cultural environment and hence influences it in some manner. The process of conscious cultural change can be conceived in such transactional terms. The more conscious the individual is of the nature of the cultural forces with which he is transacting, the more intelligently can he accept or resist them, and the more intelligently can he modify their power and their direction.[6]

The influence of the cultural environment can be envisioned as setting the broad limits within which the individual can develop and within which he has freedom of choice. This may apply to choices permitted by his physical and temperamental development. It may apply to such choices as whether or not he will read a new book and whether or not he will attempt to change the surrounding society through the advocacy of new laws. In other words, in terms of his own temperamental bent, he can accept or resist environmental pressures and can choose one line of behavior rather than another.

The more unthinkingly and mechanically the human being follows the patterns set for him by his environment, the nearer he approaches the state of the automaton. If the individual understands the important molding influences in his own past and in the history of humankind, if he becomes aware of alternative social patterns or of alternative types of happiness,

---

[6] The psychoanalysts utilize the same principle in their technique of helping the individual gain insight into the nature and influence of his past experiences. When these are brought into his consciousness and their relation to his present anxieties and obsessions is understood, he becomes capable of dealing with them rationally and is thus enabled to remold or readjust his personality. (This analogy was pointed out by Lawrence K. Frank in a letter to the writer.)

Other schools of psychology have applied this principle in the development of different techniques, for example, David C. McClelland's work in achievement motivation.

he will be better able to make choices, to dominate, and, if necessary, to remold his environment. Thus he will be in a position to exercise his will and to consciously influence his own future and the future of the society about him.

The anthropologist and the psychologist offer a critical approach to another widespread tendency: to accept the familiar or the traditional as possessing a fundamental rightness and, conversely, to consider the strange and the unfamiliar as necessarily inferior or reprehensible. Since the individual unconsciously absorbs the particular modes of behavior, views of human nature, and ideas about socioeconomic arrangements of the culture into which he is born, he takes them for granted and often cannot even imagine any possible alternatives or variations. Hence, when he does encounter another cultural pattern, as when the white person comes into contact with the African or the Samoan, he tends to look on it as inferior. An extreme illustration of this is the fact that many primitive peoples have as the name for their cultural group only the word in their language that signifies "human being." Any who do not belong to their cultural group automatically fall outside that category.

The anthropologist helps us realize that merely because we have grown up in a particular cultural pattern, we have no legitimate basis for considering it, ipso facto, the only possible, or even best possible, pattern. Much is to be gained from the knowledge that other cultures have developed working alternatives to the customs and institutions with which we are familiar. Similarly, we can compare the ethical and social ideals of our culture with those created by other cultures or other possible cultures.

Different societies, then, set up different images of the most highly desirable human satisfactions—as in the contrast cited above between those valuing violent competitive behavior and those valuing peaceful cooperation. Societies also differ in the degree to which their various institutions and customs make the valued satisfactions either more or less easily attainable. Sometimes there is a decided discrepancy between those two aspects of a culture. An example is the gradual elimination of such a discrepancy from our own society during the past few generations: sexual experience was valued, yet a frustrating atmosphere of guilt or shame was cast about it. The satisfaction of this strong, culturally reinforced need is more and more being freed from culturally imposed feelings of guilt or shame. Another example from our own society: individual self-determination, freedom of thought and speech, and self-respect are values that have received cultural sanction and have therefore become needs for which the individual craves satisfaction. Our political institutions were designed to fulfill them, but in the lives of many people conditions tend to frustrate these demands. Government has played an increasing role in fostering economic and social changes designed to narrow this gap between ideal and reality. The civil rights movement came as the culmination of a whole series of steps in this direction. That this struggle has not been immediately successful and that unremitting effort will be needed to bring lasting results do not contradict the fact of a great shift in institutionalized attitudes and expectations.

We can judge the society about us, then, in terms of the kinds of basic satisfactions it values and the degree to which it permits or stifles the attainment of those satisfactions. Self-consciousness about our cultural pattern means that we no longer need accept it as unthinkingly as the air we breathe. Probably more than any other cultural group before, we have the knowledge to consciously influence the future development of our customs and institutions.

The concept of the cultural pattern can also counteract the tendency to look on different phases of the society or different groups as distinct and unrelated. In a civilization as complex as ours, anything affecting one element in it—whether that be a geographic or economic section, an ethnic minority, or a particular category such as women or coal miners—will tend to have repercussions on the rest of society.

This view of the transaction between different aspects of the culture has been given a special interpretation by those who believe that a society's economic life—its particular methods of food getting, manufacture, distribution of goods, and property regulation—tends to determine the nature of all the other aspects of its life, such as social organization, religion, and art. Although this theory of economic determinism has often been applied in a crudely oversimplified way by the economic determinists, the economic factor is generally recognized by social scientists. The distribution of wealth among various classes in a society, for example, affects a great many different phases of life. Thus, even in the history of literature, it surely was not an accident that the type of fiction represented by the novels of Richardson, Fielding, and their literary descendants began to flourish at the time when the middle class in England was attaining increasing economic power. Moreover, the particular economic group from which a writer springs surely plays some part in his view of life, his sense of values, and his particular choice of subjects. The teacher of literature, like any other student of the products of social life, cannot ignore economic influences.

The concept of the cultural pattern is particularly rich in implications for the study of literature. Through literature we are constantly coming into contact with cultural patterns of the past or of other societies and of subcultures in our society. Often literature gives clear expression to the characteristic ways of feeling, the types of temperament and behavior valued by the group. It would be unfortunate if, in the study of literature, the student were permitted to forget that life is lived in a web of crosscurrents that tend to take on a basic pattern. Literature itself cannot be viewed in isolation from other aspects of activity in society. Moreover, the particular images of life presented in literature should be approached with a sense of the cultural complexity of our society. These questions will be discussed more fully in chapter 8.

The preceding pages have sketched only a few of the topics that enter into the problem of the patterning of human personality and human society. A great many subjects and considerations that are live concerns of present-day social scientists have not even been broached. In psychology, for instance, a center of much illumination and controversy, psychoanalytic theories concerning the role of unconscious processes and the ways in which they find expression have only been touched on. Numerous other omissions can be listed: in anthropology, the studies that undermine belief in racial superiority or inferiority or the problems involved in understanding cultural contact and change; in sociology, studies of the results of increasing industrialization and urbanization; in economics, the development of a welfare capitalism and the elimination of the cyclic nature of unregulated competitive enterprise.

The discussion may suffice at least to suggest the general way in which an acquaintance with certain basic concepts in psychology, sociology, and anthropology have a direct bearing on the subject of human personality and conduct—a subject that is an integral part of any consideration of literature. Such a structure of ideas should make it possible to turn to the literature of other ages and other societies with an open mind and to look on the expressions of our own world with critical freedom.

It is not surprising that the older approaches to human nature and society tend to persist. Even those who have come into contact with the newer theories often fail to assimilate them into their attitudes in actual life, and in their personal relationships they are still dominated by automatically absorbed prejudices and expectations. Marriage consultants, for instance, reveal that often relationships are shattered by the inability of each of the partners to recognize the causes of the behavior they dislike. The reaction is entirely one of rejection and blame. There is no sense that behavior grows out of a complex network of factors, some of them environmental, some physical, and some the result of emotional attitudes and habits whose source is in the early psychic frustrations of the individual. Spouses also fail to understand their own motivations and to see that perhaps their resentments and irritations may be due to certain factors in their environment or past history that have no validity in themselves. An attempt to understand the possible origins of the disapproved behavior may lead to modification of these causes; a changed external situation and temperamental readjustments may be brought about.

154

Contemporary behavioral scientists have substituted for the older, voluntaristic approach the effort to understand the factors that generate behavior. Given such habits of mind, the possibility of the adjustment of personalities to one another is greatly enhanced. Such an approach might also tend to prevent people from entering into relationships in which there were fundamental elements that would probably lead to misunderstanding and maladjustment.

During the past half-century, many of the concepts presented in these pages have received wide currency in college courses, in newspaper columns on child rearing, and in legal judgments and actions. On all sides, nevertheless, the student is still being bombarded with expressions of the old approach to people and affairs. In the mass media, in our governmental practices, in our law courts, and, above all, in the average home itself, this view often prevails. Hence, it is particularly important that any phase of the student's educational experience concerned with human relations should responsibly present attitudes growing out of the newer approaches to personality. The potential influence of the teacher of English is therefore considerable. Only if the teacher is himself imbued with a more reasoned approach to human personality and society, will he be able to help the student build the attitudes toward people that the psychologists and others concerned with mental health have demonstrated to be most constructive. Instead of the old defeatist notion that human nature is what it is and will never be changed, there should arise the vision of human beings as responding to many forces that can be modified and directed.

The view that insights offered by the social sciences may lead to more successful living or to a redirection of life or a remolding of society immediately raises the problem of values. For as both the moralists and the opponents of science are eager to remind us, science may give us the facts, but it cannot give us the standards of what is desirable or undesirable, good or evil. Indeed, long before the invention of nuclear bombs, it was clear that the use of scientific knowledge could raise crucial moral questions. A lesser illustration is the application of psychological knowledge to advertising that creates a demand for useless or harmful things.

The social sciences, then, are slowly building up a body of knowledge concerning important factors in the development of human personality and in the patterning of human society. But where shall we turn for some scale of values that will help us judge what kinds of personality and what kind of society are desirable?

This problem does not consciously present itself to great masses of people (and they include many of the "educated"). They have unthinkingly acquired from the cultural atmosphere their ideas concerning desirable and undesirable ends, moral or immoral acts, acceptable or unacceptable social arrangements. In other words, they are completely guided by the dominant system of values assimilated from their environment. Almost automatically they have at their disposal a yardstick by which to measure their own and others' conduct and a basis for rejecting personal or general social arrangements that deviate from the customary.

Such unthinking acceptance of any system of values or priorities is undesirable. The anthropologist, the historian, and the sociologist (as well as the philosopher) point out that many alternative systems of values are possible. This constitutes a challenge to inquire objectively into the varying effects of these different social and moral codes on the human beings whose lives they regulate.

Those who find the task of working out their own philosophy too difficult or are not sufficiently mature to assume the responsibility for their own choice of goals and moral code turn to authority—to some institution such as a church or to an individual such as a dictator. Comfortable as throwing off the burden of decision might seem, the social sciences reveal that institutions often tend merely to reinforce and crystallize the particular customs and traditional values built up by the past. They are not necessarily safe guides in a changing world. In fact, historically they often seem to stand in the way of any adjustment of old values to new conditions. Hence, a blind following of their postulates may lead to painful maladjustment and conflict and perhaps defeat the very ends of human happiness or social peace for which they first were formulated. Within such institutions today, as, for instance, in the churches and the educational enterprise, there are individuals with sufficient perspective to question whether the traditionally perpetuated codes and practices are relevant to changed conditions.

A sound system of values must guide the search for a more adequate moral code and social philosophy. The students of other societies will give us information about the personality types, the social institutions that other cultural groups may have developed. The historians of philosophy will explain to us the various value systems that societies have applied in the past or in the present age. And today's social philosophers will be suggesting new guidelines. Our ultimate choice will be influenced by all these, particularly by the philosophies that have directly contributed to our own cultural stream. Certainly, present-day attempts to solve this problem of values would be very different if the Greek and the Judeo-Christian philosophies and the ethical theories developed under feudal and capitalistic social organizations were not part of our cultural heritage. The individual will thus have available alternative schemes of value that his own culture has produced, and he may sometimes seek to import a hierarchy of values derived from another culture. The very fact that he reacts forcibly against some of the points of view in his own society may lead him to emphasize those values and ideals that they neglect. The current interest in Oriental thought—in, for instance, Zen Buddhism—suggests such a quest for alternative possibilities.

One basic value judgment has been implied throughout this discussion: Any system of values can be scrutinized in terms of its consequences for human life. Any form of conduct, any social mechanism, any custom or institution should be measured in terms of its actual effect on the individual personalities that make up the society. To use the culturally sanctioned terminology, every human being is entitled to "life, liberty, and the pursuit of happiness." This means that the human being is recognized as having value in himself and that anything that reduces him to the status of a thing, instrument, or automaton is condemned. It sets up as an ideal the social situation in which each member of society is given the opportunity for the greatest fulfillment of those culturally valued satisfactions of which he is potentially capable. The corollary of this is that if a conflict of interest should arise, no individual and no group would be justified in gaining their own satisfactions through exploitation of any other individuals or groups.

This rests on belief in the fundamental dignity and worth of the human being. It sets up the well-being and fulfillment of the individual in opposition to any abstractions for which might be claimed a superior reality or value such as the elect, the supermen, the proletariat, the nation, the race, or the state. This basic postulate of value is obviously one that receives support from many elements present in our cultural heritage. Implicit in various religious philosophies and in the democratic philosophy, it applies not only to our political but also to our social and economic life.

This fundamental principle provides a measure for individual lives, as well as the customs and institutions, the ideas and assumptions that make up our culture. It provides a standard, too, for utilizing and applying the knowledge that the scientists are so laboriously cooperating to acquire. Often only the scientist can tell us what is best for people's physical and mental health. The sciences that propose to study humankind as biological organisms and as social creatures are slowly becoming aware of their common function, their responsibility to contribute to this core of knowledge about the factors that enter into the creation of freely and fully functioning human beings. Thus the physician finds that he cannot think of a human being as a biological organism in a vacuum but must concern himself with the particular social and economic setting within which that biological organism functions. The sociologist, studying human behavior under the varying conditions created by our social and economic system, can provide information to be judged in terms of successful or unsuccessful human lives. The psychologists are increasingly aware that psychology of the individual is part of what is known as social psychology. Various specialists in the field of mental hygiene have already reached the point of being dissatisfied to merely readjust scattered individuals among the increasing numbers who are known to be suffering from nervous maladjustment and disorder. On the basis of psychiatric study of these individuals, experts will be better and better able to tell us at what points our particular cultural pattern sets up deep psychic disturbances or stifles and condemns fundamental human drives. In the field of psychology, too, preventative therapy will develop a body of information by which we can apply the basic value judgment indicated above. We shall probably be increasingly able to judge the degree to which any particular cultural pattern satisfies the requirement that it permit the greatest possible fulfillment and enrichment of human lives. Then, too, economists are studying the functioning of methods of production and distribution and of regulations concerning property in various societies, so that these practices may be judged by the standard of the maximum social welfare.

Those who are principally students or practitioners of an art, such as literature, can also place their knowledge and interests within the context of this broader system of values. Surely it is hardly necessary to speak of the joy of artistic activity and the satisfactions of the experience of art. Moreover, the artist can tell us much about ourselves. Many of the subtler potentialities of human feelings and behavior that could have been given common utterance in no other way are revealed and embodied in artistic form.

The fundamental values of democracy, the criteria of the dignity and the worth of the human being require the corollary of freedom for the artist. For not only does the artist give expression to innumerable facets of the life about him. He also has served an important function by recalling his audience to a sense of basic human needs that were forgotten under the sway of destructive symbols and slogans or the compulsion of materialistic ambitions. The opportunity for this kind of activity, at once creative and critical, is essential. Equally essential is freedom for youth—and indeed all citizens—to experience those works of art that reveal weaknesses in the contemporary world or that create a vision of greater fulfillment of human values.

Yet it may be asked, Why should the school or college be concerned with the development of emotional attitudes or with preparing the student for his personal as well as his broader social relationships? Are there not many other social agencies concerned with precisely these problems? Indeed, has not the importance of the family and community environment just been pointed out? Why then place this additional burden on the school, which in our society already has so large a task in giving information and developing skills? Why, above all, involve literature, which offers experiences that would be precious in themselves even if they had no further practical justification?

The answer is that the generations of young people now in school and college will have to meet conditions and problems very different from those their parents and grandparents faced. During periods of relative stability or extremely slow social change, the home and the community could be relied on to furnish the emotional conditioning and attitudes that would automatically fit the kind of society the child was eventually to enter. At no time, of course, has the school been entirely free from the responsibility of influencing character and mental habits. In a stable society, however, that influence would principally be a reinforcement of attitudes acquired by the child outside the school.

Present-day conditions no longer automatically provide the youth with the habits of mind and images of behavior that will be appropriate to future social conditions. The development of an urban industrial society, with all its changes in technology, and the emergence of the "global village" of the cyberspace age have produced a welter of new relationships and new images of the values to be sought for. The multiplicity of alternative choices in personal relations and social philosophy is particularly characteristic of American society. The old habitual responses, the old images of what is to be taken for granted in relations between people, can no longer be followed unquestioningly. Many of the old attitudes continue, of course, to be valid. No matter how drastic and revolutionary social change may seem, the anthropologist and the historian will remind us that the new elements are infinitesimal in comparison with the mass of cultural attitudes that persist. Nevertheless, failure to cope emotionally and intellectually with the changing political, economic, and social situation can produce much unhappiness and frustration. In a world of such vast technological change, of such a desperate sense of international tensions, the individual needs to build for himself a mental and emotional base from which to meet the fluctuating currents about him.

Since the old attitudes, the old habits of response, the old goals and images of success can no longer be automatically relied on, youth are increasingly plunged into an unprecedented self-consciousness in the choice of their patterns of life. They must be prepared to test and perhaps to modify the emotional responses their childhood environment transmits to them from the past. The home and the community, whose educational influence operates principally in undirected and unconscious ways, are being called on to contribute to such flexibility but cannot be expected to do this alone. The school, also, must step in to deliberately provide preparation for the unpredictable future.

Because in so many areas old patterns have crumbled and no clearly defined new patterns have crystallized, young people more than ever before must be sufficiently mature to assume responsibility for making their own judgments and working out their own solutions. The concept of maturity is stressed in the disciplines concerned with mental health. They see in our failure to develop a population of mature, self-reliant individuals the explanation of much of the unhappiness, the frustrations, the cruelties often characteristic of personal relationships in our society. The same lack of emotional maturity explains many of the weaknesses in the functioning of our democratic system of government. The individual who is still in the infantile state of needing an outside authority to make his decisions for him cannot be expected to participate constructively in the creation of a rational society.

The concept of emotional security is closely related to this problem of maturity. Because the surrounding intellectual and social atmosphere is in such a state of flux, the youth needs help in attaining his own intellectual and emotional base. Despite cyclical setbacks, the aim of providing employment and economic security for all, and hence eliminating one great source of insecurity, no longer seems visionary.

But there is another source of security that each individual in our culture should be able to draw on. This, the behavioral scientists tell us, depends very much on childhood experiences. If the child has been given a feeling of being wanted and loved, if he has been able to feel that he is an accepted member of the family and social group, he will tend to develop the kind of inner security that will enable him to meet constructively much of the external insecurity and struggle of later life. The less he is given assurance of affection and concern, the less strength of character and sense of self-esteem he is likely to develop. These insecurities will color his approach to the people and the world about him. The feeling of being worthless or inadequate or unloved may express itself in hostility to others and in the resort to physical force as a way of meeting the threat of life. So far as present studies indicate, the most important factor seems to be the degree of warmth experienced by the child, rather than any particular techniques of child training.

During the past half-century, many parents and teachers have been made intensely aware of the far-reaching influence they can have on the child's personality development. They recognize that he should not be made to feel guilty because he is a child and therefore cannot always live up to adult demands. Life should not be for him a formidable series of rules and prohibitions against which he is naturally a sinner. Throughout the whole course of his home and school life, he should be given the feeling that he is a person worthy of consideration. As in so many instances, the reaction against earlier authoritarianism and rigidity has sometimes led to what is now considered an excessive permissiveness. Evidence seems to suggest that the absence of rigid controls is not in itself enough. For example, inconsistency in the demands made on the child by different parents or by the home and the school may be a more important factor than the degree of authority or permissiveness.

Problems of maturity and mental security—much too complex to be adequately treated here—ultimately involve our whole economic and social setup, as well as the methods of child rearing in the home and the fundamental characteristics of our educational system. A recognition of the importance of these problems strengthens one of the main ideas on which the foregoing chapters have been based: that although the school should not force on the student subject matter and materials beyond his intellectual and emotional level of comprehension, it should permit him to function at his fullest emotional and intellectual capacity.

Particularly in the adolescent years, students are often confined to too childish a plane of thought and feeling. They too frequently are encouraged to passively accept what the teacher wishes them to think and feel, without becoming aware of themselves as personalities with definite patterns of their own. The emphasis in earlier chapters on the importance of the personal relationship between the student and the literary work, which grew out of an attempt to understand the literary experience realistically, can be related to this broader concern with the need for fostering the individual's attainment of greater maturity.

American society has steadily extended the number of years of preparation for adulthood and career. Much emphasis is placed on tapping the latent intellectual potentialities of children and youth. But there is a glaring lack of general concern, to say nothing of concerted efforts, to provide the basis for an equally successful emotional life. In both the preadolescent and the adolescent years, an emphasis on emotional development should parallel the current emphasis on the intellectual.

Here literature and the other arts can make an important contribution.

Educators seeking to deal with the student as a whole person have sometimes been frustrated by the popular tendency to conceive of education as concerned simply with impersonal skills and information and by the opposition of some reactionary groups to the very idea of students' expressing feelings. It is sheer abdication of responsibility on the part of the older generation, for example, either to ignore or to condemn adolescent efforts to discover for themselves the meaning of sex and love—efforts necessarily confused and often self-defeating in a world that offers no clearly defined satisfactory patterns and assumes that an emotional life can be postponed as easily as a profession or a career. The social scientists—the historian, the sociologist, the economist, the psychologist—deal with subjects about which cling strongly emotional, culturally transmitted attitudes. Political and economic questions, topics involving racial or national prejudices, or such matters as the relations between parents and children or husband and wife almost automatically arouse strong feeling. The social scientist has therefore tried to clear the ground for rational discussion by first eliminating or reducing any prejudices or fixed emotional attitudes that may obscure a clear view of the facts. He has striven for unemotional treatment of these explosive subjects. The general effect has been to de-emotionalize not only the scholarly investigations in the social sciences but also the teaching in those fields.

To bring the student under the dominance of the scientific spirit is a most valid aim. The means by which this is to be accomplished is another matter. One may question whether plunging the student at once into abstract considerations of generalized social conditions and problems is the best way to lead him to adopt a scientific approach to individual life and to society. May this not strengthen the tendency to deal with words as empty tokens, to brush lightly over their surface meanings without any vivid perception of the actual material and emotional elements to which they point? This abstracting, generalizing, and devivifying tendency will not be counteracted by the type of materials usual in social science courses. In reading his psychology textbooks, for instance, the student may tend to dissociate theories or phenomena from the thought of actual human beings. In his history classes, mass movements and national changes may be thought of without ever being translated into terms of the individual human lives that made up these vast historical sums. The information drawn from sociology and economics courses may also be kept on the plane of the general and the impersonal.[7]

If the purpose of the social science courses in high school and in college were solely to give information, complete objectivity might be an end in itself. The teaching of such courses, however, seems to imply a more practical aim than information for its own sake. The assumption seems to be that such understanding will enable students to handle better their own observations and experiences. Should it not be assumed that a comprehension of the forces at work in society may

[7] This tendency to deal with abstractions called social forces apart from any sense of the human beings who embody these forces may explain why so many adolescents seem to have derived only a pessimistic view of the individual and society from their social studies courses. They have developed the feeling that the individual is merely an impotent puppet at the mercy of inexorable forces. This result might largely be averted through a more human presentation of social theory. This is an illustration of the extent to which the so-called form in which ideas are presented actually determines the meaning that they will have for the student.

help them play a more socially useful role? Therefore, without abandoning the emphasis on unbiased scientific knowledge, the educator still has to inquire whether such understanding is being conveyed in a form that will affect social attitudes and influence social behavior.

The aim, surely, is to enable the student to make intelligent judgments. In the choices open to him, he needs to be guided not by the blind reflex of unconsciously absorbed prejudices but by ideas based on scientifically valid facts. Can the unemotional, impersonal recital of facts and the objective scientific analysis of problems be counted on in themselves to give the youth the power of rational choice? Will the information thus acquired outweigh the force of irrational attitudes absorbed from the lagging social atmosphere? In its simplest terms, the question is, Will this objective knowledge affect his actions, inside and outside the school today, and will it influence his actions in later adult life as a member of a family and as a member of a national and world community?

Investigations of changes in attitude resulting, for example, from courses in the social sciences have usually proved nothing more than that the students changed their articulate opinions. They no longer echoed jingoistic sentiments but approved international cooperation; they advocated racial tolerance; they rejected the "devil take the hindmost" theory in favor of the idea of community responsibility. Whether these opinions had struck deep enough to affect emotional response and actual conduct under the pressure of practical circumstances is a highly debatable matter and a question seldom investigated.

Impersonally presented information, thoroughly understood, may influence behavior. For one thing, there are individuals who respond most readily to abstract ideas. Yet, even in this case, those abstract ideas are practically worthless unless the student is led to recognize their application to specific concrete situations. The fact remains that the influence of this type of impersonal, theoretical instruction is not as obviously visible or as profound as one might hope. How often even high school and college graduates seem unable to resist the pull of disingenuous slogans, specious appeals to emotion, or the contagion of mob hysteria!

It must not be forgotten that the student—no matter whether he is a young child or a college boy soon to enter adult life—is already functioning in society. He has to make choices; he must set up goals for himself in his daily life; he must develop a sense of priorities. And these demands he will continue to meet throughout his life. The pressure of actual living does not permit prolonged meditation and analysis in precisely those person-to-person and general social situations where such reflection is most needed. Hence, in moments of indecision the emotionally rooted attitudes come to the surface to guide behavior.

The young man in school or at college may have become thoroughly acquainted in his courses in history or sociology with, for instance, the more modern ideas concerning woman's potential equality with man. He may even have become convinced of the desirability of the new ideal of marriage as a partnership and a mutual give-and-take, in which sometimes one and sometimes the other will be dependent or dominant. The success with which he carries out his program for a modern marriage, however, will largely depend on the degree to which these intellectual convictions have been translated into emotional attitudes and have displaced the old automatic sets. Probably, from his family background and many other sources in the society about him, he would earlier have absorbed the image of woman as weaker, more dependent, more emotional than man. He is still being indoctrinated with this image daily in the society about him. If these older, deeply ingrained images still persist, he will unconsciously demand those qualities from the women with whom he comes in contact. He may often find himself irritated at the absence of the conventional feminine qualities in his mate. Particularly in moments of tension, the older, culturally weighted attitudes will tend to assert themselves. He may find himself seeking the sense of dominance and superiority associated with the early acquired image of the husband.

When such moments of conflict and irritation arise, they can be handled successfully only if he and his wife are able to recognize his reaction as the irrational following of deeply grooved patterns that may no longer be justifiable. To overcome this, he must possess some strong emotional impulsion toward achieving the kind of marriage that his reason approves.

The gap between the individual's intellectual perceptions on the one hand and his emotional attitudes on the other must be bridged. If such a linkage of opinion with the emotional springs of action does not occur, there are two dangers. First, in moments of crisis the individual may be dominated, not by his rationally worked out opinions, but by the no longer appropriate attitudes absorbed from his childhood environment. Or, if the critical point of view has succeeded in breaking down the old attitude, he may be capable of only a negative approach to the situation. To revert to the illustration, the family: Have we not all encountered the "emancipated" man or woman, whose only attitude toward marriage was a sense of all the things it must *not* be?

The objective study of human society should do more than illustrate the absence of a valid basis for many of the attitudes and images surviving from former social conditions. There should also be provided a valid emotional basis on which to build more appropriate and more successful patterns of thought and behavior. Only then can we hope that the present knowledge concerning humankind and society will bear fruit in more rational social development and in happier, more complete human beings.

This phase of the problem, the transmutation of scientific knowledge and critical opinion into emotional attitudes guiding behavior, has usually been either neglected or evaded by the social science teacher as well as by the others. Obviously it offers difficulties and even some possibilities of abuse. Yet to go on blithely with objective de-emotionalized procedures is a betrayal of the practical value of social understanding. The young boy or girl still under the sway of anachronistic compulsions will be a ready victim of the emotional appeals made by less scrupulous, less disinterested social agencies, such as the biased media or partisan groups. The cause of youth's confusion and sense of futility today is often that they recognize the inadequacy of the old images and yet lack any clearly felt emotional drive toward new choices and new patterns of behavior. The quest for new images and social goals must be given sufficient emotional sanction to carry the younger generations through to a more successful solution of their problems.

Education in this era of social transformation must serve both critical and constructive ends. On the one hand, youth need the knowledge and the intellectual tools required for critical appraisal of ideals and social mechanisms—new and old. On the other hand, youth need to develop positive emotional drives that will quicken intellectual insight. Thus they will be enabled to free themselves from antisocial attitudes and will be impelled to achieve a world that will safeguard human values.

The educational system is only one among the many socioeconomic influences—such as the family, the community, the mass media, the political climate, peer groups—that shape the individual, but it is crucially important. A much-ignored cliché is that a school dominated by the principle of unquestioning obedience to hierarchical authority—in relations between teachers and students or in relations between teachers and administrators—cannot reasonably be expected to develop people capable of functioning in a democracy. Equally censurable is a disorganized, understaffed, poorly equipped school environment that does not foster in students either self-respect or respect for others. All teachers have the professional responsiblity—and should demand the opportunity—to share not only in developing the curricula of their respective fields but also in shaping the total educational environment. And like all citizens, they have the political responsibility to participate actively in the creation of the economic and social supports essential to the schools' role in fulfilment of our democratic ideals.

Teachers of literature share these responsibilities with all others in the educational enterprise. The theory of literary experience presented earlier explains why the literature classroom can serve these broader aims while fulfilling its aesthetic purposes. The following chapters will consider some of the ways in which this can be accomplished.

172

CHAPTER 7

PERSONALITY

Literary materials—the poem, the short story, the novel, the drama, and, by extension, the motion picture and television—can contribute powerfully to both phases of the twofold educational process that we have outlined. Contemporary psychology encourages the belief that "the really important things in the education of youth cannot be taught in the formal didactic manner; they are things which are experienced, absorbed, accepted, incorporated into the personality through emotional and esthetic experiences" (Frank 214).

Of all the elements that enter into the educational process—except, of course, the actual personal relationships and activities that make up the community life of the school—literature possesses the greatest potential for that kind of assimilation of ideas and attitudes. For literature enables the youth to live through—and to reflect on—much that in abstract terms would be meaningless to him. He comes to know intimately, more intimately perhaps than would be possible in actual life, many personalities. He vicariously shares their struggles and perplexities and achievements. He becomes a part of strange environments, or he sees with new emotions the conditions and the lives about him. And these vicarious experiences have at least something of the warmth and color and immediacy of life.

Any insight or clarification the youth derives from the literary work will grow out of its relevance to certain facets of his emotional or intellectual nature. The whole personality tends to become involved in the literary experience. That a literary work may bring into play and be related to profoundly personal needs and preoccupations makes it a powerful potential educational force. For it is out of these basic needs and attitudes that behavior springs. Hence, literature can foster the linkage between intellectual perception and emotional drive that is essential to any vital learning process.

The criterion for judging the success of any educational process must be its effect on the actual life of the student; its ultimate value depends on its assimilation into the vary marrow of personality. What, then, are the results in terms of personality and behavior to be expected from the kind of literary experience and training that has been defined as desirable?

This question will be answered first in the light of the individual student's relation to books. The present chapter will thus deal with the potential influence on personality inherent in literary experiences themselves. Chapter 8 will then apply this question to the type of literature study outlined in the first half of this book. Both of these chapters will reflect the view of personality development sketched in the preceding chapter and will indicate how an awareness of the suggested approach to human relations may grow out of the experience and study of literature.

We are now venturing on ground that is thorny with unexplored difficulties. Much emotion has been expended on this problem of the influence of literature, but little careful or controlled study has been made of it. The following discussion is offered principally for the purpose of focusing attention on this extremely important problem. The aim is to arouse an increased awareness of some of the elements that enter into this question, rather than to suggest a set of neat formulas. As teachers themselves become aware of the dynamic and complex nature of the literary experience and as students of literature give it added attention, a body of more accurate information on this phase of the problem will slowly be built up.

If we keep in the center of our attention this view of the transaction between the individual mind and the literary work, we shall not be misled into thinking that only books read in the most solemn and pedantic manner will have an influence. The power of literature to offer entertainment and recreation is, despite the pedants and moralists, still its prime reason for survival. Books read solely for entertainment satisfy, after all, definite needs and answer definite preoccupations. Such works have therefore a potential capacity to influence the reader's personality and behavior, perhaps even more than those he may read in the course of the school routine. The discussion that follows envisages any writings that elicit a vivid personal response from the young reader.

Prolonged contact with literature may result in increased social sensitivity. Through poems and stories and plays, the child becomes aware of the personalities of different kinds of people. He learns to imaginatively "put himself into the place of the other fellow." He becomes better able to foresee the possible repercussions of his own actions in the life of others. In his daily relations with other people, such sensitivity is precious. Through literature the individual may develop the habit of sensing the subtle transactions of temperament on temperament; he may come to understand the needs and aspirations of others; and he may thus make more successful adjustments in his daily relations with them.

This increased ability to imagine the human implications of any situation is just as important for the individual in his broader political and social relationships. Many political blunders or social injustices seem to be the result not so much of maliciousness or conscious cruelty as of the inability of citizens to translate into human terms the laws or political platforms they support. Political slogans tend to take on an emotional coerciveness regardless of their human implications. Whole nations have been, and indeed are today, so dominated by such dogma in their political and social life that they follow its dictates no matter how disastrous the consequences to themselves or others. A democratic society, whose institutions and political and economic procedures are constantly being developed and remolded, needs citizens with the imagination to see what political doctrines mean for human beings.

It has been said that if our imaginations functioned actively, nowhere in the world would there be children who were starving. Our vicarious suffering would force us to do something to alleviate their plight. The reading of the morning newspaper with its accounts, say, of war, famine, the suppression of human freedoms, the death of scores of people here

176

and there in automobile accidents may take place with hardly an emotional quiver on the reader's part. He registers only the abstract sense of the words and may never even glimpse what they mean in actual human experience. This habit of mind has its immediate value, of course, as a form of self-protection. Yet this callous shell is there to be dealt with in any attempt to inculcate new understanding and new attitudes. Because of the reluctance of the average mind to make this translation into human terms, the teacher must at times feel the responsibility for stimulating it. Anything said about the need for reflection on the reading experience applies also to the audiovisual media, since their very immediacy creates an even greater impetus toward a self-protective shield.

Many young people today seem to have withdrawn into some such defensive attitude of callousness. Not to feel anything very deeply, not to care about anything too much, is one way of dulling the effect of quite possible defeat or disillusionment. In a highly competitive world, it also seems necessary not to think too much about the feelings and needs of others. The way the youth in many countries has lent itself to a philosophy of force and vicious sadism is proof of the great social dangers inherent in that kind of disillusioned cynicism and flight from altruistic feeling. The totalitarian ideologies capitalize on this when they callously preach that their ends justify any means, no matter how brutal.

Lack of such imaginative sympathy is probably back of many of our present-day difficulties. No matter whether the problem is just distribution of taxation or universal civil rights or federal-state relations, the basis of any ultimate decision should be its meaning for actual human lives. It is easy enough to understand the possible effect of a point of view on ourselves and on the human beings with whom we feel the kinship of family, class, nation, or race. We must also develop the capacity to feel intensely the needs and sufferings and aspirations of people whose personal interests are distinct from our own, people with whom we may have no bond other than our common humanity.

If there has been any progress during the past few centuries, it has fundamentally resulted from a certain extension of this kind of imagination. For is not humanitarianism ultimately the result of this sense of the prime importance of the human being, based on the ability to transcend selfish interests and to feel the needs of others? Despite the horrible persistence of war, the record shows an extension of increasingly humane social practices.

It would be absurd to suggest that literature was the cause of this (*Oliver Twist* and *Uncle Tom's Cabin* notwithstanding!), for the writing of such works was in itself the result of social conditions conducive to increased humanitarianism. Yet it can be maintained that literature undoubtedly contributes to the diffusion of more humane sentiment. And this applies not only to works like *Oliver Twist* that preach such sensitivity but also to works written without propagandistic social or moral aims. The ability to enter vicariously into the experience of others can be fostered by a great many different kinds of literary experience.

Constant reading of a wide range of literature may in itself, without any contribution from the teacher, tend to develop social sensitivity. The teacher, however, can have an influence: he can help the student retain his living sense of the experiences through which he has just passed or, by pedantic "literature study," lead him to dismiss them as unimportant. By helping to focus the student's attention on the actual emotions through which he has entered into the lives of others, the teacher can reinforce the power of literature to develop social imagination. Hence, in attempting to foster a vital personal relationship between the student and the literary work, the teacher will also be making an important social contribution.

Literature can play an important part in the process through which the individual becomes assimilated into the cultural pattern. Just as the young child and the adolescent acquire images of behavior and ways of thinking and feeling from the actions and lives of the people about them, so they may assimilate such images from the experience offered by books—from sharing the emotions and ideas of the poet, from participating in the lives of the people created by the novelist, the dramatist, or the biographer. The child and the adolescent often learn from books the culturally appropriate emotional response to types of situations or people (see p. 86). Similarly, they may absorb from their reading ideas concerning the kinds of behavior or types of achievement to be valued, and they may acquire the moral standards to be followed under various circumstances.

Undoubtedly, the human influences encountered in the family, the school, and the community tend to be the most powerful and lasting. In recent years, however, it has been increasingly recognized that television, the radio, the motion picture, the newspaper, and the literary work often take their place beside other social agencies in the important task of molding the individual. Probably not enough attention has been given to the fact that literature is one of the important media through which our cultural pattern is transmitted.

Any individual born into a society must somehow learn not only its language, its gestures, its mechanics but also the various superstructures of ideas, emotions, modes of behavior, and moral values that this society has built on the basic human relationships. It has been maintained, for instance, that if it were not for literature most people would never even have suspected the possibility of romantic love. The whole super-structure of affection, admiration, idealization of the loved one, desire to sacrifice oneself for his or her welfare, and all the other attributes of the romantic relationship does not inevitably and automatically grow out of the basic fact of sex-ual attraction. These are ways of feeling and behaving that in some parts of our culture have become associated with this basic physical factor. After all, even within Western culture there are groups who dispense with much of this idealizing aura cast about the sex relationship. They see it associated with the need for a mate who can bear healthy children or cooperate in the business of life on a farm or bring the neces-sary wealth or social prestige. In any case, the feelings and attitudes associated with the basic fact of sexual attraction will have been learned.

Even in the case of romantic love, it would be ridiculous to suppose literature the sole agency through which it was prop-agated. It would never have found expression in literature if there had not been present in the society the social and eco-nomic conditions out of which such a complex of attitudes could have flowered. And there are many other agencies through which this view of love can be inculcated. Yet undoubtedly literature, oral and written, has played an important part in its perpetuation.

This theory does, at any rate, emphasize one of the social effects of literature—its inculcation of images of behavior and accompanying emotional attitudes. This applies potentially to all the phases of human life and aspirations that have found expression in literature. With the increase of literacy and the wider dissemination of books, it can be expected that literature may play an increasingly important role in helping the individual to assimilate the superstructure of attitudes that he must erect on the basis of his fundamental human impulses.

Much more important than explicitly stated general ideas are the kinds of personalities and the emotional overtones ascribed to particular situations or conduct in literary works. In contrast to abstractly phrased statements concerning humankind or abstract formulations of moral codes that may be encountered in books, the peculiar power of the literary work of art resides in its influence on an emotional level, analogous to the kind of influence exerted by people and situations in life. Yet precisely because the literary experience is imaginary, it can be reflected on more judiciously.

The very things most taken for granted in a work may have the most powerful influence on the adolescent reader. He is avidly curious about what it means in intimate personal terms to fulfill various adult roles. In literature the adolescent finds, for instance, certain traits of temperament, certain kinds of emotions, certain ways of achieving prestige associated with women characters that are very different from the traits or satisfactions associated with the concept of the male character. Again, certain kinds of physical expressions of emotions such as fear, anger, or love are encountered, or certain emotional reactions are presented as appropriate to specific situations. Because of the personal quality of literary experience, it can be an important force in the transmission of the culturally shaped images and options of behavior.

The power of literature to transmit those elements of our culture that are most taken for granted may be more easily seen operating in a past age. The image of the delicate Pamela with her tiny waist and her hands too tender to scour a pewter dish had many even more exaggerated counterparts in eighteenth-century literature. Innumerable maidens of fragile physique, too ladylike to engage in even the slightest practical activity, sighed and wept and fainted their way through the pages of interminable eighteenth-century novels. Letters and biographies of women of the time, particularly of those women who came to revolt against this image, demonstrate how inextricably these attributes came to be associated with the idea of being a lady.

Veblen, in his *Theory of the Leisure Class*, treats some of the social and economic factors that probably produced this ideal of the lady; the novelist did not create her out of whole cloth, for obviously he was reflecting standards in process of crystallization. The novelists, however, clearly did much to perpetuate and disseminate this image. It has tended to persist in slightly modified form long after the conditions that produced it had changed. It began as a picture of the aristocratic or upper-middle-class woman, but with changing social conditions and with the extension of literacy, women of the lower classes sought to approximate this picture in their appearance and behavior. That this was not necessarily the aim of the novelists who created such heroines does not minimize the incidental influence of this image.

Thus, notions of complex patterns of behavior, such as courtship, or moral and social attitudes can be assimilated from books. Goethe's *Werther* and Byron's poems influenced whole generations. Scott's novels undoubtedly played a part in the hold of feudalistic ideas on the South. This kind of influence may reinforce acceptance of rigid class differences or suggest the possibility of overcoming them. Books may propagate stereotypes; consider the influence, for instance, of the fact that for so many generations the child usually encountered the black character presented as an object for laughter or at best a prized servant, as in so many of the novels of the South purporting to show the kindness of masters. The repeated impact of such images in poems, novels, plays, and biographies surely added to the complex pressures acting on the individual and leading him to crystallize his sense of the world about him and of the appropriate attitudes to assume toward it.

Thus far, parallels have been drawn between the nature of the influence exerted by literature and the nature of the influence of the family or community environment. Literature, however, possesses special characteristics of its own. In so-called primitive societies, only those elements of the culture present in the minds of specific human beings at that time can possibly be transmitted to the child born into the culture. The only chance for him to suspect the existence of any other way of life is through particular individuals in the society who may have had contact with other cultural groups. The basic factor that distinguishes our own society from primitive societies is that we possess a written literature. Books are a means of getting outside the limited cultural group into which the individual is born. They are, in a sense, elements of societies distant in time and space made personally available to the reader.

Books are one important means of transmitting a much more complex cultural pattern than could be derived from any particular family or community environment. Without the additional contribution offered by the written or printed word, it would be impossible for the personal or community agencies of cultural transmission to give to youth an adequate sense of the complex fabric of our society. (Any kind of systematic education through the electronic image still remains a hypothetical thing of the future, and even this would undoubtedly incorporate the written word.) Hence, the illiterate or unread person usually participates only in a very narrow and limited subculture in our society.

Literature offers a release from the provincialism of time and space. In this way it may exert a powerful influence on the youth's future behavior. In a heterogeneous, democratic society more and more explicitly seeking to create new social and economic patterns, literature can perform an increasingly important function. Any new synthesis, any integrated American culture must be more than a mere aggregate of its many, often conflicting, social and economic groups. More than ever before it is essential that the individual be liberated from the provincialism of his particular family, community, or even national background. Democracy requires a body of citizens capable of making their own personal and social choices. The corollary of this is that they should be emotionally and intellectually aware of the possible alternatives from which to choose.

A third generalization concerning the potential influence of literature is, then, that literature offers an important source of awareness of possible alternatives. This constitutes the social value of that enlargement of experience that the college girls quoted in chapter 2 attributed to literature.

Books can be a liberating influence in many ways. They may reveal to the boy and girl that there can be modes of life different from the ones into which they have happened to be born. They can learn about the extraordinary diversity of subcultures to be found within the framework of our society, with its sectional, economic, and social differences. Their reading can early make them aware that there are families organized very differently from their own. They will discover in our complex society culturally accepted patterns of behavior and socially approved formulations of personal and social goals completely alien to their own background.

Particularly important is this discovery that various groups within our society hold up diverse images of success and that there are kinds of work despised or ignored by one's own group that others consider socially valuable. This diversity of patterns is undoubtedly one of the most valuable aspects of American society. The artisans, the technologists, the artists, the scientists, the scholars offer personal goals and value systems often strongly in contrast to those represented by the dominant image of the successful business executive. Literature may often provide the first emotionally vivid realization of these facts. Young readers glimpse types of temperament, kinds of work, intellectual and moral atmospheres very different from anything they have known. They come to realize that there are wide possibilities for choice open to them within the framework of American society.

Vicarious participation in different ways of life may have an even more broadly liberating influence. The image of past civilizations or of past periods within our Western civilization, as well as images of life in other countries today, can help the youth to realize that ours is only one of a great variety of possible social structures. The individual is thus able to look at the society about him more rationally. He can evaluate it, judge what elements should be perpetuated and what elements should be modified or rejected.

Literature not only makes possible the experience of diverse patterns of the past and present; it also offers the opportunity to envisage new and more desirable patterns. Wilde's dictum that "nature imitates art" is after all only a paradoxical expression of the fact that the artist often makes people aware of new aspects of life and new angles from which to view it. Perhaps Wilde was quite accurate in calling a sunset a poor Turner painting. Without Turner his contemporaries might never have learned to look for and perceive certain effects of light and color in that sunset. Surely the same thing applies to what the artist and particularly the writer can reveal about new emotional overtones in relations between human beings, new aspirations toward greater fulfillment of human personality, or new points of view, moral and aesthetic, from which to judge experience.

Thus the writer often becomes the medium through which the future is forecast. Often especially sensitive to the new tendencies at work in the society about him, he disseminates images of new goals. These images may kindle in his readers emotional drives toward setting up new patterns of conduct and new social structures. As the history of literature reminds us, writers have set forth scathing revelations of the life about them or have created attractive images of alternative ways of life. Of course, their writings have had influence because many other factors in the society at that time were conducive to it. Conversely, writers have many times created images of life that their own age and succeeding ones were not yet ready to understand or to assimilate.

This latter consideration should allay the typical fear that literary works may incite the youth to rush into all sorts of untried modes of behavior. This view is based on the unrealistic idea of the social effects of literature that is usually associated with Victorian moralism. The Victorian critic often seemed to believe that the mere reading about particular actions in a book would in itself lead to the performance of the same actions in life.

Fortunately or unfortunately, the human being is not plastic enough to be easily moved to any new action simply by reading representations of it. The Victorians mistakenly thought of the reader as a blank photographic plate on which was projected the series of images offered by a literary work. Some of the factors that make the individual reader anything but such a blank photographic plate have been noted in earlier chapters. Various influences in his environment have already left their imprint on him. For the youth especially, literature can be only one of the many elements that help channel the intensely dramatic process that is so casually called growing up. Books contribute an additional influence that must take its place beside the others.

In the interplay of forces acting on the individual, the literary work, unaided, will probably have little weight if its emphasis is opposed to images that many of the agencies in the society about him are reiterating. If the work does not fit in with dominant conceptions, the reader may indignantly reject what the book offers. In fact, the great body of literature probably exerts its most powerful influence in reinforcing and perpetuating the cultural pattern. Therefore the images or ideas presented by literature function in the context of other environmental influences.

The reading of a book, it is true, has sometimes changed a person's entire life. When that occurs, the book has undoubtedly come as a culminating experience that crystallizes a long, subconscious development. In such cases the book usually opens up a new view of life or a new sense of the potentialities of human nature and thus resolves some profound need or struggle. The probability of any particular work's having so profound and transfiguring an effect cannot, however, be predicted or planned for. It would result from the convergence of a great many intangible factors. The possibility that literature may offer such inspiration should, nevertheless, make us eager to stimulate our students to roam freely through a great many types of literary experience.

Literature characteristically operates in less direct and sudden ways. The influence of literature will usually be the result of the cumulative effect of a long series of literary experiences, interacting with, or parallel to, the many other forces acting on the young person.

Only in rare cases would the literary image of a new and aberrant interpretation of a personal role outweigh the influence of frequently encountered conventional images of that role. When the power of the old patterns sanctioned by society is surmounted, it is probably because conditions have so changed that there is a pressing need for a new adjustment. Moreover, even then the new image probably must be reinforced by constant repetition over a long period of time. The emancipated woman, for instance, appears in literature at least from the time of Shelley and Mary Wollstonecraft, very infrequently at first and only with any significant frequency after about 1880. Yet it was not until early in the twentieth century that that image caught the imaginations and was translated into the practical lives of an appreciable number of women.

This may seem a decidedly pessimistic estimate of the possible contribution of literature to constructive social change. That is not the case. Yet it is evident that no oversimplified theories about literature's influence can be accepted. Since any one literary work is only a strand in a complex fabric of influences, the social situation out of which the reader turns to a particular book will, in large part, determine its possible impact on him.

The rather negative implications of the preceding paragraph are counterbalanced by the overarching fact about our age: we are living in a time of extraordinary social flux. Because there is such a lack of unanimity in our society, because even the agencies committed to transmitting the conventional images are often self-contradictory or at cross purposes, the individual is freer than in other periods to accept or to reject the images offered by literature, which may reflect actual life or present alternatives. Hence the insight of the adolescents who claimed that "enlargement of experience" is an important function of literature. Because conditions are ripe for it, people today are eager for the new vision and new sensitivities that books may stimulate.

Someone has said, "The fool learns only through experience. The wise man anticipates experience." This suggests two essential traits of literature: its power to give vicarious experience and its delineation of a great diversity of personalities and conduct. Is not the capacity for imagination—the ability to picture oneself in a variety of situations and to envisage alternative modes of behavior and their consequences—the thing that gives the wise man his advantage? C. S. Peirce, in stressing the value of "ideal experimentation" (3.527), was referring to the same thing. In imagination we rehearse various possibilities of action in a given situation. We go through a process of imaginative trial and error, trying out different modes of behavior and working out their probable effects. When the situation arises in actual life, we are better prepared to act successfully.

Literature permits something resembling ideal experimentation because it offers such a wide range of vicarious experiences. We can live different kinds of lives; we can anticipate future periods in our own life; we can participate in different social settings; we can try out solutions to personal problems. We are able to apprehend the practical and emotional results, the reactions of others, the social praise or blame that may flow from such conduct; we find some of these temperamentally more satisfactory than others. Literature may thus offer us a means of carrying on some of the trial-and-error experimentation that might be disastrous in real life. *Hence the emphasis in earlier chapters on the necessity for equipping the student to evaluate the diverse images of life that he encounters in books.*[1]

The vicarious experiences offered by literature can have a particularly significant effect when they are related to

[1] See also page 250 for comment on the fact that literature does not simply mirror life.

problems and conflicts intimately involving the reader. The students mentioned in chapter 2 remarked that often in books one comes across people like oneself or people with problems similar to one's own: other adolescents carry on the struggle to achieve a new working relationship with their families; other husbands and wives live through irritations and misunderstandings; other men and women seek recognition and the opportunity to exercise their talents in an indifferent world. The very fact that the reader's situation is not unique, that it at least parallels what others evidently understand and have lived through, gives him some perspective. Through seeing his problems apart from himself, he is helped to think and feel more clearly about them. This constitutes another phase of the potential influence of literature.

Lawrence K. Frank has suggested in a letter to the author that ideally a series of literary experiences could perform something approaching a psychoanalysis if the reader were encouraged to react fully and freely. In large part, the psychiatrist serves his patient by helping him to bring into consciousness various experiences, attitudes, or impulses that have been repressed or "censored." The patient is then encouraged to look on them as rationally explicable and hence manageable. Thus he is led to free himself from his fears and obsessions. In order that he may readjust his environment as well as himself, he is also helped to see at what points his environment imposes unnecessary frustrations. The experience of literature may effect a similar liberation. Vicariously experiencing the life of a character in fiction or participating in another's emotion expressed in a poem may enable the reader to bring into consciousness similar elements in his own nature and emotional life. This may provide the basis for a release from unconscious fears and guilt.

The adolescent particularly may be helped to interpret his own acutely self-conscious emotions and motivations. As a child he has built up a sense of himself in relation to other people. Now he finds that self undergoing various modifications and expansions. Often he feels that he must be abnormal because of unsuspected tendencies within him. Often, too, he develops a sense of guilt, a feeling that he is highly sinful because his fantasies lead him into forbidden fields or because he resents restrictions on his behavior. If he has been brought up to have religious belief, the growth of agnosticism may lead to intense inner turmoil and disillusionment. The young boy or girl frequently hesitates to confide these conflicts or fears to adults because they might view them as rejections of their standards. Sometimes such anxieties create nervous tension and neurotic distortions of the personality. Literary experiences may at least militate against the growth of neurotic tendencies.

Books may help the adolescent perceive the validity of his own temperamental bent, even when that bent may not be valued by his own environment. Thus, the young boy and girl may find encouragement to set up for themselves goals undreamed of in their own families. For example, a contemplative youth in a family of extroverted business executives or an individual in an uneducated or indifferent milieu who has discovered the wonders of science might be particularly in need of encouragement. This sense of aloneness or estrangement creates much adolescent insecurity. Through books each of these youths might learn that other milieus valued their kind of temperament and ability. For the first, works such as Cather's or Mann's stories or Joyce's *Portrait*, and for the second, works such as Michael Pupin's autobiography, the books about George Washington Carver, or David Newton's account of Watson and Cricks's discovery of the double helix might offer the sense of sharing common values and goals. In the literature of both the past and the present the youths might have found strong contrasts to the norms of their environments.

The range of human temperaments that have been admired and held up as a standard are perhaps best revealed through literature. The autobiography of a Franklin with its disciplined, prudent narrator may be contrasted with the reckless, swashbuckling heroes of romance or with the sensitive, introspective characters in a Henry James novel. The passionate, impulsive folk of Elizabethan drama may be compared with the intellectualized, cynical creatures of Restoration plays, their most vigorous act some sharp thrust of phrase, or with the characters in contemporary dramas such as Shaw's, O'Neill's, or Williams's, where dramatic conflicts often take place within the mind and are revealed through a technical device. Portrayals of the successful man of power may be placed beside characters whose success lay in self-abnegation or in spiritual and intellectual achievement. The poets, too, offer a wide gamut of temperaments that we can come to know intimately.

The adolescent worry over the need to conform to the culturally dominant pictures of the temperamental traits, types of work, and modes of behavior appropriate to each of the sexes can be lessened through a wide circle of literary acquaintances. The young girl may need to be liberated from the narrow view of the feminine role imposed by her milieu. It hardly seems necessary to point out that through literature of earlier periods an extraordinarily broad range of feminine temperaments and a great variety of views of woman's place in society may be encountered: Pamela's determination not to offend the social code, the common sense conformity of Elizabeth Bennet, the passionate struggles of Meredith's Diana, the striving for independence of Hardy's Sue. Plays by Shaw and Ibsen, the works of Virginia Woolf could offer further instances of the attack on patriarchal attitudes. Since the 1960s, an outpouring of short stories, novels, poems, and plays has contributed to making woman's role a national social and political issue. Works by minority group writers, such as Amy Tan's *The Joy Luck Club* and Sandra Cisneros's *The House on Mango Street*, even while warmly evoking their ethnic backgrounds, join in the rejection of traditions of women's subservience. Feminist aspirations also merge with the ongoing broader struggle for human rights.

For the younger adolescent, we have seen, the concern with normality extends even to the problem of conformity to a particular physical type. Here, again, literature may show what a great diversity of physical traits have been admired and that physical characteristics, even those considered handicaps, need not prevent successful and happy lives. If one approaches fiction from this rather special angle, one is amazed to find how many novels and stories do reflect this concern with conformity to physical standards. Cyrano de Bergerac and Falstaff by no means stand alone. Thomas Wolfe recounts the experiences of an extremely tall man, or Vardis Fisher, in "April," tells the story of a girl who thinks herself hopelessly unattractive.

Frequently literature is the means by which the youth discovers that his inner life reflects a common experience of others in his society. He finds that the impulses and reactions he feared are normal, that they are shared by many others in our society, and that there may merely be a convention (or a conspiracy) of silence about them. In this way, a particular poem or an autobiographical novel may provide liberation from blind fears or guilt. Having learned that others have lived through and dominated these supposedly strange impulses, the adolescent can achieve sufficient objectivity to proceed to work out an integrated sense of his own emotional nature. This kind of influence is especially difficult to document. All that psychologists and psychiatrists have been telling us recently about adolescent conflicts, however, tends to suggest that it may be very important.

A point introduced earlier in another connection is especially relevant. Often the reader, without necessarily being aware of it, projects his own present emotional preoccupations on fictional situations and personalities that seem on the surface very remote. The reader responds not so much to the situation presented in the work as to the structure of emotional relationships it implies. Thus, *Mutiny on the Bounty* or *Catcher in the Rye* might strike a responsive chord because a boy was passing through the process of psychological weaning from the authority of his parents. Or the relationship between Othello and Iago may have significance because of the boy's own preoccupation with the need for loyal friends. Similarly, the biography of a great statesman may symbolize the reader's own struggle to make others sympathize with his aims and enthusiasms.

This basic emotional parallelism is most obvious when an author selects a legend like the Prometheus myth or a story set in the past, such as the tale of Tristan and Iseult, and infuses into it values and emotional overtones significant in terms of contemporary life. (Perhaps emphasis on the underlying emotional structure would counteract recent tendencies to be satisfied with the classification of works according to their archetypal or mythic categories. The labeling should be incidental.) Each age finds new significance in the structure of emotional relationships in works like *Hamlet* or *Faust*. It is not usually recognized that in responding to a work of literature, even one that deals with contemporary people and situations, the reader may also be transposing its emotional patterns into his own special situation.

Talking about these matters in terms of the situation in the book merely makes it easier for the reader to bring his inner problems into the open and to face them or seek the help of others without the embarrassment of explicit self-revelation. Thus he often reveals what he cannot or will not say about himself. The teacher cannot afford to ignore this tendency to respond to the implicit emotional pattern of poems or novels or plays. Even books that seem to have little to do with the externals of a student's life may provide vicarious experience and occasion discussion that will lead to increased self-understanding for the student.

This is a perfectly valid way of responding to literature—in some ways the most valid, since it means that the work has profound importance to the reader. However, the aims of the literature classroom dictate a prime qualification: If in projecting his own situation into the work the reader has actually created something alien to its intention, he should be helped to discover this. The major task of the teacher (see part 1) will consist in such clarifications through group discussion of alternative responses and interpretation. Actually, in thus learning to read the text more closely, the reader often becomes aware not only of unnoticed verbal clues but also of his own biases or blind spots.

In recent years there has been much discussion of literature as a means of sublimation of socially disapproved impulses. The desire for violence and cruelty; the wish to dominate others; the need for sexual expression when, as in the case of the adolescent, society prevents it; the impulse to strike back at those who place restrictions on us—these are tendencies for which literature is said to provide an outlet. Certain aspects of this theory are related to the function of literature set forth in Aristotle's much-debated remarks about the catharsis, or purgation, of the emotions of fear and pity that results from the experience of tragedy.

Literature may perform an even more constructive service for the individual. It can suggest to him socially approved channels for expression of his impulses. A young boy whose fantasies had taken a consistently antisocial form might be directed through fiction and biographies toward goals that society would consider highly valuable. Domination of others might be sought not through physical violence but rather through the possession of superior knowledge and even the ability to help others, as through the knowledge of medicine.

In some rare cases the teacher might consciously attempt to use literature in this way. One extremely perceptive teacher who has had training in psychology reports that she has done this. She has been able to create an unself-conscious relationship with the students and has led them to express themselves very freely in their writing for her classes. Thus she is often able to glimpse some of their conflicts and obsessions. In one instance it became apparent that the boy's sympathy for his mother and antagonism toward his father were the source of strong feelings of guilt and were creating much friction. The teacher casually suggested that the boy read such books as Bennett's *Clayhanger* and (admitting its meretricious elements) Deeping's *Sorrell and Son*. These helped to bring directly into consciousness the problem of his own relations with his father. He was sufficiently freed from his sense of guilt to be able to discuss the matter and to work out a more adequate handling of it.

Unless the teacher is in an almost psychiatric relationship with the student, however, any attempt to use literature in this way would probably create more conflicts and tensions than it solved. Many teachers might be led into officious meddling with the emotional life of their students. (Unfortunately, like members of any other group, many teachers are themselves laboring under emotional tensions and frustrations. Given the right to meddle in this way, they might be tempted to find solutions for their own problems by vicariously sharing the student's life. They might also project on the student their own preoccupations and lead him to think that he was suffering difficulties and frustrations that in reality were the teacher's.) Assuredly, even worse than the old indifference to what is happening psychologically to the student is the tampering with personality carried on by well-intentioned but ill-informed adults. The wise teacher does not attempt to be a psychiatrist. The essential thing, he knows, is to be a complete human being in his relations with his students—bringing to bear in his work with them all the sensitivities that he would bring to bear in his relations with people outside the classroom.

On the whole, then, the teacher should avoid any too literal application of what might loosely be called the psychiatric possibilities of literature. It is highly important, however, to recognize that books may often perform such functions for young people. The teacher's responsibility is to provide a wide selection and to help the student develop sufficient independence to seek out those works for himself. Thus there may be at least the chance of his coming upon those that will be psychologically helpful. Moreover, if the teacher is aware of the conflicts and anxieties that recur most frequently among adolescents in our society, he will be able to make available works that have some relevance to these tensions. If a segment of our youth today take an almost completely negative stance toward the adult world, this may be because they have encountered in literature classrooms, as elsewhere, materials consistently irrelevant to their own concerns and needs. Above all, the adolescent should have a wide range of alternative experiences in works that speak to him as he now is. In an earlier day, the need was mainly for a certain iconoclasm; today, the need is not only for challenge but also for the frank treatment of themes that may lead beyond rejection toward affirmation of new and more socially satisfactory attitudes.

These considerations were an additional reason for the discussion of adolescent needs and conflicts in chapter 5. Since any vital literary experience is possible only when the work strikes some responsive chord, the teacher should present to the student literary works that have this personal import. Such literary experiences will make it possible for him to grow in critical ability. At the same time, they may have valuable psychological repercussions. Probably in most cases the wisest thing for the teacher is to keep his attention focused on the relationship between the text and the student. If he does this part of his job well, in the spirit outlined in the earlier chapters of this book, he can probably feel assured that he has created the basis for a great deal more than purely literary insight.

The consideration of psychological values that may be derived from literary works suggests a related problem that causes many teachers difficulty. They are aware that, both during school days and afterward, the great mass of the American people feed on shoddy reading matter. The stilted academic approach to good literature in the schools may contribute to the student's feeling that he can get little personal enjoyment from it, so he turns to a type of writing about which there hangs no academic aura. The more generally assumed reason for American reading habits is, however, that they reflect the desire for escape. Undoubtedly, the causes for this wish to escape from reality are deeply rooted in our society.

It is sometimes argued that the teacher's condemnation of cheap escape fiction is merely an expression of professional snobbery. If this "trash" gives pleasure and momentary release from pressures or permits the compensation, at least in fantasy, for personal lacks and frustrations, why should the reader be denied this? An earlier comment is relevant here: The criterion for discriminating between helpful and harmful kinds of escape is that escape through literature should not leave the reader less able than before to cope with reality.

Someone dealing with extremely maladjusted individuals would probably use various means, including this type of literature, for even a temporary effect. In such cases, however, the literature performs only the function of a drug that momentarily releases tension. The work of returning the patient to mental health, of giving him greater capacity for meeting situations in life, still remains to be done. Repeated indulgence in the drug of escape fiction can lead only to an increased craving for such escape.

To be sure, it is not always trashy fiction that provides escape. The reader who immerses himself in medieval romance or reads and rereads the works of Scott as a steady literary diet or turns constantly to such works as Trollope's stories of quiet cathedral towns may be indulging in the same flight from reality as the girl who avidly reads the stories about the international set on the Riviera. In either case, there has undoubtedly been a period of pleasant escape from the difficulties and disappointments of the present-day world. Surely, only the most ascetic of Puritans would wish to cut us off completely from this relaxation and enjoyment.

In most cases, however, the escape function is served by writings that present a false image of life. The obstacles placed in the way of the characters are oversimplified. The ease with which problems are solved or the absence of any real problems probably constitutes one appeal of this type of writing. Even more subtly enervating are the emotions undiluted with thought and lacking in individual quality. Purportedly successful personal relationships in marriage or business are usually presented in naively simple terms. And the crudest elements in our society—the ruthless competition, the emphasis on wealth, the respect for the winner no matter what his methods—often provide the framework of the story. The reader will return to life from this kind of fare probably less capable than before of understanding and coping with the complex situations, the mixture of frustrations and satisfactions, that life offers. Such fiction fosters the notion that the level of vitality required for a full life is lower than is actually the case.

A striking phenomenon in recent years has been the widespread sale of writings purveying crude images of violence, sadism, and sexuality. Such materials jostle the classics on the paperback shelves and fill magazine racks in stores throughout the country. The other mass media also manifest this trend, which has been interpreted as a reflection of the tensions and violence characteristic of twentieth-century life. Psychiatrists have disagreed about the effect of such materials on young readers. Some have suggested that these provide an outlet for aggression, while others have found that they contribute to delinquent behavior. Under different circumstances and with different individuals, both these effects seem possible. Much more systematic study of the problem is needed, with both literary critics and psychologists contributing.

Some have justified such writings by pointing to the presence of violence and eroticism in serious contemporary works, such as those of existentialist and "absurd" writers. The necessary rejoinder is that the presence or absence of such elements is not in itself a basis for judgment. Such writings may serve a function as expression for the author; whether they serve the needs of a particular reader remains a legitimate question. The educator, who knows that freedom is essential to the health of any literature, will oppose censorship. His responsibility is all the more clear—to develop discriminating readers able to evaluate the human import of the literary fare offered to them. When the teacher and the school seriously carry out such professional responsibilities, they have earned the right to exercise them without external censorship.

The fundamental social causes for this national craving for the drug of escape literature are beyond the scope of the classroom. At least the literature class can counteract the tendency to follow the path of least resistance. One way is to discuss examples of poor fiction. It is wise, after all, to start with the student at whatever level of understanding and appreciation we may find him. There is no point in just condemning the reading he most enjoys. He will only develop a feeling of shame about it without being able to resist indulging in it. Reading forbidden books in the attic or behind the barn or whatever the modern equivalent may be seems one of the persistent traits of our culture. Condemnation or prohibition alone can have only pernicious effects.

For adolescent students, a calm analysis of the appeal of this kind of reading might lessen its attraction. A critical attitude toward its silly, dishonest, and sensational pictures of life can have a wholesome influence. The contrast between cheap and honest treatments of similar themes can help accomplish this. This will help students judge by other criteria of happiness the picture, for example, of wealth as equivalent to success. In contrast to love as limited to the physical, they will be made aware of the many values that can be integrated into the love relationship.

Without assuming a holier-than-thou attitude, the teacher should keep in mind the adolescent psychology that leads students to this low-grade fiction and should try to provide more wholesome and invigorating satisfactions for these needs. Educators and parents have come to recognize the importance of this in the field of sex education. They realize that the attempt to prohibit any knowledge about sex causes the adolescent to seek it from undesirable sources, often sensational fiction. They admit, therefore, that it is better to provide this information in more wholesome ways and to permit the adolescent to read literature that deals frankly and honestly with sex as a fundamental and enriching element in human life. This principle should not be restricted to the field of sex knowledge, however. There is certainly something wrong with a literature curriculum if the students turn from it to magazines and books purveying violence and the crudest sexuality under a veneer of cynicism. Adventure and vigorous action, on the one hand, and honest treatment of the sex relationship, on the other, are to be found in abundance in good literature. Probably in many cases the school is still too much dominated by nineteenth-century ideas about the literature that the cultivated person should read, even though it would be very easy to find equally good literature that has the swift pace and vigorous action the student craves. Of course, even when such books are read in a classroom, there still remains the danger that they may be drained of all their tang and zest by routine study.

Victorian notions about the influence of literature led to a rigid censorship of books by publishers and critics as well as by parents and teachers. Particular books were valued because they offered approved models of conduct which young people were expected to imitate. The view of literature presented here has led to a rather different emphasis: in a democracy, the more varied the literary fare provided for students, the greater is its potential as an educationally liberating force. In this way, through literature, the necessarily limited scope of the student's environment will be supplemented and corrected by contact with expressions of other phases of society and other types of personality.

This means that the student will not be restricted to one kind of literary diet. He will not read exclusively the works of the past or the present. He will not be nourished entirely on the literature of England and America. Instead, he will be permitted an insight into ways of life and social and moral codes very different even from the one that the school is committed to perpetuate.

These generalizations about the choice of books apply to several specific problems that can be mentioned only briefly. Very often in school, children are required to read works that demand a constant effort at comprehension because the vocabulary and sentence structure represent the next stage toward which they are being led. Or they may be required to read works written in an archaic language, very different from the language that they hear about them or that is used by accepted contemporary writers. Few adults—even college professors!—impose on themselves the task of constantly reading works with a vocabulary that is strange to them or with a complicated style that demands unusual efforts of attention. Only rarely do they undertake such tasks. Most of the time their reading is at the level of their present vocabulary and powers of attention. In our zeal to give our students the proper literary training, we constantly set them tasks a step beyond their powers or plunge them into reading that practically requires the learning of a new language. Belated efforts to help the disadvantaged child have revealed that standard English is indeed often a strange dialect, to be learned almost as a second language. No wonder that many students, both middle-class and disadvantaged youths, do not learn to read or read only the simplest of crude escape literature!

The question of command of language leads to another controverted subject: the literature of the past versus contemporary literature. When one objects to intensive study of words and syntax as withering any possible love of the classics, the answer is usually that the students will not otherwise understand what they are reading. If a work presents such linguistic difficulties, one may question whether a direct attack on the linguistic problems offers a solution. By the time the student has acquired enough understanding of the unusual language, the work as a whole has probably lost its power to affect him. If the work presents experiences and ideas highly relevant to the student's own preoccupations, his interest will often carry him over the hurdle of the language difficulty and give him sufficient motivation to infer meaning. Many of the great classics have elements of vivid action, strong emotion, and suspense that may provide an incentive for the more mature or the more secure student to clear away the obscurities due to unfamiliar language or literary forms. Too often, however, the classics are introduced to children at an age when it is impossible for them to feel in any personal way the problems or conflicts treated.

Difficulties in understanding, as indicated in chapter 5, are usually not merely a matter of words and syntax, for words must be apprehended in some context of experience. The teacher who feels that if he can only get the students to understand the individual words he will have eliminated all obstacles is often mistaking the symptom, the language difficulty, for the real seat of the trouble, which is the student's lack of readiness for what the work offers.[2] For the great majority it would probably be much wiser to postpone such reading and to gradually build linguistic flexibility through

[2] Obviously, this does not imply a neglect of any of the means by which the student can acquire a clearer understanding of words themselves. The dictionary can become a very interesting book for the student, if what he gets from it is not left on the purely verbal level but is functionally assimilated.

See pages 105–08 for other references to this problem of understanding. There has been widespread interest in this basic problem of meaning, owing to the influ-

the use of more familiar materials. When the students are more mature, more experienced, they will then be able to apprehend enough of what the great classics offer to be willing and eager to clarify any linguistic obscurities.

When one thinks of all that great literary works can yield, one is horrified to see them so often reduced to the level of language exercise books for the young. The antipathy of many students to Latin and Greek arose from this use of masterpieces beyond their powers of appreciation as texts for acquiring the language. Those who cram the classics down students' throats long before they are ready are careless of the fate of the great works of the past.

Even though the majority were to graduate from school and high school without having encountered many of the great authors, we should not need to be alarmed if they had the ability to read with understanding and had acquired zest for the experience that literature can give. Those who try to crowd into the school years everything that "ought" to be read evidently assume that the youth will never read again after school years are over. People who read for themselves will come to the classics at the point when particular works have particular significance for them. To force such works on the young prematurely defeats the long-term goal of educating people to a personal love of literature sufficiently deep to cause them to seek it out for themselves at the appropriate time.

The difficulty presented by works of the past is that not only the language but also the externals of life and the manners

ence, for example, of the writings of C. S. Peirce, Bertrand Russell, P. W. Bridgeman, I. A. Richards, and Gilbert Ryle. Two highly influential works have been *The Meaning of Meaning* by C. K. Ogden and I. A. Richards and *Philosophical Investigations* by Ludwig Wittgenstein.

and morals represented may seem so peculiar that the student's attention is focused almost completely on these aspects rather than on the major experiences the authors sought to convey. Even those works that deal with personal emotional problems still vital today are often clothed in an atmosphere and deal with ways of life that make the whole thing seem artificial and remote. Many teachers are aware that before the student can enjoy a work, he must feel that it has some relevance to his own experience. They therefore often devote much time and energy to indicating the equivalents in our own society of the different aspects of life represented in the work. Like all background information, however, this should not obscure their purpose, to reveal the basic emotional patterns of the work itself.

There are many works of the past in which the strange mores do not block comprehension of the basic emotional relations; the older work may offer just as intense a personal experience as would a contemporary work. The friendship of Achilles and Patroclus might seem as personally important to a boy as would a treatment of friendship such as in John Steinbeck's *Of Mice and Men*. The story of Lear and his daughters might seem as near to a girl as the family relations in E. M. Forster's *Howards End*. *Dombey and Son*, just because it was written at a time when problems of parent-child and husband-wife relations were still drawn in their broadest terms, might, at a certain stage, be more comprehensible than the treatment of similar problems in a book by Virginia Woolf. The fact that some writers of this century, like James Joyce or T. S. Eliot, are themselves so much the product of a long literary heritage might make them less comprehensible to the young reader than a nineteenth-century writer would be.

The student himself needs to go through the experience of relevant literature of the past before he can understand some contemporary writers.

Nevertheless, most contemporary authors offer no such difficulty but write about a life that the student can understand. For instance, Stephen Vincent Benét's *John Brown's Body* would be more easily understood than *The Idylls of the King*; Carl Sandburg and Langston Hughes would have more personal impact than Matthew Arnold; George Orwell and J. D. Salinger than William Makepeace Thackeray and Nathaniel Hawthorne. The question of literary comparisons must wait until the students can handle the historical obstacles to participation in the older works.

Certain other considerations relate to the use of classical or contemporary literature. It is usual to think that classics survive a winnowing process that guarantees them to be repositories of the accumulated wisdom of the race. There is much in this view. Even so, it is hard to find any great work that has been consistently recognized as such. Shakespeare has had his ups and downs, as have lesser writers. And when different ages agree in their exaltation of a work, it may be for widely differing reasons. Moreover, in any work, the elements of "lasting truth" are intermingled with much that was special to the particular age in which it was written. This is as true of the work of Shakespeare, Milton, and Goethe as it is of Jane Austen.

Surely, many works that every person "should" have read lend powerful reinforcement to emotional attitudes and assumptions about human nature that our contemporary life and our contemporary thinkers have discarded as outmoded and false. What is the possible influence of a steady diet of literature produced out of social systems and ethical philosophies very different from our own? Ideas about the relations between men and women, between employer and employee, between citizen and state, and indeed between human beings and the universe, as they are reflected in much of the older literature, would seem to exalt much that the person of average enlightenment today considers reactionary or limited. Are the students offered literary fare that provides opportunity only for imaginative identification with images of behavior irrelevant to actual life or whose relevance they are not equipped to see? Is literary training in the schools contributing to the persistent hold of images and ideals no longer appropriate to our present-day life and knowledge? To what extent, for example, can the influence of literature be held responsible for the fact that many women today find within themselves emotional obstacles to their sincere ambition to be independent emotionally and intellectually? Throughout their entire experience with literature, they have been led to identify themselves most often with the older image of woman as temperamentally, as well as economically, subordinate and dependent. (See chapter 8 and the index for further discussion of gender roles.)

Obviously, these questions are presented in oversimplified form. Books, it has been seen, do not function in a vacuum, and their influence is always part of a complex network of social factors. For instance, the boy who has come into contact with the present-day skeptical scientific attitude will naturally be less likely to absorb the authoritarian point of view that permeates much of the writing of the past. Yet in a conflict between the two attitudes, a steady fare of such literary experiences might tend to strengthen subservience to intellectual authority. It is realistic to think of particular literary works as tending either to reinforce or to weaken attitudes and images the young person may encounter through other social influences.

It is generally recognized that students should read works of both the past and the present. That a work is written by a contemporary is certainly no automatic proof of its value. Still, in the mass of literature produced today there is much that represents those areas of thought and experience that are the points of growth and change in our own age. If the youth is to develop a critical understanding of his world, he must be exposed to contemporary expressions of personal and social attitudes. The novel, the poem, the play—whether encountered on the printed page or in other media—provide a sense of the adult world he must enter. Through the processes of Peirce's "ideal experimentation," they help him forge some of the necessary intellectual and emotional tools.

This leads back to the principle so often reiterated in these pages, that the test of what books the child or adolescent should read is his intellectual and emotional readiness for what they offer. The classics will be more appropriate than some esoteric contemporary author, but in many cases comparatively recent works will speak more profoundly and constructively to the boy and girl than will much "greater" works of the past.

We should not, then, set up arbitrary ideas in this matter of classic and contemporary works. The teacher should be eager to find those books of the past and present that will have a live meaning for his students. In most schools and colleges even today, this principle would lead to a greater liberality in introducing contemporary literature into the curriculum. For the teacher's desire will be to give the youth as wide a range of relevant experiences as possible at his level of development.

To sum up: Because the literary work of art is a form of personal experience, literature has many potentialities. A favorable educational environment and dynamic and informed teaching are needed to effect their full realization:

Literature fosters the kind of imagination needed in a democracy—the ability to participate in the needs and aspirations of other personalities and to envision the effect of our actions on their lives.

Literature acts as one of the agencies in our culture that transmit images of behavior, emotional attitudes clustering about different social relationships, and social and personal standards.

Literature can reveal to the adolescent the diversity of possible ways of life, patterns of relationship, and philosophies from which he is free to choose in a heterogeneous, rapidly changing democratic society.

Literature may help him make sound choices through imaginative trial and error or experimentation—through experiencing in the literary work the consequences of alternative actions.

Literary experiences may enable the reader to view his own personality and problems objectively and so to handle them better.

Literature, through which the adolescent reader encounters a diversity of temperaments and systems of value, may free him from fears, guilt, and insecurity engendered by too narrow a view of normality.

Literature may suggest socially beneficial channels for drives that might otherwise find expression in antisocial behavior.

The role of the teacher and the teaching process sketched thus far can now be viewed in terms of its potential influence on personality and behavior. This will involve, too, a consideration of how the study of literature may create an understanding of the various basic social concepts discussed in chapter 6.

CHAPTER **8**

EMOTION AND REASON

The teaching process outlined in earlier chapters consists in helping the student develop the habit of reflecting on his primary transactions with books. Having created the environment for evoking an experienced meaning and reacting freely to it, the teacher then seeks to create a situation in which the student becomes aware of possible alternative interpretations and responses and is led to examine further both his own reaction and the text itself. In this way he is helped to understand his own preoccupations and assumptions better. He considers whether he has overlooked elements in the text. He thus becomes more aware of the various verbal clues— the diction, the rhythmic pattern, structure, and symbol—and develops or deepens his understanding of concepts such as voice, persona, point of view, genre. This process of reflection leads the student to seek additional information concerning the work, the author, and their social setting as a basis for understanding of himself and of literature. These new techni-

214

cal, personal, and social insights may ultimately lead to a revision of his original interpretation and judgment and may improve his equipment for future response to literature.

Now if we were to substitute the words *situation* or *personality in life* for *text* or *work* in the preceding paragraph, the description would apply equally well to the kind of thinking that is most fruitful whenever an individual meets a new situation in life or must adjust to a new kind of personality. His first need is to understand his own emotional response to the person or situation. He realizes that preoccupations and prejudices may have led him to exaggerate some things and ignore others. He has to bring his basic moral or psychological assumptions out into the open to test the validity of their application to this new situation. He may find that his past experience and information must be supplemented before he can make an adequate judgment or plan appropriate action. The result of these considerations may be a rejection or revision of his original reaction. Through this process of self-scrutiny, he may have come to understand himself, as well as the outside world, better. A certain inner readjustment may have started that will modify his response to the next person or situation encountered.

In both the literary experience and the life experience, a process such as the one outlined constitutes reflective thinking. If the individual is stimulated often enough to engage in this kind of reflection, it may tend to become habitual. There will have been set up a readiness to reflect on his own attitudes toward people and situations as a prelude to passing judgment or deciding on action.

It seems reasonable to suggest, therefore, that in building up the habits of mind essential to the attainment of sound literary judgment, the student will also be acquiring mental habits valuable for the development of sound insight into ordinary human experience.

There is more than a verbal parallel between the process of reflective thinking arising from response to literature and the process of reflection as a prelude to action in life itself. John Dewey and other pragmatist philosophers remind us that in actual life constructive thinking usually starts when there is some conflict or discomfort or when habitual behavior is impeded and a choice of new paths of behavior must be made. Such thinking, therefore, grows out of some sort of tension and is colored by it. The tension contributes the impetus to seek a solution, but intelligent behavior results from thought brought to bear on the problem. Moreover, the validity of the thought will usually depend on whether emotion has been controlled and has not obscured the actual situation. "Impulse is needed to arouse thought, incite reflection and enliven belief. But only thought notes obstructions, invents tools, conceives aims, directs technique, and thus converts impulse into an art which lives in objects" (Dewey, *Human Nature* 170–71).

Educators are more and more recognizing this view of constructive thinking. It is comparatively easy for the student to think rationally about difficult human problems when impersonal academic treatments make them abstract subjects of thought. Unfortunately, that kind of thinking is probably not very useful; it lacks the conflicting impulses or emotional perplexities out of which thinking usually grows in real life. Reason should arise in a matrix of feeling:

> The conclusion is not that the emotional, passionate phase of action can be or should be eliminated in behalf of a bloodless

reason. More "passions," not fewer, is the answer. To check the influence of hate there must be sympathy, while to rationalize sympathy there are needed emotions of curiosity, caution, respect for the freedom of others—dispositions which evoke objects which balance those called up by sympathy, and prevent its degeneration into maudlin sentiment and meddling interference. Rationality, once more, is not a force to evoke against impulse and habit. It is the attainment of a working harmony among diverse desires.   (Dewey, *Human Nature* 195)

That kind of rationality may be fostered by literature. The literary experience may provide the emotional tension and conflicting attitudes out of which spring the kind of thinking that can later be assimilated into actual behavior. The emotional character of the student's response to literature offers an opportunity to develop the ability *to think rationally within an emotionally colored context*. Furthermore, the teaching situation in which a group of students and a teacher exchange views and stimulate one another toward clearer understanding can contribute greatly to the growth of such habits of reflection.

Several specific classroom discussions may serve to illustrate this. The students who discussed Ibsen's *A Doll House* (see p. 115) provide an example of processes that might also be evoked by many more recent works. After they had clarified their historical approach to the play, they still found themselves involved in a lively difference of opinion. "Nora should never have left her children, no matter how unhappy she was," declared one. "Her main duty was toward them and toward maintaining a home for them." This was vigorously opposed by others who claimed that Nora's duty was first of all toward herself. She needed to develop her own mind so that she might consider herself truly an individual. Without this she could be of little service to her children.

The young women had obviously identified very strongly with Nora; the discussion seemed to have personal immediacy for them. The rights of a woman to self-expression and personal dignity were thoroughly canvassed. Nevertheless, all the students, even the most decided individualists, hesitated to say that Nora had no responsibilities toward her children. A number of the students found it difficult to take one position or the other. Their sympathies were involved in Nora's gesture of independence; they shared her desire to stand completely alone; yet they were equally ready to see the value of marriage and children. At this point an emotional tension had developed.

Although the discussion seemed to be moving in circles, the teacher did not rush the class over this hurdle. Finally, one of the students pointed out that Ibsen's ending had not provided a solution to Nora's problem but had only underlined her dilemma. Certainly an individualism that entailed the sacrifice of important relationships could not be very desirable. A valuable kind of independence for Nora would have permitted her to be a complete human being yet to remain in the home and to function as a wife and mother. Another student added that it is often necessary to sacrifice certain satisfactions—such as the right to complete, untrammeled independence—in order to satisfy other needs in our nature. It was agreed, however, that the role of wife and mother should not have required submergence of Nora's personality. Furthermore, as one student pointed out, even if Torvald had been an ideal man, there still would have remained the need for adjustment between the personalities of the husband and wife as equals.

The students here were groping toward ideas that authorities on family problems and mental hygiene consider extremely important. Those experts remind us that to achieve an integrated personality the individual must reconcile or adjust conflicting impulses and aspirations within himself. Moreover, much friction would be avoided by recognition that any personal relationship necessarily entails compromises between different temperaments. The family group, for example, should provide scope for each of the personalities within it; yet if it is to be a smoothly functioning group, each individual must to a certain extent be willing to adapt himself to the others. The adolescent, in his present family or in future relationships, will be better prepared to make the necessary adjustments if he has thoroughly assimilated this approach.

In the discussion about Ibsen's play, there was not only a clash of opinion among various students; certain students discovered conflicting emotional attitudes within themselves. Thus these students lived through something analogous to the inner conflict that must often attend choices in life.

Furthermore, in this phase of their discussion the students were not considering the demands and responsibilities only of the marriage relationship. They also achieved some understanding of the complex adjustments required in any relationship. And each individual, they concluded, should seek to reconcile his different needs; he must attempt to satisfy the most important with as little sacrifice as possible of other valued tendencies in his nature. Such insights were much more valuable than any conclusion that the students might have reached concerning the rightness of Nora's final act.

More significant than any statements made by the students was the fact that these ideas grew out of emotional tension and lively personal feeling. There is no proof that the insights achieved were retained. But it can safely be said that they were more likely to be retained than if the same ideas had been encountered in an impersonal way in a traditional psychology or sociology course.

That Ibsen's *A Doll House* is a "problem" play may possibly obscure the point. A similar process might have grown out of the experience of a play that was in no way designed to focus attention on a controversial problem. Works that are read solely because of their literary significance may arouse interest in such issues.

For example, in a discussion of *Antony and Cleopatra* carried on by a freshmen literature class in a women's college, the play was rejected by the majority of the group. Their dislike for the tragedy, it became apparent, grew out of their antipathy to Cleopatra. As one student put it, "I hate that kind of woman. She is selfish, conceited, grasping for power. I am not interested in what happens to her." Like most students, they had responded to the character as they would in real life. The instructor's job was to help them maintain that personal sense of the work and yet react to it in rational terms.

The students were challenged to consider the basis for their antipathy. It finally became obvious that theirs was the point of view of the average woman to whose marital peace a person like Cleopatra would be a decided menace. (When this episode was related to an authority on adolescent psychology in charge of guidance in a large California high school, she commented that the students' reaction to Cleopatra was as much in terms of their present adolescent relationships as of any future adult situations. We tend to forget, she pointed out, that adolescents in their boy and girl relationships are already engaged in an intense emotional life parallel to adult experiences. They are already, for instance, experiencing the disillusionments and triumphs of sex rivalry.)

The students felt that their judgment of Cleopatra's ruthlessness and egotism was justified by the text. This led them to inquire what her function was in the play. Obviously, the reader was being led to feel that the fate of Cleopatra and Antony was important. Much as the class might disapprove of Cleopatra in real life, they came to perceive that her very vices and weaknesses, like those of Antony, are intermingled with traits that make their struggle and their downfall significant. Although morally some of Cleopatra's actions merit condemnation, she possesses great vitality, the ability to feel and act on a grand scale. Approaching the character in this way, students were able to comprehend the intermingled childish and queenlike actions that characterize her. They responded more perceptively to the verse. Shakespeare, the students concluded, helped them grasp the complexity of such a character; there is understanding to be gained from living through the fugue of emotions that the play presents, to their resolution in those noble last scenes.

From this discussion of Cleopatra there emerged, first of all, a clearer understanding of the aesthetic attitude. Cleopatra's significance for them was obviously not what it might have been if she were part of their own lives. They could set aside their practical reaction toward her and participate in the complex and heightened form of experience that the play offered. One student phrased in her own terms the value of aesthetic distance, which made this possible.

These literary perceptions tended to modify the students' initial reaction. They came to see that their practical judgments on people, in either a play or real life, need not be the limit of their insight. They might attempt to comprehend the human drives that lead people to act in ways potentially injurious or repugnant to them. In some cases, they realized, their own aims and satisfactions might seem equally alien or objectionable from the point of view of other people.

Implied in this discussion, therefore, was the germ of a new moral attitude, as well as the development of critical objectivity. Instead of simply approving or condemning, one might seek to understand. Instead of being based on fixed rules of conduct unconditionally applied to all under all circumstances, judgment should be passed only after the motives of the behavior and the particular circumstances had been understood. One might condemn the act and yet wish to understand what produced it. Moral judgment itself would thus become more humane.

Much less complex works than Shakespeare's plays may lead to similar insights. A class in a coeducational southern school was reading plays and short stories. The group was at first content to condemn the possessive mother in Sidney Howard's *The Silver Cord* or to talk about how much they disliked the vain posturing of Mr. Reginald Peacock in Katherine Mansfield's story. Because of the way the anthology for the course was arranged, they tended to speak in terms of types of people, such as the boor, the sadist, the gossip. One or two of the students tried to suggest some excuse for these characters' behavior; the discussion ultimately veered toward the idea that, after all, the important thing was not to condemn but rather to find out what produced such personalities and behavior. The students felt that their reading had led them to observe themselves and other people much more carefully. That in itself was useful because one might then learn how to live with them. It might also be better not to think that one necessarily has the right to try to change other people or that mature personalities are easily modified. However, one might at least attempt to see what explained behavior in order to help create conditions that would in the future produce more socially valuable people.

The class had started with a decidedly moralistic attitude, sitting in judgment on the characters encountered in their reading. Their point of view changed appreciably in the direction of greater human sympathy and objectivity. Instead of thinking of the characters only as individual human beings, they saw them in relation to the social forces that had molded them or that gave them scope for expressing their special temperaments.

The question of censorship is relevant here. For example, the demand in some quarters that the *Merchant of Venice* be barred from the schools. In a class in which a number of students were Jewish, it is argued, Shylock would create self-consciousness and resentment in that group and reinforce the prejudices of the rest of the class. This argument assumes a number of things that the preceding discussion has rejected. The first assumption is that the class would read the play and react to the character of Shylock without any interchange among themselves or with the teacher. The second assumption is that even if they did express themselves, their original ideas would remain unchanged.

The desirable kind of classroom situation outlined in the preceding chapters would negate both these assumptions. If the literary experience offered by this play did give rise to decided reactions to Shylock, that should then serve as the beginning of a process of clarification such as was described earlier. Obviously, the kind of classroom atmosphere predicated, reflecting a relationship of confidence, would be extremely important. The students would not be encouraged merely to express their attitude toward Shylock. The discussion would become a means of leading them back to the text, to understand Shylock's situation, to see the adverse conditions against which he struggled, and to recognize the connection between that and his behavior. In other words, that part of the play would have enabled them to live through the experiences of a member of a minority group and to understand his behavior even when it was distasteful or ridiculous to them.

It might be contended that Shakespeare shared the prejudices of his age and that therefore this excursion into the development of racial understanding would be irrelevant to the play. Even if one grants the view concerning Shakespeare's attitude (his text provides its own antidote to that attitude), the English teacher could not justifiably ignore the fact that the students are reacting to the play in terms of their own present-day lives. He could not shirk the opportunity to contribute to a more rational, unprejudiced approach to human beings. Young people in school function as whole personalities; they are not creatures that can be neatly divided into literary or sociological segments, each segment to be ministered to by a different teacher. Hence the English teacher must feel some responsibility for dealing with whatever repercussions, no matter how controversial or nonliterary, the experience of such a play may have. That the play is "great literature" may have determined its selection in the first place, but that means nothing unless the play has human significance today.

Some will concede that the school and the teacher have the responsibility of developing constructive attitudes toward human relations but will ask, Why suggest this round-about way of transmitting such insight? Why not give the first group lectures on the need for adjustment of the different temperaments within the family? Why not present to the other groups a clearly worked-out exposition of the factors conditioning personality and behavior? Why take the time of a literature class for discussions suggested by the haphazard accidents of student reactions? Topics may not be brought into the discussion in any logical order, and there may be important subjects that the students may not introduce in their discussions at all. Would it not be preferable to eliminate any such topics from the literature classroom and to depend on a more orderly method of presenting this information to the students?

The considerations set forth in the first five chapters of this book offer an answer to one aspect of these questions. The student's personal response to literary works will be primarily colored by his attitudes toward the characters and situations they present. To attempt to ignore these student reactions would destroy the very basis on which any greater *literary* sensitivity could be built. Even when the English teacher's responsibilities are interpreted in the narrowest terms, the discussion of such topics remains relevant to the literature classrooms.

If, however, one were not at all concerned with whether students developed sounder literary appreciation, one should nevertheless recognize literature as a potential means of developing social understanding. A formal course in psychology or social problems could not perform quite the function illustrated by the discussions in literature classes reported earlier in this chapter. Their special characteristic was the element of personal emotion that permeated the students' treatment of these topics. In the argument about *A Doll House*, some sort of identification with Nora had occurred. Yet the students felt free to show their feeling because ostensibly they were talking about Nora, not themselves. The discussion of any general topic concerning human nature or social relations arose from the students' own vicarious experience and their feelings about it. Their concluding insights grew out of a process accompanied by definite emotional pulls toward various points of view. The whole discussion was *felt* as well as thought.

If the literary works had had little emotional impact, any discussion would have been empty verbiage. The discussions reported above were fundamentally attempts by the students to work out some rational understanding of their reactions. They were involved in the task of managing their emotions—something very different from ignoring or repressing them. In this way, they were encouraged to bring thought to bear on emotional responses—the starting point for intelligent behavior.

Thus, discussion of literary experiences makes possible rehearsals of the struggle to clarify emotion and make it the basis of intelligent and informed thinking. This possesses a certain parallelism to those situations in life that engender conflicting inner attitudes. The insights and ideas that result from such an experience tend to be assimilated into the individual's active equipment because they are embedded in a matrix of emotional and personal concern. Hence, literature provides an educational medium through which the student's habits of thought may be influenced. When this is more widely recognized, we may expect that literary materials will be introduced into many different phases of the curriculum.

The emotional quality of literature has sometimes caused the social scientist to look askance at it as something that strengthens the student's natural tendency toward undisciplined emotion. Dewey offers the rejoinder that rationality does not exist in opposition to emotion but rather represents the attainment of a working harmony among diverse desires. The social scientist should recognize that literature may provide a means of helping the student achieve a functioning rationality.

The power of literature to develop capacity for feeling, for responding imaginatively to the thoughts and behavior of others, was treated in earlier chapters. This chapter has considered how, through discussion and reflection on his response to literature, the student may learn to order his emotions and to rationally face people and situations he is emotionally involved in. Power to transmit understanding of society in terms that will be personally assimilable is lacking in traditional social science teaching methods. When literary experiences are made the material for reflective thinking, they may be one means of providing this sorely needed linkage between feeling, thought, and behavior.

Teachers of the social sciences usually demonstrate a rather limited view of the value of literary treatments of their subjects. History textbooks append references to historical novels, or students are assigned short stories and novels about foreign countries or about different types of social background. If the French Revolution is being studied, for example, *A Tale of Two Cities* is read. The idea seems to be that the literary work adds sharpness to the information that the teacher wishes to convey. The student is helped to "understand" the information better through the more vivid and detailed descriptions; a novel, for instance, helps him visualize the people and scenes mentioned in his history book. That, certainly, may be one of the contributions of literature. But the matter is usually left on this level, with literature considered merely a tool for vividly conveying facts.

The repercussions of such understanding gained through vicarious experience do not end there. From enhanced perceptions may flow a sense of the human and practical implications of the information that has been acquired. This information is no longer words to be rattled off; the words now point toward actual human situations and feelings. Thus, the reading of John Hersey's *Hiroshima* or Zora Neale Hurston's *Their Eyes Were Watching God* will bestow emotional reality in terms of human beings, their suffering, their needs and struggles. The meaning attributed earlier to the term *understanding* transcends the view of literature as a pedagogic device for giving sugar-coated information.

The teacher of social sciences as well as the teacher of English should hold firmly to this fact that literature is something lived through, something to which the student reacts on a variety of interrelated emotional and intellectual planes. Therein lie its many educational potentialities.

This stress on the value of the literary experience in no way rules out the organized study of psychological and sociological subjects. On the contrary, students should be given even greater opportunities for that kind of knowledge. The social sciences, however, could be made more practically fruitful than they are at present. The question as stated at the end of chapter 6 is, How can the student come to assimilate the scientific approach to humankind and society so thoroughly that it will translate itself into the very attitudes, decisions, and actions that constitute his own life? Unfortunately, this has too seldom happened. Many even of the college graduates among present adult generations tend to think only of the conditions that affect them most directly. They do not reconsider their own opinions in the light of social, economic, or psychological theory, nor do they attempt to imagine the human effects of the social measures they espouse as immediately beneficial to themselves.

The will to learn, it has been said, rests on a state of dissatisfaction with present knowledge. The interchange of ideas in class discussions can lead the student to dissatisfaction with his present knowledge about human relations, since lack of information limits his ability either to participate in the experience offered by the book or to fit the experience into some rational structure of ideas. The reading of literature, therefore, might be made a means of arousing the will to learn. Furthermore, sociological or psychological information sought in this way is more likely to be integrated into the stream of the student's thought and behavior.

The social science teacher must, of course, determine the extent and manner of his use of literary materials, questions beyond the scope of this book. There are similarities between literary experience and direct observation through field trips, another source of personal response to social facts.[1] His special concern will be to bring about a perception of the general implications of what is experienced vicariously through literature. The purposes of the social science classroom require the transition from concern with particular instances to concern with the general social conditions or basic factors involved.[2]

The teaching processes described in part 2 of this book and in the present chapter can further that transition to general concerns. Conversely, social science discussions of general ideas should more frequently be translated back into terms of individual human beings. Such a shuttling back and forth between the abstract and the concrete, the general and the specific, which the use of literary materials might foster, would

---

[1] Literature, for instance, might be used as a substitute when such direct observation is not possible. Literary materials might even be an excellent means of introducing the student to the subject or problems to be studied, as a preliminary to direct observation of actual conditions. The analysis in the preceding chapter of the development of social sensitivity through literature is also relevant here.

The case history is another approximation toward personal experience. Its value will depend, probably more than is recognized, on the literary effectiveness with which the case history is presented. In addition to the more scientifically controlled and studied case history, the social science teacher should probably utilize the surer emotional and intellectual effects of literary treatments of the general social conditions with which his particular science concerns itself.

[2] The teacher whose main responsibility is the development of literary sensitivity will be less impatient for this transition to occur and will depend on repeated literary experiences and discussions to accomplish it. The social science teacher will probably consider this too time-consuming, given his desire to impart a body of relevant information. To read a book like Claude Brown's *Manchild in the Promised Land* and then to study Harlem might contribute to such generalization.

Students will need to question whether the picture is an accurate one and whether there may not be contrasting or contradictory considerations that he did not offer. This will illuminate the value of the impersonal scientific investigation based on the study of as many cases as possible.

give social science study immediacy and lasting value. The student would develop the habit of recognizing that behind any particular situation there exists a general social situation whose causes and effects should be understood. Equally important, he would be aware that any generalizations or statistical data about society, politics, or economics refer to the behavior of living, feeling people.

The preceding remarks reflect the belief that the social science teacher shares with the literature teacher, and indeed with all other teachers, the responsibility toward the student as a complete person. The emphasis and methods of the social science teacher may be different; he is interested in initiating his students into an understanding of the methods of research in his particular field and in giving his students some knowledge of the nature of its materials. Ultimately, however, these techniques and this information must become a part of the equipment with which the student encounters actual life situations. In the functioning personality, there should not be any conflict between the attitudes toward people and toward society engendered by literature and by the social sciences.

Teachers of different subjects will be helped by an understanding of how their various contributions toward a common goal are related to one another. The view that the literature teacher should have some knowledge of the fundamental methods and concepts of the social sciences implies with equal force that the social studies teacher should have some understanding of the special nature of the emotional and intellectual experience provided by the literary work of art. The social science teacher should also make students aware of the extent to which writings in the social sciences are colored by rhetorical devices.

The necessity for such mutual understanding among members of the different disciplines has been demonstrated where teachers have worked together in an integrated course. They need to share a common approach to literature and human relations. The great weakness in such courses has been that a lack of insight into the special nature of the literary experience has caused both social science and literature teachers to reduce the literary work of art to the status of social document.

The classroom discussions of *A Doll House, Antony and Cleopatra,* and other works are isolated instances representing a wide variety of possible illustrations. The intention has been to avoid any suggestion of a routine procedure through which students are docilely led to predigested slogans about social understanding. One of the banes of educational systems today is the pressure on the teacher to work out neat outlines of the ideas about literature that his students are to acquire. Once such a plan is made, there is a great temptation to impose it arbitrarily. The teacher becomes impatient of the trial-and-error groping of the students. It seems so much easier all around if the teacher cuts the Gordian knot and gives the students the tidy set of conclusions and labels he has worked out. Yet this does not necessarily give them new insights. Hence the emphasis throughout this book on the teacher's role in initiating and guiding a process of inductive learning.

A teacher of English in a high school, unusually aware of the adolescent's need to understand human development, decided to give his class a period of several weeks in which they could read novels that presented a life history, ranging from *David Copperfield* to *Sons and Lovers.* He began by lecturing on the main points in developmental psychology. He provided an outline of some of the major problems and influences that enter into the development of any personality. The students were then required to write essays on each novel read, discussing the hero's development in the terms provided by the teacher's outline. The essays indicated that the pupils had read the novels with the aim of finding details to illustrate just those points mentioned by the teacher. The papers gave little indication of what the novels had meant to the youngsters themselves. The whole thing took on the nature of an exercise in which they attempted to apply the teacher's labels to each novel as it passed in review.

Despite his admirable initiative in breaking away from the usual routine of literature teaching, this teacher's aims were defeated by his unfortunate tendency to be satisfied when students had learned a vocabulary. He did not let the desire for organized understanding grow out of the reading of the novels. The pupils should have first been permitted to read these books in ways significant to themselves and thus to have participated emotionally in the growth and aspirations of the heroes and heroines. The class should have become involved in an interchange of ideas and feelings produced by their experience of the novels. Discovering certain similar problems in the lives of these characters, the students would then have been ready for the analysis of life patterns that the psychologist can offer. The perception that the development of a personality is not a haphazard process would have grown out of the reading, not have been imposed on it. The teacher would have played an extremely important role in fostering this. The students themselves would have played an equally important role, however, and they would have achieved insights related to their own tensions and their own world.

Given the spontaneous and largely unpredictable character of specific literary experiences and the great diversity of temperaments and backgrounds in most student groups, any discussion will tend to develop a special character and focus. To take advantage of this, the teacher will not impose a routine but will let the discussion grow out of the ideas and the perplexities formulated by the students themselves. However, this does not imply sheer improvisation. To see the possibilities present in the students' responses, the teacher needs to have a firm grasp of the work and the major concepts relevant to it. He will then be able to carry on an inductive process, in which the students are stimulated to raise questions and to arrive at understandings that have personal significance.

The necessity for presenting isolated classroom illustrations may do injustice to another very important point. Certainly a few scattered discussions of literature could have little or no influence on students' attitudes toward people. Any such influence would be the cumulative effect of many experiences with literature, many free interchanges of opinion among students and teachers, many such emotionally motivated insights. Moreover, the intellectual tone of the school and the habits of thinking fostered by the entire school experience will modify the nature of the discussion in any single class. And within the class, the basis for such spontaneous discussions must be slowly and steadily built up. The give-and-take of ideas and the interplay among different personalities will in itself have a liberalizing influence. If under the repeated stimulus of literature the students have again and again been able to start from their emotional uncertainties and work through to some rational understanding, it is probable that a gradual revision of their habits of feeling and thinking will occur. They will at least have been set on the path that leads to the development of rational approach to experience.

The personal nature of the learning process places a decided responsibility on the teacher. In seeking to create a vital relationship between his students and literature, he will become imbued with a feeling for the complex process by which social insights can grow out of response to literature. The areas of intellectual and emotional ferment are the points at which growth is possible in the student's mind and personality. The teacher who learns not to become insecure when lively discussion arises will also learn to sense the right moment to introduce new concepts relevant to these growth points. The thesis of chapters 1 and 6 can now be seen more clearly in its educational context: The teacher can perform his function successfully only when aware of the attitudes toward human nature and society that he is helping his students to assimilate.

This view of literature study is completely alien to the old notion of character building through literature, which consisted in giving the student, without any regard for his needs and state of mind, a series of models of behavior to imitate. Equally unacceptable are attempts to treat literature as a body of documents that may be brought forth to illustrate various subtopics under the heading of human relations. Lists of books dealing with topics such as family, war, labor relations—let alone such moralistic topics as noble characters or great deeds of the past—will not in themselves do the job that has been formulated in this book.

The teacher's responsibility would be much reduced if he could think entirely in terms of the subject matter of literature. His task then would be principally the assembling of such lists of books. That is not the situation. Literature offers not merely information, but experiences. After all, the important thing is not whether a particular book presents a picture of contemporary marriage relations or describes the activities of the Eskimo but the way these subjects are treated by the author and the context into which they are integrated in the reader's mind. Does the image of marriage relationships present an attitude of resentment toward one or the other sex? Or does it offer the possibility of sensing the subtlety of temperamental adjustments involved in the achievement of happily shared lives? The significant thing is not that a book tells how the Eskimo fishes, builds his house, and wins his mate but whether the book presents the Eskimo as a remote being of a different species or as another human being who happens to have worked out different patterns of behavior.

To catalog the great body of literary materials according to the basic attitudes they might convey would be a colossal task. It would be almost impossible to find general standards of judgment, principally because the effect of any book will vary with the attitudes and assumptions that each reader brings to it. Although in the following pages terms drawn from the social sciences will be used, the focus is on the subtler, least easily cataloged modes of social understanding that literature makes possible.

There is a tendency to feel that one can create social understanding by simply assigning to students a group of novels or plays dealing with a social science topic. The value of book lists depends on how they are used and whether the teacher selects from them in the light of his students' or his classes' needs.

Moreover, it is necessary to reiterate that the teacher must play an active part in the development of social understanding. He himself needs to possess an enlightened sense of human relations in order to help his students derive new sensitivities from literary experience and evaluate it in personal and social terms. In the long run, therefore, this kind of illumination cannot be prescribed for by means of book lists, outlines, and routine procedures. It will depend in each case on the particular personalities and backgrounds of each group of teacher and students as well as on the nature of the particular school setting.

The preceding qualifications should prevent the misinterpretation that sometimes arises when ideas illuminated by literary materials are emphasized. Moreover, given the point of view and the teaching process set forth in part 2, literary history, biographical information, and critical analysis of technique will not degenerate into routine studies considered as ends in themselves. They will have value because they throw light on the total literary experience, with all that it implies of personal emotion and social awareness.

The study of literary history, for instance, is often insufficiently motivated. The student learns about the sequence of literary movements and memorizes the chronology of authors and works, but only because this seems to be information arbitrarily demanded. He learns it for examinations but forgets it very quickly. Despite the study of periods and chronology, Chaucer, Swift, and Thackeray come to inhabit the same vague region.

The history of literature recounts the social activities of people in one special realm, just as does the history of politics

or of industry. The various approaches to the study of literature parallel the approaches to the study of people's activities
and institutions. Failure to emphasize this partially explains
the usual sterility of the study of literary history in school
and college.

The study of literary history constitutes a study of social
history in two ways: First, since the writer is always a member
of a particular society and of a particular group within that
society, his work grows out of the various social, economic,
and intellectual conditions of his time. Literary scholarship
has generally assimilated this approach. Especially in the treatment of American literature, the writer is studied as a member of society, and his work is viewed in relation to the
various social and intellectual pressures of his time.

Second—and this is the point that is least often recognized
or exploited—the various *processes* of social history may often
be studied more dramatically through literary history than
through any other phase of human activities. Literature is a
social institution in the sense that the family or church is a
social institution, each with its own history. Because a society's literary behavior takes the explicit form mainly of a body
of written or printed works, its history is perhaps somewhat
more clearly delimited. Yet it seldom is utilized to initiate students into an understanding of general social mechanisms.
Literary history reveals clearly the nature of the individual's
relations to the social group, as well as the nature of the forces
molding the group itself. The student should be helped to
apply to other phases of life the ideas concerning historical
processes derived from literary history.

Literature is not a photographic mirroring of life but the
result of a particular socially patterned personality employing

particular socially fostered modes of communication. Much of what is considered purely literary, technical, or textual criticism involves definitions of the special temperamental attitudes of the author, the precise emotional tone of his work, and its particular philosophic approach. All this is essential to appreciate the literary merits of his work. The study of his manipulations of literary technique (to which the term *literary criticism* is often too narrowly limited) is incidental to the desire to apprehend the special qualities of the novel or poem or play. Walter Pater, the apostle of aesthetic criticism, limited his duties as critic to a clarification or definition of the impression produced on him by literary works. Yet in a study such as his "Wordsworth," this aim encompasses social and psychological considerations.

From these literary concerns should arise an added awareness that any individual—writer or bricklayer—with his special traits and techniques is the result of transaction with his environment.[3] This concept is often presented to the student only in the study of such topics as crime, juvenile delinquency, or politics. Yet this view of the individual is illustrated just as dramatically in the creation of the artist as in the acts of criminals or government leaders. By seeing how a concept of this sort applies throughout the whole range of his studies—social,

---

[3] "Environment" here necessarily includes physical nature as well as the cultural setting. Various geographical determinists at the end of the last century exaggerated the influence of natural environment; nowadays we may tend to underestimate its influence, particularly on literature. See Aldous Huxley's entertaining essay "Wordsworth in the Tropics," on what the poet's sense of nature might have been if he had lived in the tropics rather than in the gentle atmosphere of the Lake Country.

scientific, or artistic—the student will be able to build up an integrated approach to human relations.

One of the usual approaches to the study of literature is the history of different forms—the novel, the drama, poetry, the essay. The student learns that in different periods these forms reflect different literary traditions. He is not made aware that literary traditions represent one type of crystallized social behavior. After all, environmental influences operate as much in an author's treatment of literary form and choice of theme as in any other phase of human activity. The imagination of the Elizabethan dramatist, for instance, necessarily functioned within the framework of the conventions and dramatic formulas of his day. Knowing them can help us differentiate between what in Elizabethan plays the contemporary audience accepted as dramatic convention and what reflected the actual life about them. The very themes the dramatist selected were similarly nourished by the intellectual climate of his time. From study of a particular literary form at different periods there can arise the perception that the individual's activities and ideas in any sphere are necessarily directed by attitudes and patterns absorbed from his cultural environment.

Similarly, the study of a literary period as a whole may illuminate this concept of the shaping pressure of the environment on the individual. If he lives in a time when prose forms are highly valued and poetry neglected, he will tend most readily to express himself in prose. If he lives in an age when the drama is the dominant form, he will probably express himself through that medium. Or if he uses some minor form, it will probably be selected from those admired in his milieu, as in the case of the Elizabethan sonnet. Indeed, the pressure of literary conventions is even more pervasive than that. Having grown up at a time when the heroic couplet is the common poetic mold, he will tend to express himself in its balanced and measured phrases, and freer patterns will seem rough and unpleasant to his ear. The study of eighteenth-century poetry or of eighteenth-century criticism of Elizabethan literature can serve to illustrate this concept of cultural conditioning.

It is often hard for the student to realize in a vivid or personal way that the ideas and behavior he accepts most unquestioningly derive their hold on him from the fact that they have been unconsciously absorbed from the society about him. He can be led from a perception of how this happens in literary activity to an understanding of the similar process that crystallizes the individual's ideas concerning ways of behavior and ideas of right and wrong. Having observed so explicit a demonstration of how even the most gifted and intelligent authors are shaped by their environment, the student may come to recognize similar pressures on all other phases of human thought and activity. He should see that the existence of literary periods with marked characteristics of style and subject matter is the reflection of a general sociological phenomenon.

The student who becomes acquainted with this concept of cultural conditioning may often tend to exaggerate its implications. He may think of the individual as completely at the mercy of the dominant forces in the environment about him. This is as erroneous, of course, as is the earlier notion that the individual has complete free choice and self-determination. The study of Shakespeare in relation to the other Elizabethan dramatists may illuminate this problem in a way highly interesting to students. They have accepted the idea of Shakespeare as a supreme genius. Their introduction, however, to the tragedies of blood, and particularly to Thomas Kyd's

Spanish Tragedy, usually brings keen disillusionment. They find that much in Shakespeare's *Hamlet* follows the outlines of earlier plays that also use ghosts calling for revenge, avengers who are mad or feign madness, heroes who hesitate and soliloquize. They discover that Shakespeare often followed very literally the theatrical conventions of his own day. The student's first reaction is usually to remove Shakespeare from his pedestal and to exclaim that he was merely a man of his own time, after all.

Reflection, however, brings revision of this judgment. They begin to see that Shakespeare was thoroughly a product of a particular environment, and yet, working within the patterns set by his time, he modified them and put his unique stamp on them. A comparison between his plays and contemporary ones of the same type, such as the romantic comedies or the tragicomedies, reveals the pervasive influence of the literary environment, but it also reveals his ability to create something new and superbly individual out of the elements provided by his age. Moreover, these unique creations will influence writers who come after him. Through the study of easily recognized literary details, the student can be led to perceive within a limited sphere something of how in all phases of human life the average individual, too, not only is molded by but also molds his environment.

Even more striking is the light that the study of literary history may cast on the process of social change. This should be understood as a process in time, involving the constant adjustment and readjustment of particular individuals to particular cultural patterns. This human view of social changes can grow out of a study of the modifications over a period of time in authors' selections of subjects and choices of literary forms. The study of English literature from 1750 to 1830, for instance, offers the student dramatic possibilities for developing a sense of the complex factors involved in any change in human ways of thinking and behavior.

For example, the concept of cultural lag applies as much to literature as to any phase of history. A study of verse forms, poetic diction, and themes shows how attitudes and social patterns tend to persist even when they no longer serve a vital need. The hold of the heroic couplet, the endless minor variations on themes fully exploited earlier in the eighteenth century, the development of tricks of poetic diction to the point of absurdity illustrate very forcibly the tendency of the average mind to follow already channeled grooves.

Against this background of persisting habits and conventions, the study of the beginnings of the Romantic movement in the eighteenth century and its flowering in the early nineteenth century can illustrate the slow cumulative process of social innovation—the few signs earlier in the century of a slight departure from accepted attitudes toward humanity and nature in a poem here and there by a Lady Winchilsea or a Parnell; the evidence of an increasing body of sentimental minor poetry, like the "graveyard poems," that hints at new tendencies; the partial break with tradition represented by the Wartons or by Thomson; the harking back to literary precedents of the Middle Ages and the Renaissance to sanction rejection of the contemporary conventions; the curious transitional quality of Gray's poems or of Wordsworth's earliest verse; the full revolt bursting forth in the *Lyrical Ballads*; the resistance that Wordsworth, Keats, Shelley, and the others met from critics and readers still dominated by the Pope tradition in poetry; the slow education of an audience that would understand and appreciate their work.

These literary materials give vivid evidence that social change often comes about slowly and almost imperceptibly. At first a few minds here and there free themselves from the worn-out attitudes and procedures that no longer satisfy new needs. Gradually the number of these nonconformists increases; their influence spreads; and ultimately their ideas may become the dominant ones automatically assimilated by young authors and readers, as in the case of the Romantic view of poetry. Thus, in his study of the rise of Romanticism, the student can find dramatically portrayed the pull and tug of contending social phenomena. The tendency to hold on to old attitudes, on the one hand, is opposed by the struggle, on the other hand, to find fresher and more completely satisfying patterns. In other words, the relation between the processes of cultural lag and social innovation is revealed as legitimately in literary history as it is in the history of technology or of political institutions.

The anthropologist's idea of the interdependence of the various aspects of any culture can be related to the history of literature. An understanding of what happens in the realm of literary activity requires the study of the accompanying economic, social, and political conditions. It would, for example, be false to explain the Romantic movement entirely in literary terms as a revolt against eighteenth-century formalism. (Of course, this popular view of eighteenth-century literature is also oversimplified.) It is necessary to be aware also of the political ideals, the emphasis on a static and stratified society, which paralleled the eighteenth-century concern with balanced form and disciplined emotion. Romantic exaltation of free expression of individual feeling often arose from rejection of social as well as literary limitations.

Similar interdependence can be noted no matter what period is studied. What, for example, were the forces at work in Elizabethan society that helped to make possible the flowering of the drama? What were the economic and social conditions that created so heterogeneous an audience for the theater? How did the fact that the court still played so central an economic and social, as well as political, role influence the drama? How did the religious and philosophic developments affect the sense of significant human problems? The history of literature cannot be viewed as completely separate from other aspects of society.

The anthropologists point out also that through this interaction of its different elements, a culture tends to develop some degree of integration, a recognizable basic cultural pattern. For historical or social reasons, it may retain or produce groups with differing customs and values. The United States has from its political inception recognized that its unity arises out of plurality. Always a nation of immigrants—the Indians are said to have been the first to come from elsewhere—America has become increasingly multi-ethnic. Whole literatures have been produced reflecting the interplay between the cultural past brought to these shores and the society established by the predecessors. Often these literary works present the inequalities between the dominant and minority groups and the tensions between less and more assimilated generations. The problem is to fulfil our democratic goal of equal justice for all without regard to differences and yet to maintain respect for such differences. In the schools the aim is to develop students' respect for their own ethnic or group background and for the cultural traits of others and at the same time to prepare the students for constructive citizenship in our democracy. The current movement termed *multiculturalism* is having widespread impact, but at times seems to be heightening the sense of difference and conflicting interests among groups. In 1915 Horace Kallen with the support of Alain Locke introduced the term *cultural pluralism* and substituted for the metaphor of the melting pot the metaphor of the orchestra, with each instrument likened to a cultural group making its special contribution to the symphony of civilization. Such a symphony, such a sense of common human interests that transcend differences could determine the character of personal and political relations within our society and ensure its survival as a democracy (Rosenblatt, "Whitman's *Democratic Vistas*").

Within the history of even a single literature, we may encounter the reflection of a number of different cultural emphases—in the literature of England, for example, the sharp contrast between earthly and otherworldly values in medieval society, with its intense appreciation of both; the greater flexibility of Renaissance institutions, with the attendant zest for free expression of individual personality; the increasing importance of materialistic bourgeois values in the eighteenth and nineteenth centuries, with accompanying stress on property and on social prudence; the paradoxical reflection of bourgeois economic individualism in the Romanticists' demands for personal freedom and their break with the utilitarian bourgeois view of life when the Romantic artists translated their individualism into aesthetic and spiritual values; the development of the physical and biological sciences' creating a crisis in religious thought through their reinforcement of a naturalistic interpretation of humankind and the universe; and the increasingly frequent expression today of a philosophy that stresses the individual's inescapable bonds with other human beings. The societies that express themselves through English literature seem to have developed varying degrees of integration. In some ages, one perceives a number of clear-cut subpatterns, or even a number of contradictory patterns in a state of unstable equilibrium; in other ages, many aspects of the society seem to reflect similar or parallel emphases.

Even such a sketchy listing indicates that a literary work reflects or refracts the characteristic emphases of its own age. The literature program has always included works produced in a great many different periods and social settings. Students read (or should read) books that treat both contemporary and past American life; British, French, German, Russian novels; modern versions of the Scandinavian epics; and Greek drama. An increasingly large body of Oriental literature is becoming available in translation. In addition, a growing body of fiction shows the persistence of cultural traits in the lives of different ethnic groups in America. The student encounters diverse temperaments and images of personal success in the literary works of different ages or even in the literature of a single period. He tends to take these differences for granted, without recognizing the extent to which each work implies a framework of values, mores, and modes of expression particular to some one cultural setting.

Students are not usually helped to recognize that in any literary work the diverse values of a society are incorporated into the personalities and lives of individual men and women. Mark Twain utilized this insight in *A Connecticut Yankee in King Arthur's Court*. The Yankee embodies the sense of values of one cultural pattern; the Arthurian knights reflect a different pattern. Much of the humor of this book arises from the perspective thus created, so that both cultures are viewed satirically—and, of course, Twain ultimately uses this to question certain values of his own society. Orwell's *1984* is another work that forces readers to ponder the system of values of a whole society and to consider its meaning in terms of individual lives.

Problems in values thrust themselves on the reader even more urgently in the works of those contemporary novelists, dramatists, and poets who look on human life as absurd. Many young people respond intensely to this image of human beings born into an indifferent world, shorn of all former external props, and confronting the inevitability of death. Such works as Camus's *The Stranger* or Beckett's *Waiting for Godot* undoubtedly provide a catharsis for many youthful readers. Still, the very sense of alienation may be the beginning of a movement toward positive commitment to society and toward the feeling that a person creates himself by his choices. In *The Plague* Camus explores the many different hierarchies of values people affirm through their choices in a crisis. Many contemporary writers, for example, Saul Bellow (*The Dangling Man, Herzog*), Bernard Malamud (*The Fixer*), Ralph Ellison (*Invisible Man*), or John Knowles (*A Separate Peace*), develop such a theme.

Yet surely it is not only in contemporary works that the issue of choices in values imposes itself. As in life itself, questions of values are always implicit in any poem, novel, or play. Characters are faced with the necessity for choice and by those choices affirm or deny the values of their world; the voice of the persona in a poem or narrative, by one clue and another, creates a scale of values by which the reader is asked to measure the mood or the world that has been evoked. Far from the old didacticism is this recognition that all literature affirms or denies values and that an important part of literary criticism is the clarification of such values. The youth today is confronted by necessity for choice among a vast range of alternatives. Contemporary works relevant to the adolescent's quest for identity will generate receptivity to all that literature, of both the past and the present, has to offer him.

Just as the student will recognize in the literature of the past reflections of dominant drives and emerging alternative attitudes, so he will view contemporary literature as the expression of many minds working, slowly and often at cross purposes, toward the creation of a new and more satisfactory system of common values. Through the experience of literature of the past he will be able also to come into contact with diverse views of the satisfactions to be derived from human life and society. These will serve both as contrast and as commentary on present-day emphases and on any newly offered alternatives for personal and social arrangements. Perhaps such perspective may also lead him to discriminate between works that merely reflect a general mood of disillusionment and those that reveal minds seeking new and positive alternatives.

The introduction of new types of personalities into literature, the picture of new types of relationships, or the assertion of new values in life by the writer will have their repercussions on the practical social and political life of an age. Even those works that are in opposition to the dominant attitudes of their time—for instance, the writings of Dickens, Arnold, and Ruskin—are as much a part of their age as the writings that reflect its dogmas. Subtract the works of Dickens and the others from the Victorian age and it would be something different from that age as we now understand it. The tendency to speak in terms of the social and political background of literature is misleading, since it implies that the background existed apart from the literature. This contradicts the view that aspects of any culture tend to act and react on one another.

Another point requires clarification: Literary works do not inevitably "hold the mirror up to nature." Often the work can best be viewed, with Zola, as "a slice of life seen through a temperament." The poem, play, or novel reflects the social philosophy of the author, or it may present a picture of people and situations dictated by the dominant literary conventions of the age in which the author lived. Again, it may be that only the life of a limited group in the society finds any sort of reflection in the literature of a given period. (Typical examples are Restoration comedy or the triangle situations in French novels.) Often, moreover, certain literary trends (for example, the novels of Sir Walter Scott, the great mass of Romantic poetry) may represent an attempt to escape from the realities of the society in which the authors live.

Part of a sound equipment for understanding and judging literature is a knowledge of the possible factors—personal obsessions, class bias, political aims, pendulum-swing reactions—that may color the world the writer chooses to create. It would be as absurd for students to think that the novels of futility, such as those of F. Scott Fitzgerald, reflected the whole picture of life in the nineteen-twenties as to believe that Elizabethan drama is a literal transcript of life in England at that time. Learning to sense the angle of vision of the author, the young reader will come to see in contemporary literature the inverted Victorian prudery of some of the clinical descriptions of sex and to differentiate these from the works seeking to do justice to its central role in a mature life.

The student has to be provided with the tools for weighing the various images of life that he encounters in books. This means that he must often turn from the literary work to other sources of information, whether those be the materials offered by the historian, the literary scholar, the sociologist, the anthropologist, or the psychologist. Both from the point of view of literary criticism and from the point of view of preparation for actual living, he should be stimulated to evaluate the ethical and social implications of the images of life encountered through literature. To evade this responsibility out of fear of falling into didactic moralism is to narrow the study of literature to a sterile formalism.

The preceding remarks on cultural criticism have led to a transition from general social processes working themselves out in literary history and methods of literary creation to those processes as they are exemplified in the images of individual lives offered by specific literary works. Chapter 6 reported the behavioral scientists' emphasis on the concept that the human being is a complex of qualities and habits that are the result of a great many different forces converging on and transacting with the individual organism.

Ideas about human growth and development are the very stuff of literature. The process of cultural conditioning is seen operating in the images of life that the author places before us. In the course of a year, the student usually reads works dealing with personalities in a wide variety of environments, but he is not always led to think about this. The personal strivings, the ethical problems, the social conflicts he shares through books are often part of social patterns very different from his own. With Macbeth, Jane Eyre, Becky Sharp, Lawrence's Paul Morel, Dreiser's Clyde Griffiths, Faulkner's Quentin Compson, he struggles vicariously with social codes reflecting diverse environments. Because Hardy placed the problem of the influence of environment in the center of attention, students are often led to associate this question only with his works. Any writer, particularly any novelist or dramatist, treats some aspect of this basic process by which the individual human being lives out his life in terms of the social structure, the moral code, and even the emotional habits he has acquired through transaction with his specific environment.

As we become more clearly aware of forces that pattern our lives, we acquire a certain power to resist or modify these forces (see p. 148). Hence the importance of an understanding of the concept of cultural conditioning. The student may derive this valuable insight from almost any work of literature. To return to *Hamlet* as an illustration: On the one hand, students will perceive in personal terms relevant to life today the nature of Hamlet's problem (such a modern interpretation as, for example, that he is a contemplative man caught in a situation demanding action). On the other hand, they should not ignore the fact that Hamlet's problem is bodied forth in specific terms of the code of eye for eye, tooth for tooth—a code archaic in Shakespeare's day as well as our own. Obviously, no play about a man of Hamlet's social and intellectual status in our own time would present him as assuming that society expected him personally to kill the murderer of his father.

The fear has been expressed that constant reading of literature of the past might tend to perpetuate the hold of anachronistic images of behavior. Perhaps one way of counteracting this is to make the reader aware that in literary works he submits vicariously to a cultural pattern and code of behavior often different from his own. This may develop some immunity to archaic images and some objectivity toward the cultural situation in which he himself is immersed. If the Jungian concept of an archetypal pattern or myth is brought to bear, it will be used with similar objectivity. Thus without inner confusion or maladjustment to contemporary reality, he will be able to profit from the breadth of experience, the flexibility of imaginative insight, and the sensuous enrichment that literature can impart.

The various other concepts concerning human growth and development sketched in chapter 6 are also implicit in the great body of literary works. Numerous novels follow the hero or heroine from birth to maturity. Works such as *Tom Jones, Great Expectations, The Way of All Flesh, Of Human Bondage, Sons and Lovers, A Portrait of the Artist as a Young Man, The Last Puritan, Pelle the Conqueror, Jean-Christophe* imply the whole developmental approach to personality. As the student shares the life of the hero or heroine, he perceives some of the psychological processes involved in the transaction between the growing human creature and his environment: the child in a world of adults, taking on their behavior and standards, extremely sensitive to their acceptance or rejection of him; the emergence of the child's sense of himself as a separate person and his struggles to attain some kind of integrated personality; the environmental aids or obstacles to the attainment of this personal and social independence; the necessity for resolving problems and conflicts created by the fact that he is a member of a particular economic and social group; the impact of different religious and ethical systems; the need to make some kind of sexual adjustment; the way all these factors affect the individual's image of himself and the crystallization of his

attitudes toward others; how the individual's sense of the satisfactions worth striving for is formed; the variety of possible
attitudes of acceptance or rejection toward the dominant conventions of his environment; the fact that a life viewed from
one angle may be a failure but viewed from another may be
highly successful; the element of continuity in any life history.

Such a developmental approach to personality is equally
applicable to biography. We have seen how the traditional
study of literary history can be given general significance and
intellectual motivation. Similar pointedness could be given to
the traditional study of writers' lives. Too often, studying an
author's biography consists merely in learning the chronology
of events. If the personality was in conflict with his environment or maladjusted in any way, as in the case of Shelley or
Keats, the student tends to think this a peculiarity of artists.
The highly marked personalities of many literary figures,
their sensitivity to the world about them, and their articulate-
ness make their biographies particularly vivid material for
viewing the complex factors that enter into the crystallization
of personality.

A study of various biographies of the same person is another
means of making the student conscious of different interpretations of what are the important factors in personality development. Such a point of view would do much to vivify the
usual routine and quite irrelevant study of authors' lives—as it
would, of course, illuminate the study of any biographies,
whether of world leaders, scientists, explorers, or teachers.
There has been a revival of interest in biography—all the
more reason for helping students develop from this reading
some general framework of ideas concerning the growth and
development of the human being.

The province of literature, we have said, is all that humankind has thought and felt and created. It would be possible to multiply examples of how literary works embody one or another phase of social life or reveal one or another potentiality of human temperament or clarify one or another process of individual or group development. There is, for example, the great body of works that express the broad gamut of social arrangements, temperamental adjustments, conflicts and disillusionments, joys and fulfillments that have grown out of the relations between man and woman. Literary works whose theme is love, courtship, and marriage may give the adolescent reader not only an emotional outlet and psychological preparation but also a historical and cultural perspective.

Suggestions might be offered about how various bodies of literature throw light on human life—in, say, the relations between races, nations, classes, and ethnic groups or groups such as the artists and their public. Or how through literature we can apprehend the meaning, for the individual life, of different religious and philosophic attitudes. What it means to the individual to live in an agricultural or an industrial economy, in a rigid or flexible class system; how variously family relationships can be patterned; what problems face members of different groups in our own society today—artists, laborers, farmers, Jews, African Americans, women, youth; what social and economic philosophies inspire people today—these and innumerable other questions about human beings and society are illuminated through literature.

The study of American literature offers the student abundant opportunities for social insights especially relevant to his own problems. He can derive from our literature valuable understanding of the social conditions and processes that are

characteristic of our extraordinary history. Our whole literature bears the stamp of a new country only gradually being
created out of humankind's struggle with nature. The works
of American authors from Puritan days to the present reveal a
cultural heritage drawn from various Old World sources, particularly from England, taking on new overtones, absorbing
new values, being slowly merged in a new cultural synthesis.
The emphasis throughout this book on the social values and
insights implicit in literary experience seems self-evident in
relation to American literature. Our writers, almost every
one, have in one way or another been conscious of their
unique cultural setting and have sought to reflect it, to utter
its essential spirit, to castigate its weaknesses, to sing its hopes
and aspirations. Even those writers who have seemed to stand
aside from the life about them have usually sought to create
something of the beauty or the subtlety they found lacking in
their environment.

The problem of the American writer has been to utilize
everything of value in his literary heritage without letting it
screen from him the special qualities of the new way of life
about him. Seeking to remain a part of the splendid current
of European literary tradition, he has at the same time struggled to grasp and make articulate the nature of the unique
American experiment. With varying degrees of success, our
writers have sought to use or remold the traditional forms in
order to express the energetic spirit of a pioneer society.
American literature reveals the convergence of a number of
cultural trends produced by the intermingling of many peoples under the conditions imposed by a new land, during a
period of economic, social, political, and philosophic readjustment throughout Western civilization. It has been the task

of our writers to give utterance to the complex problems of a society in process of creation and yet to place these problems in their larger setting of changing scientific, political, and philosophic thought in the modern world.

The development of programs of American studies in undergraduate and graduate institutions has fostered concern with American literature in its cultural setting. Studies of various writers have illuminated different facets of this process of the creation of a new society. Many writers have given sensitive expression to the problems of immigrants, in their adjustments both to the new environment and to the cultural gap between themselves and their Americanized children. Even the great body of regional literature makes vivid the heterogeneous and complex nature of America. Or again, many recent works express the strains and stresses of our society and the plight of minority groups. There is the recurrent theme of aspiration toward an ever more democratic and humane way of life. Works such as these can aid the student in understanding the nature of the past out of which the society has grown and in becoming aware of the forces at work in it today.

Many other areas of human relations could be cited to illustrate this general philosophy of literature study. As the teacher himself comes to view his own literary experiences in this way, he will be able to make the study of any literary work a means for fostering in his students the capacity for such comprehension of humankind and society.

Essential to this approach is the gradual discovery of ideas and insights by the student through actual literary experience and reflection on it. Hence the focus on general social concepts rather than specific informational topics such as family relations, labor relations, juvenile delinquency, or war. By seeing how certain basic concepts apply throughout the range of his studies, the student will be able to build up an integrated approach to human relations. In this way he will develop fundamental understandings and critical attitudes that he will be able to apply even to those fields or unforeseen situations that his school courses have not covered.

Such recognition of recurrent basic concepts encountered through a variety of approaches to knowledge is probably the soundest kind of disciplinary correlation. It is not half so important that the student acquire history, sociology, and literature simultaneously as it is that he see exemplified in each of these fields certain unifying concepts concerning human nature and society.

Similarly, outlines of integrated courses are much less important than the teacher's possession of an understanding of how the particular body of knowledge with which he is concerned is related to the rest of human life. Certainly there is much to be gained from breaking down rigid subject-matter divisions. But the success of any such procedures must depend ultimately on whether or not the teachers themselves have assimilated such an integrated and humanistic point of view.

After all, even in schools and colleges where there are rigidly separate departments, the individual teacher can do much to prevent compartmentalization in the students' minds. The teacher can communicate to his students a sense of his particular subject in its living context. In his class, they can encounter echoes and new incarnations of ideas gained in other classes. They can be made to feel the human implications and overtones of a particular body of knowledge. Learning can be made a process of perceiving wider implications and of relating them to the central core of human values.

As more of his fellow teachers acquire such insight, they will eventually develop external procedures and curriculum arrangements more expressive of their sense of the organic nature of knowledge. Only those integrated courses or core curricula that have grown out of such attitudes have much chance of success. If such experiments are sometimes unsatisfactory, the fault is not with the idea of integration or synthesis but with those who have sought to execute it. Concern about flexible and integrated curricular patterns has tended to obscure the prime essential—flexibility and an organic approach to knowledge in the teacher's own mind.

The literary experience has been shown to reside in the synthesis of what the reader already knows and feels and desires with what the literary text offers—the patterned verbal signs through which the author has sought to communicate sensations, emotions, and ideas, his sense of life. Our eyes must always be directed toward that dynamic transaction between the work of art and the personality of the reader. The aim will be to increase the student's ability to achieve a full, sound reading of the text and to broaden the personal context of emotions and ideas into which this response will be incorporated. The development of literary appreciation will depend on a reciprocal process: an enlargement of the student's understanding of human life leads to increased aesthetic sensitivity, and increased aesthetic sensitivity makes possible more fruitful human insights from literature. Efforts to heighten the student's appreciation of the formal qualities of the literary work will be organically related to the effort to enrich his sense of human values.

Awareness of the highly personal nature of the literary experience protects against the deadening influence of routine; the student may derive from literature intimate benefits perhaps not visible, yet more precious than anything didactically imposed. Literary works may help him understand himself and his own problems more completely and may liberate him from his secret self-doubtings and personal anxieties. Literature's revelation of the diverse elements of our complex cultural heritage may free him from the provincialism of his own necessarily limited environment. Books may often provide him with an image of the kind of personality and way of life that he will seek to achieve. A major contribution toward these potential benefits can be to provide him with as broad a gamut of literary experiences as possible.

Even more important is the scrupulous effort to avoid any academic procedures that may hinder a spontaneous personal response. Because aesthetic reading involves both the intellect and the emotions in a manner that parallels life itself, the literary experience provides the opportunity for the student to develop the habit of reflective thinking within the context of an emotionally colored situation. Hence the insights attained through literature may be assimilated into the matrix of attitudes and ideas that constitute character and govern behavior.

This book has attempted to reveal how much the experience and study of literature have to offer that is relevant to the crucial needs of personalities involved in the conflicts and stresses of life in our changing society. Indeed, literary experiences might be made the very core of the kind of educational process needed in a democracy.

If we only do justice to the potentialities inherent in literature itself, we can make a vital social contribution. As the student shares through literary experience the emotions and aspirations of other human beings, he can gain heightened sensitivity to the needs and problems of those remote from him in temperament, in space, or in social environment; he can develop a greater imaginative capacity to grasp the meaning of abstract laws or political and social theories for actual human lives. Such sensitivity and imagination are part of the indispensable equipment of the citizen of a democracy.

Moreover, literature may serve the student in the two phases of his development usually neglected by orthodox educational procedures but essential for successful life in a heterogeneous, democratic society seeking to create more satisfactory ways of life. First, imaginative participation in the wide variety of alternative philosophies and patterns of behavior accessible through literature and the development of the power to reflect on them can liberate the student from anachronistic emotional attitudes.

Second, having freed himself from the tyranny of attitudes and ideas ill-adapted to modern life, the youth should not be left in a state of paralysis of the will. The organic nature of the literary experience provides some assurance that new insights will be assimilated emotionally as well as intellectually. Hence literature can also nourish the impetus toward more fruitful modes of behavior. Literary experiences may help to fasten his emotions on new and happier types of relationships or on the images of new and more socially valuable satisfactions to be derived from life. Thus he may acquire the sympathy and insight, the critical attitudes, and the sense of human values needed for his creation of new ideals and new personal goals.

Only as literature teachers actively promote these latent possibilities can they hope to approximate this ideal picture. A preeminent condition for success is that teachers themselves possess a lively sense of all that literature offers. They should avoid inculcating their own assumptions about human beings and social values and should support the student in his efforts to understand himself and the forces that pattern society. He needs to create for himself a humane system of values and the flexibility to apply it under the complex and fluid conditions of contemporary life. One source of such strengths can be literature—the ordered sensuous, emotional, and intellectual perceptions embodied in the literary experience.

Our society needs not only to make possible the creation of great works of art; it needs also to make possible the growth of personalities sufficiently sensitive, rational, and humane to be capable of creative literary experiences. In the pursuit of such ideals, the teaching of literature can become a function worthy of the humane nature of literature itself. Literary experiences will then be a potent force in the growth of critically minded, emotionally liberated individuals who possess the energy and the will to create a happier way of life for themselves and for others.

CODA:
A PERFORMING ART

Those who seek to praise the riches of literature have often been well-served by Keats's image of the reader as a traveler "in the realms of gold" coming on a great work like "some watcher of the skies / When a new planet swims into his ken."[1] But this suggestion of a remote object gazed on with awe may reinforce the current, almost hypnotically repeated, emphasis on the text or the work itself as distinct from author and reader. Fortunately, in "On Sitting Down to Read *King Lear* Once Again," Keats provides a counterbalancing image, which does justice to the reader's involvement in the literary work:

This essay, reprinted from the *English Journal*, November 1966, with the permission of the National Council of Teachers of English, is added here to perform the function of the coda in music—a few closing measures introduced at the end of a composition to emphasize the major chords.
    [1] "On First Looking into Chapman's Homer."

> . . . once again the fierce dispute
> Betwixt damnation and impassion'd clay,
> Must I burn through. . . .

Imaginative literature is indeed something "burned through," lived through, by the reader. We do not learn *about* Lear, we share, we participate in, Lear's stormy induction into wisdom. In *Huckleberry Finn*, we do not learn about conditions in the pre–Civil War South; we live in them, we see them through the eyes and personality of Huck. Even while we chuckle at his adventures and his idiom, we grow into awareness of the moral dimensions appropriate for viewing that world. Whether the work be a lighthearted lyric of Herrick's or a swiftly paced intellectual comedy of Shaw's or a brooding narrative of Hardy's, a reading is of necessity a participation, a personal experience.

The literary work is not primarily a document in the history of language or society. It is not simply a mirror of, or a report on, life. It is not a homily setting forth moral or philosophic or religious precepts. As a work of art, it offers a special kind of experience. It is a mode of living. The poem, the play, the story is thus an extension, an amplification, of life itself. The reader's primary purpose is to add this kind of experience to the other kinds of desirable experience that life may offer.

No one else can read a literary work for us. The benefits of literature can emerge only from creative activity on the part of the reader himself. He responds to the little black marks on the page or to the sounds of the words in his ear and he makes something of them. The verbal symbols enable him to draw on his past experiences with what the words point to in life and literature. The text presents these words in a new and unique pattern. Out of these he is enabled actually to mold a new experience, the literary work.

It is this experiential aspect that differentiates the literary work of art from other forms of verbal communication. *Imaginative* literature happens when we focus our attention on what we are sensing, thinking, feeling, structuring, in the act of response to the particular words in their particular order. Even the most modest work—a nursery rhyme, say—demands attention to what the words are calling forth within us. In its highest form, as in Keats's reading of Shakespeare, such absorption in what we are evoking from the text produces feelings of being completely carried out of oneself.

As the reader submits himself to the guidance of the text, he must engage in a most demanding kind of activity. Out of his past experience, he must select appropriate responses to the individual words; he must sense their interplay on one another; he must respond to clues of tone and attitude and movement. He must focus his attention on what he is structuring through these means. He must try to see it as an organized whole, its parts interrelated as fully as the text and his own capacities permit. From sound and rhythm and image and idea he forges an experience, a synthesis, that he calls the poem or play or novel. Whether for a nursery rhyme or for *King Lear*, such an activity goes on, and its complex nature can only be suggested here. The amazing thing is that critics and theorists have paid so little attention to this synthesizing process itself, contenting themselves usually with the simpler task of classifying the verbal symbols and their various patterns in the text.

In the *teaching* of literature, then, we are basically helping our students learn to perform in response to a text. In this respect we are perhaps closer to the voice teacher, even the swimming coach, than we are to the teacher of history or botany. The reader performs the poem or the novel, as the violinist performs the sonata. But the instrument on which the reader plays and from which he evokes the work is—himself. The final lines of Yeats's "Among School Children" are sometimes used out of context to suggest the fusion of so-called form and substance in the work of art itself.

> O body swayed to music, O brightening glance,
> How can we know the dancer from the dance?

In this image of the dancer, who under the spell of the music makes of his own body the formed substance that is the dance, we can also prefigure the reader: under the guidance of the text, out of his own thoughts and feelings and sensibilities, the reader makes a new ordering, the formed substance that is for him the literary work of art. The teacher of literature, especially, needs to keep alive this view of the literary work as personal evocation, the product of creative activity carried on by the reader under the guidance of the text.

Critical theory during the past few decades has made this emphasis suspect, however. Building on one facet of I. A. Richards's work, the New Critics and their sympathizers did much to rescue the poem as a work of art from earlier confusions with the poem either as a biographical document or as a document in intellectual and social history. A mark of much twentieth-century criticism became its avoidance largely of the social and biographical approach to literature. This, moreover, was paralleled by a reaction against impressionist criticism. Walter Pater, for example, became the exemplar of the reader too preoccupied with his own emotions to remain faithful to the poem itself. The reaction from impressionism fostered the notion of an impersonal or objective criticism, which, avoiding also the historical and social, busied itself with exploitation of the techniques of close reading. This tended to treat the poem—or any literary work—as if it existed as an object, like a machine, whose parts can be analyzed without reference either to the maker or to the observer (or reader). Those who have been indoctrinated with this critical emphasis are especially shocked at insistence on the literary work as experience. They misinterpret this as an invitation to irresponsible emotionalism and impressionism.

There is, in fact, nothing in the recognition of the personal nature of literature that requires an acceptance of the notion that every evocation from a text is as good as every other. We need only think of our successive readings of the same text, at fifteen or thirty or fifty, to know that we can differentiate. Undisciplined, irrelevant, or distorted emotional responses and the lack of relevant experience or knowledge will, of course, lead to inadequate interpretations of the text. The aim is to help the student toward a more and more controlled, more and more valid or defensible response to the text.

This does not imply, however, that there is one single correct reading of a literary text. This raises very complex and thorny problems concerning the criteria of soundness to be applied to any interpretation. However, this question is much more difficult to settle in theory than to face in practical interpretation of particular texts. We may not be able to arrive at a unanimous agreement concerning the best interpretation of, say, *Hamlet* or "The Second Coming," but we can arrive at some consensus about interpretations that are to be rejected as ignoring large elements in the work or as introducing irrelevant or exaggerated responses. Recognition that there is not a single interpretation that the teacher can impose still leaves room for a very stringent discipline. This can be carried on at the simplest or the highest level.

First, we can always move from our personal responses and interpretations back to the text. What in the text justifies our response? This is what the scientist would call our control, the means of avoiding arbitrary and irrelevant interpretations.

Second, we can make clear the criteria—the framework of ideas or knowledge or the standards of evaluation—that we are bringing to bear on our experience. We may sometimes find that differences are due not to readings of the text but to very different sets of expectations or bases of judgment.

More is involved than just the need for a reaction from current pseudoscientific "objectivity" or "impersonality." More is implied than merely reinstatement of the social, historical, philosophic, or ethical approaches to literature. We must place in the center of our attention the actual process of literary re-creation. As teachers of literature, our concern should be with the relation between readers and texts. This would change the emphasis in much that we do.

We would not forget, of course, that the text was an event in the life of an author, that he produced it at a particular moment in his life and in the history of his world. But we would not forget, either, that the poem becomes an event in the life of each reader as he re-creates it from the text.

What, then, are some of the implications of this emphasis on the personal nature of literary experience? Above all, our business is to contribute to a continuing process of growth in ability to handle responses—linguistic, emotional, intellectual—to literary texts. This means that our aim is to improve the quality of our students' actual literary experiences. We must seek to bring to our students at each stage of their development sound literary works in which they can indeed become personally involved.

This may seem simply to repeat a cliché of education, that students should be given works suited to their interests and level of maturity. Often, however, the search for appropriate works is perfunctory, and habit or convenience or economy intervenes. Sometimes, the notion of interest is oversimplified or superficial, as when works dealing only with teenage problems are offered to adolescents or when youngsters are allowed to go on indefinitely following one type of reading— science fiction, say. Nowadays, for the advanced-placement youngsters especially, the error is to look only at the works and to be pleased at the number of "great" works or works of high technical complexity being read, rather than at the *quality of the actual reading experiences.* (I hear, alas, of *The Waste Land* in the ninth grade and *The Magic Mountain* in the eleventh— extreme instances, perhaps, but symptomatic.)

It may be that the youngster reading *National Velvet* or *Johnny Tremain* will have a fuller, more sensitive, more responsible literary experience than the student who is so unready to handle the demands of *The Divine Comedy* or even Henry James that he falls back on criticism of criticism of criticism and never develops a literary technique of reading and assimilating for himself.

Those struggling to face the challenge of education for the culturally disadvantaged have been least able to ignore the fact that the reader can read only out of past experience and present interests. Here, however, the danger is to focus too exclusively on the external life of the reader. What he brings to the text is not only an external environment and special dialect but also fundamental human emotions and relationships. Probably many of the works that do treat essential human relationships but are considered remote from the interests of the disadvantaged reader are not so at all; they are made inaccessible by being expressed in a "standard" dialect that the youngster must learn almost as a second language. Materials treating the immediate environment and problems of the slum child have their important uses, but mainly as bridges, leading the young reader to learn how to enter through the printed page into the whole culture surrounding him.

When the young reader is confronted with the text— whether it be *The Pearl* or *The Scarlet Letter* or *Hamlet*—first of all we should seek to foster his having a personal experience with it. His efforts and his attention should be focused on re-creating it sensitively and responsibly. He should be encouraged to bring to the text whatever in his past experience is relevant: his sensuous awareness, his feeling for people and practical circumstances, his ideas and information, as well as his feeling for the sound and pace and texture of language. We know that in a reliving of the work, he does not read coldly, arriving first at something called the meaning or the paraphrasable sense and *then* starting to feel or think about it. In an actually creative reading, all these things may go on either at the same time or in many different phases: emotional response, the formulation of ideas, and tentative general views about the emotional attitudes, the characters or the situations that the work treats. The young reader needs to learn how to suspend judgment, to be self-critical, to develop and revise his interpretation as he reads.

To do justice to the text, then, the young reader must be helped to handle his responses to it. Yet the techniques of the usual English classroom tend to hurry past this process of active creation and re-creation of the text. The pupil is, instead, rushed into peripheral concerns. How many times youngsters read poems or stories or plays trying to memorize as many random details as possible because such facts will be the teacher's means for testing—in multiple-choice questions— whether they have read the work! Or students will read only with half a mind and spirit, knowing that this suffices for filling in the requirements of a routine book report: to summarize the plot, identify the principal characters, describe the setting, and so on. Even the search for meaning is reduced too often to paraphrase that simply dulls and dilutes the impact of the work. The concern with theme often relies too much on high-level abstractions, while the analysis of techniques becomes a pre-occupation with recognizing devices—the scanning of verse, the labeling of types, the listing of symbols, the recognition of recurrent myths.

Our assignments, our ways of testing, our questions about the work, our techniques of analysis should direct attention to, not away from, the work as an aesthetic experience. In applying the accepted treatments to the work, we must remember that all the reader has to deal with is whatever he himself lives through in his interchange with the text.

Hence, we should have the courage to admit to our students that the actual business of re-creating a work is difficult and tricky and sometimes frustrating but always exciting and challenging. Instead of hurrying the youngster into impersonal and so-called objective formulations as quickly as possible, the successful teacher of literature makes the classroom a place for critical sharing of personal responses. Awareness that others have had different experiences with it will lead the reader back to the text for a closer look. The young reader points to what in the text explains his response. He may discover, however, that he has overreacted to some elements and ignored others. Or he may learn that some word or image has triggered a fantasy or awakened some personal preoccupation quite alien to the text. (I. A. Richards, long ago, reported in *Practical Criticism* on the many pitfalls awaiting the reader.) Such exchange of ideas, such scrutiny of the reasons for response will create awareness of the relevance of critical terminology and will develop ability to handle more and more demanding texts. Discussion of personal responses, of the text as lived through, can thus give rise to a truly inductive study of literature.

The more we teachers understand the linguistic demands of a particular work, the better able we shall be to help the young reader. But we cannot do this by espousing formulas for reading or by simply requiring the mouthing of the right answers to the right questions. Passive acceptance of the teacher's interpretation can bring only pseudounderstanding, verbalizing about, rather than experiencing, the work. Even the skills and knowledge to be imparted can so easily become substitute ends in themselves. The identification of the persona of the poem or the definition of the nature of irony or the statement

272

of the theme or the recognition of a mythic pattern (the journey, the Oedipus situation)—it is hard to keep in mind that these are not the ends or the justification of our teaching. These are means by which the reader can handle or describe his response to the clues offered by the text. But their value as means lies always in their helping the reader enter more fully into the total experience by which he organizes, re-creates, the work for himself.

We may not always be able to look over his shoulder while the student is having a real literary experience, but we can do at least two things. First, we can be very careful to scrutinize all our procedures to be sure that we are not in actuality substituting other aims—things to do *about* literature—for the experience *of* literature. We can ask of every assignment or method or text, no matter what its short-term effectiveness: Does it get in the way of the live sense of literature? Does it make literature something to be regurgitated, analyzed, categorized, or is it a means toward making literature a more personally meaningful and self-disciplined activity? And, second, we can create in our classrooms an atmosphere of give-and-take and mutual challenge; through this, we shall surely find indirect evidences of the real literary experiences, the sources of growth.

A consequence of such an approach is that as the student clarifies his sense of the work, he becomes aware of his own attitudes, his own notions of what is important or desirable; he broadens his awareness of alternatives of behavior and aspiration. Willy-nilly, the English classroom, if it is a place where literature really resides, becomes the arena for a linkage with the world of the student. What he brings to literature, what he undergoes through the medium of the literary text, how he is helped to handle this in the classroom will affect what he carries away from it in enhanced sensitivities to language and to life.

When some remarks of this nature were made at a meeting of college teachers of literature, one of them exclaimed, "Good heavens! You don't propose to have kids read stories in order to learn that they mustn't steal cars! Or concentrate on stories about teenage dating?"

He was echoing what has been generally a wholesome reaction against certain kinds of too-literal use of literature: for example, the emphasis on extracting a message or moral or lesson or the use of stories as a springboard for getting youngsters to talk out their problems and release tensions. This use of literature has probably not been as widespread as some think, and actually no one denies the therapeutic potentialities of such use of literature by people trained in such matters. Nor is the reading of poetry as an art threatened because John Stuart Mill found in Wordsworth's poetry the experience through which he overcame a severe mental depression. However, such didactic or therapeutic aims should not replace directly literary concerns. Yet the antiseptic reaction of the extreme disciples of the so-called purely literary approach, who fear any moral or psychological concern, also negates the full nature of the literary work of art. The teacher of literature seeks primarily to help students read so well that they may derive any and all possible benefits from literature.

Here, then, is another important implication of the emphasis on the essentially personal character of literary experience: it forces us to recognize that in the classroom, if we are to keep literature alive, we cannot completely separate the technical, the aesthetic from the human meanings of the work.

Perhaps a very simple and modest illustration will suffice, drawn from a discussion by a group of verbally not very gifted high school seniors, most of whom were destined for vocational or technical colleges or institutes. One of the girls responded with intense indignation to the story of a man who had left his wife and child and run off to sea. The other pupils objected to her unqualified condemnation. They pointed out the many clues to the father's unhappiness, his boredom with monotonous routine work, the dreary apartment, his nagging wife, and his yearning for the romance of far-off exotic places. Some of these clues were in descriptive details, in items like a picture on the wall that took on symbolic meaning in relation to all the other details. The story was certainly not very complex, but it sufficed to provide the occasion for what amounted to a group process in close reading. By the time the discussion ended, the girl realized that, no matter what her opinions about a husband's responsibilities, she had missed the insights the story offered into personality and the conflicting needs of husband and wife in the situation.

From one point of view, the girl's learning was merely a matter of becoming aware of literary devices and narrative development. From another angle, she had to some slight degree simply acquired a sounder moral stance, in which passing of moral judgment was tempered by understanding of motives and human needs. These are two indivisible facets of the same process of growth in ability to read and respond in a balanced way to the literary work. (Probably none of the youngsters in that group was ready to be amused at the trick ending of the story or to decide on whether it was a sound ending—which again, even for so frail a literary work, would involve the human implications of the story as well as its technical dexterity.) When we are helping students to better techniques of reading through sensitivity to diction, tone, structure, image, symbol, narrative movement, we are also helping them make the more refined responses that are ultimately the source of human understanding and sensitivity to human values.

When there is active participation in literature—the reader living through, reflecting on, and criticizing his own responses to the text—there will be many kinds of benefits. We can call this growth in ability to share discriminatingly in the possibilities of language as it is used in literature. But this means also the development of the imagination: the ability to escape from the limitations of time and place and environment, the capacity to envisage alternatives in ways of life and in moral and social choices, the sensitivity to thought and feeling and needs of other personalities. The youth will need to grow into the emotional and intellectual and aesthetic maturity necessary for appreciating the great works of literature in our own and other languages. As he does this, he grows also into partnership in the wisdom of the past and the aspirations for the future, of our culture and our society. The great abstractions—love, honor, integrity, compassion, individuality, democracy—will take on for him human meaning.

Keats, you recall, ends his sonnet on reading *King Lear* with the lines:

> But when I am consumed in the Fire
> Give me new Phoenix-wings to fly at my desire.

Keats saw himself about to be completely "consumed," absorbed in, the reliving of the play. But he anticipated that he would emerge reborn to even greater freedom and creativity. This is indeed the paradox of the intensely personal nature of the reading of a literary work: it is a kind of experience valuable in and for itself, and yet—or perhaps, therefore—it can also have a liberating and fortifying effect in the ongoing life of the reader.

PART FOUR

REAFFIRMATIONS

RETROSPECT AND PROSPECT

I have been asked to explain how a young woman came to write *Literature as Exploration* in 1935–36. What prepared her to present ideas in diverse fields that in some instances have only recently been generally accepted? How was the book received? How does it relate, they ask, to what she has written in subsequent years? When I seek to respond, I find that various aspects of her experience before 1935— family background, undergraduate years at Barnard College, doctoral work at the University of Paris, postdoctoral study of anthropology at Columbia University, teaching at Barnard College—converged to provide the matrix for the book.

Family upbringing was of overarching importance. Intellectually influenced mainly by ideas drawn from antiauthoritarian

This essay is a slightly altered version of "Retrospect," which first appeared in *Transactions with Literature*, edited by Edmund J. Farrell and James R. Squire. ©1990 by the National Council of Teachers of English. Reprinted with permission.

European sources and such American writers as Emerson and Thoreau, it would at a later date have been called progressive. Accordingly, I was saved from acquiring lingering Victorian attitudes—especially about gender, class, and ethnic differences. Instead of the social Darwinism of the struggle for survival, I was introduced to Peter Kropotkin's ideas about mutual aid even in the animal world. At Barnard College also, my experience was not conventional. As part of an experiment probably modeled on the British universities, I became an honor student during my last two years and was released from the traditional liberal arts English program, with its array of period courses. Reading mainly on my own, intensively in English and American literature and widely in the social sciences, I conferred once a week with a professor. A week-long series of written examinations at the end of the senior year rendered the usual work for the MA superfluous.

Returning to my files in connection with these reminiscences, I came across a paper written in my junior year that may have some interest in this context. Having cited an article by the philosopher Horace Kallen that found tragedy to reside mainly in the destruction of values, I went on to discuss what this meant in terms of the relationship between the writers and their readers or audiences! I argued that Shakespeare could take for granted that he and his audience shared the same value system, whereas Ibsen had to build into his plays a way of changing his audience's values before they could share his tragic vision.

My choice of graduate specialization also involved important preparation for later concerns. At graduation from Barnard, I had hesitated between continuing the study of literature and electing graduate work in anthropology, a lively interest since my sophomore course with Franz Boas, the great founder of American anthropology. My compromise was to study in France and ultimately to seek acceptance as a doctoral candidate in comparative literature at the University of Paris. My dissertation, *L'idée de l'art pour l'art*, published in 1931, on the espousal by English and French writers of the idea of art for art's sake, foreshadowed *Literature as Exploration* by its concern with the relationship between writers and society in the context of comparative cultures and the philosophy of art. After I had received the doctorate from the Sorbonne, and while I was teaching at Barnard, I enrolled in graduate work in anthropology with Boas and Ruth Benedict, whose *Patterns of Culture* (1934) is still widely read. The combination of training in literature and in anthropology and other social sciences led in 1935 to my being appointed to the Commission on Human Relations.

The title page of the first edition of *Literature as Exploration* contained, after the author's name, the phrase, "for the Commission on Human Relations, Progressive Education Association." The relationship between the book and those agencies was not, however, as simple as the title page might suggest. Much as I was in sympathy with their general aims, the book was largely the product of other connections and, in a sense, was written on the rebound from completing the work for which I was appointed to the commission.

For several years a group of social scientists at the forefront of their fields had been meeting for interdisciplinary discussions and had conceived the idea of two commissions, one on secondary education and the other on human relations. Since the General Education Board of the Rockefeller Foundation, which funded the projects, did not subsidize individuals, the grant was administered through the Progressive Education Association. The task of the Commission on Human Relations was to produce a group of books addressed to older adolescents—late high school and early college students—on important subjects such as human development and the family. My contribution was to draw on my literary and social science background for the planning of the books. Others, skilled at popularizing the social sciences, were to do the actual writing.

The work with the commission, for which I took a leave of absence from Barnard, gave me the opportunity to meet with the social scientists who had initiated the project, to read widely, and to visit some schools and colleges—especially those seeking to innovate. This was perhaps the heyday of the progressive education movement. I had been aware of its existence and, because of the influences mentioned earlier, was already imbued with the progressive point of view. John Dewey's *Human Nature and Conduct* and *Art as Experience* confirmed my sympathy for that general approach. My completely liberal arts education and work had not, however, brought me into contact with schools or with specialists in education. I entered enthusiastically into the work for the commission under the progressive rubric, but perhaps because the roots of my thinking were elsewhere, I maintained a certain objectivity.

The commission agenda contained no plans, and no commitment, for a book by me or for a book on the teaching of a particular subject. Given my role, my work was completed when the responsibility for producing the books on the various areas of human relations was turned over to the writers. As I reflected on the books planned, I felt that their expositions of the latest developments in the social sciences would be valuable contributions toward students' understanding. But I also came to the conclusion that the kinds of discussion of human relations that went on in my own literature classes could also perform a unique and vital function.

My teaching experience had made me increasingly disillusioned with the discipline represented by university departments of English. Even introductory literature courses were geared to the needs of future majors in English and reflected the approaches dominating the graduate curriculum, which in turn reflected the pseudoscientific model of the German universities. Literary history, philology, or a watered-down, moralistic didacticism mainly constituted the study of literature. My training—excellent, I must admit, in its terms—had prepared me for historical and theoretical research but had not prepared me, I felt, for helping the average student discover why one should read literary texts, given all the other interesting things in life. Although the lecture method prevailed at Barnard—sometimes in a rather relaxed form, it is true—and I gave some advanced lecture courses, I had been able to develop in my introductory courses what has come to be called the reader-response discussion method.

The reading of texts such as the commission proposed—texts that expounded, even though in popular style, sociological and psychological ideas about, say, family relationships—was, I decided, very different from the reading of *Romeo and Juliet* or *Great Expectations*. The informative texts were ultimately needed, perhaps essential, but they were to be read impersonally and objectively. In contrast, my work for the doctorate had taught me, and Dewey had confirmed, that literary works of art exist in unique personal experiences. The reader attends not only to the formal aspects of the work but also, perhaps primarily, to the situations, thoughts, and emotions called forth during the reading. Generational conflicts and tensions over family loyalties lived through in reading *Romeo and Juliet*, for example, can give rise to personal responses that can be reflected on and expressed. Thus the literary experience provides the opportunity to help students think rationally about issues with which they are emotionally involved. When the desire arises to hear what others, such as social scientists, have to say, it can influence, and be assimilated into, personally felt attitudes and expectations.

I had visited classes in schools and colleges where teachers had thoroughly eliminated the traditional exposition of standard interpretations of literary works for students to echo on examinations. There was lively expression of opinion and the excitement of freedom from conventional methods. Yet I felt that I could contribute something constructive—a philosophic or theoretical foundation for revising the teaching of literature, a foundation for setting up a process that would make personal response the basis for growth toward more and more balanced, self-critical, knowledgeable interpretation. Moreover, I could draw on my literary and interdisciplinary studies to provide students with frameworks for thinking about the social, psychological, and aesthetic assumptions implied by the literary work and by their own and others' responses. Much as I agreed with rejection of the traditional methods, my approach, especially in its emphasis on growth based on personal experience, constituted an implicit criticism of what I had observed in some experimental classes. I later discovered in John Dewey's *Experience and Education* (1938), published in the same year as my book, an explicit criticism of the divergence of some so-called progressive educators from his own broader vision.

I dictated a first draft of the book, much of it while on vacation in Connecticut, and completed it after returning to teaching at Barnard. Since I had received secretarial assistance, I gave the book to the commission. When the Progressive Education Association disbanded in 1955, whatever royalties were produced went to designated professional organizations. The copyright reverted to me in 1965. The second edition appeared in 1968 (1970 in England); the third edition in 1976; the fourth edition (Modern Language Association publication) in 1983.

Various people have recently expressed satisfaction that the book has finally received recognition, but they underestimate the strength of the progressive current in educational thinking at the time of its publication. Actually, in 1938, *Literature as Exploration*, despite its challenge to accepted practices and philosophies, received a surprisingly wide favorable response. A leading authority on American literature at Harvard (who gave the book high praise) and the Shakespeare authority at Columbia invited me to join with them in writing a statement for an MLA committee on the teaching of literature. At a meeting during the convention of the Modern Language Association, a group of eminent scholars voted to approve the statement, which was published in the November 1938 issue of *PMLA*. This was the very university establishment whose influence on the teaching of literature in colleges and schools I was seeking to combat!

Equally astonishing to me was that at the national meeting of the National Council of Teachers of English in New York, I found myself on the stage of the Manhattan Opera House, addressing thousands of teachers. (After the book had appeared, Dora V. Smith, then president of NCTE, had asked me to have lunch with her, and the invitation to speak had followed.) I discovered an organization that welcomed all who were concerned with the teaching of English in all its modes and at all levels, from kindergarten to graduate school. And in the NCTE I also found leaders seeking to promote an educational process aimed at developing critically minded, socially productive individuals.

The NCTE became the professional organization to which I mainly devoted my energies over the next half-century— because I felt that the teaching of English to all our people was of paramount importance, an importance that few of my liberal arts university colleagues recognized or felt to be their concern. Over the years, I found myself involved in many NCTE committees, commissions, conventions, and publications. In these days of articulate minority voices, I especially recall editing the June 1946 issue of the *English Journal*, devoted to furthering the concept of cultural pluralism set forth in *Literature as Exploration*. (Thomas Mann, Ruth Benedict, Alain Locke, James Farrell, Ernst Kris, Horace Kallen, among other leaders in their fields, wrote essays for the issue.)

Historians of education in the post–World War II period record, on the one hand, the capture of English departments in the colleges by the formalist and elitist New Criticism. On the other hand, the increasing number of students and the extension of school-leaving age reflected the fact that our society had undertaken the noble—and unparalleled—responsibility for educating all our children. The early response to mass education fostered the "life adjustment" movement. Unfortunately, this anti-intellectualistic effort to prepare pupils to serve, to "adjust" to the needs of the status quo, was confused with the progressives' concern for meeting the needs of students. The progressives sought rather to help them to develop their capacities to the full, a view of education assuming a democratically mobile society.

The historians are correct in reporting the continuing prevalence of generally conservative methods, but they fail, it seems to me, to do justice to the persistence and gradual acceptance of many of the ideas generated during the twenties and thirties. In the mid-century decades, colleges and universities simply rejected students "unprepared" to carry out their traditional programs. The teachers in the elementary and secondary schools could not evade the task created by our increasingly democratic educational system. No matter what the changes in the society and in the schools and no matter what elitist ideas dominated in the universities, there have always been teachers, I have found, who understand the need for a new approach.

The New Criticism prevailed after World War II through the wide adoption of college textbooks such as Cleanth Brooks and Robert Penn Warren's *Understanding Poetry* (published, ironically enough, in the same prewar year as my own book). Surely one reason for their success was that their approach fitted in with the postwar glorification of science, fueled by fear of Soviet scientific superiority. The New Critics and I seemed to start out on the same path by deploring the neglect of literature as an art resulting from the traditional preoccupation with literary history and "the message" of the work. But we parted company in our understanding of the nature of art. The New Critics treated the poem as an autonomous entity that could be objectively analyzed. This approach suited an intellectual

climate of narrow empiricism in which behaviorism dominated psychology and logical positivism reigned in philosophy.

Moreover, the methods of close reading that the New Critics propagated were easily merged with traditional methods
of formal analysis and categorization of the text. The New
Critics' dogmatic attack on the "intentional fallacy" and the
"affective fallacy" diminished the importance of the author
and decried concern with the reader's feelings and ideas. In
the universities, recognition of the reader did not begin until
the late sixties and early seventies.

Despite the hegemony of the New Criticism, whose for-
malistic methods of analysis are reflected in literature classes
even today, I never felt completely isolated. I continued to be
invited to present papers at NCTE meetings and to be active
in its committees. I served on various state and national educational panels, was called on as a consultant, was one of the
thirteen members of the College Entrance Examination Board
Commission on English. My differences with the formalists
or my urging of a different idea of the reading process from
the theory being taught by reading experts in my own School
of Education simply acted as stimulants to further thought
and writing and served as the basis for a continuing and sometimes effective criticism of dominant practices. When in 1948
I joined the New York University School of Education,
which included content courses as well as pedagogy in its programs, I was able to develop an undergraduate curriculum
and a doctoral program combining English and education that
reflected my philosophy. Indeed, my own courses, such as Literature and the Crisis in Values and Criticism and the Literary
Experience, provided the empirical basis for further refinement of my theories.

In 1968, the publication of the second edition of *Literature as Exploration* was cited as one of the signs of the growing reaction against the New Criticism. The 1970s were to see a proliferation of diverse alternative theoretical positions in the academic and critical journals. By 1980, when two anthologies of reader-response criticism were published, both editors cited *Literature as Exploration* as the first to set forth the importance of the reader. (For whatever reason, however, neither anthology includes my article "The Poem as Event," published in *College English* in November 1964—so far as I know, the first explicit attack on the New Critics that called for a criticism based on the reader's response.)

My 1978 book *The Reader, the Text, the Poem: The Transactional Theory of the Literary Work* was not intended as a substitute for the earlier work; indeed, I think of the two books as complementary. *Literature as Exploration* not only deals with implications for teaching but also presents more fully the cultural and social aspects of the reading event. Decades of studying student responses had led me to develop a theory of the reading process that is both general and rounded. The later book deals systematically with such questions as validity in interpretation, the nature of the literary experience, and the relation of evocation, interpretation, and criticism.

In 1949, John Dewey had suggested that, instead of *interaction*, which implies separate entities acting on one another, the term *transaction* should be used to designate relationships between reciprocally conditioned elements. I adopted the term because it underlines what was already present in my 1938 declaration that there are no generic readers or generic interpretations but only innumerable relationships between readers and texts. Most reader-response exponents still seem ultimately to conceive of the reader and the text in the traditional ways—as already defined entities acting on each other—and hence tend to situate the meaning of a work either in the reader or in the text, instead of recognizing the dynamic to-and-fro relationship that gives rise to the work. The transactional phrasing places the stress on each reading as a particular event involving a particular reader and a particular text recursively influencing each other under particular circumstances.

As I explained earlier, a conviction about the difference between "literary" reading and other reading led to my writing *Literature as Exploration* in the first place. In *The Reader, the Text, the Poem*, I work out more fully the theoretical explanation of what the reader does in a potential continuum from predominantly nonliterary, or, to use my terminology, *efferent*, reading, to predominantly literary, or *aesthetic*, reading. Strangely enough, this distinction has been the most difficult to communicate. The habit of explaining the literary qualities of a work (such as rhythm, imagery, metaphor, and departures from ordinary diction) by pointing to elements in the text has prevented the realization that the reader must first of all adopt what I term an *aesthetic stance*—that is, focus attention on the private, as well as the public, aspects of meaning. Reading to find the answer to a factual question requires attention mainly to the public aspects of meaning and excludes, pushes into the periphery, personal feelings or ideas activated. To call forth a literary work of art from the same text, the reader must first of all permit into the focus of attention not only the public linkages with the words but also the personal associations, feelings, and ideas being lived through during the reading. Traditional and formalist methods of teaching literature treat it as a body of information to be transmitted, rather than as experiences to be reflected on.

I find this matter of the reader's stance toward the contents of consciousness vital not only to the solution of various persistent problems in literary theory but, to put it bluntly, essential to the survival of the reading of literature as an active part of our American culture.

In both kinds of reading, efferent and aesthetic, the reader focuses attention on the stream of consciousness, selecting out the particular mix of public and private linkages with the words dictated by the purpose of the reading. Teachers often forget that if students know that they will be tested primarily on factual aspects of the work (often by multiple-choice questions), a full aesthetic reading is prevented, and the mix swings toward the efferent end of the continuum.

Why, some have asked, am I so concerned about my differences with the other so-called reader-response exponents? Don't we all start by rejecting the idea of a single determinate meaning in the text? Despite this agreement, I believe that our differences in epistemology, theories of the nature of language, and views of the reading process lead to very important differences in educational and political implications.

In education, the period since World War II has been in many ways a reactionary one. The authentic philosophy of progressive education as Dewey had envisioned it has, for various reasons, never been fully realized, while narrow partial versions have brought the very label into disrepute. Behaviorist psychology reinforced practices that provided what seemed like answers to the demands of mass education. Increasing dissatisfaction with the results has led some critics to propose a so-called literacy achieved through rote acquisition of skills and facts. Other critics yearn for education based on the classics for the benefit of a narrow elite. Still, as I have said, progressive ideas concerning human development and the learning process have persisted and are being implemented in many schools throughout the country. The diverse approaches to education are increasingly coming into conflict, and economic considerations are often confusing the issues.

The explosion of writings on literary and critical theory in the 1970s and 1980s reflected a similar diversity. The term *reader response* took on such broad usage that some theorists, though giving lip service to the reader, end up with positions even more remote from mine than was the New Criticism.

Looked at in terms of educational and political implications, the division in literary theories falls elsewhere than between the old historicism and formalism on the one hand and the new reader-response approaches on the other. Reader-response theories such as the psychoanalytically based ones tend to overemphasize the reader and to treat responses primarily as a means of self-interpretation according to Freudian or some other theory of personality. Poststructuralists or deconstructionists, in contrast, range themselves with the New Critics and the traditionalists in overemphasizing the text. They are concerned with abstracting the underlying system of codes and conventions that the text possesses for a particular "interpretive community." Author and reader become mere carriers of cultural conventions, and both fade away under the extreme relativism of the deconstructionists and some cultural critics. Even some of those theorists who phrase the reading process in terms of an interaction between reader and text tend in practice to postulate the text as an entity ultimately determinate of meaning.

The critical processes and teaching procedures that serve this overemphasis on the text result in neglect of the personal aesthetic experience. The stress is placed on efferent analysis, whether of codes and conventions, logical self-contradictions, or ideological assumptions. The advocates of these textually oriented theories find no problem in continuing the teaching practices of the traditionalists and the formalist New Critics.

My insistence on the term *transaction* is a means of establishing the active role of both reader and text in interpretation and ensures that we recognize that any interpretation is an event occurring at a particular time in a particular social or cultural context. *Once the work has been aesthetically evoked*, it can become the object of reflection and analysis, according to the various critical and scholarly approaches.

Without accepting the notion of a single correct interpretation, the transactional concept and pragmatic theory of warrantability provide the basis for developing, in a particular context, criteria for discriminating the relative validity of differing interpretations. The importance of the culture is recognized (here, *Literature as Exploration* is especially pertinent), but, I point out, personal choice and variety derive from the fact that cultural conventions are individually internalized. This especially differentiates my theory from the poststructuralism that sees the individual as caught in the prison house of language and culture.

Again, I am especially concerned with differentiating the political implications of my position from others who claim to start from reader-response premises. Since 1938, I have urged that students be made aware of the implicit underlying cultural and social assumptions of any evoked work and that they be helped to make these the basis for scrutinizing their own assumptions. Those who term themselves cultural critics seem to share this emphasis. The difference lies in what often seems to be an overarching negative attitude toward our Western culture. Reading thus becomes a defensive action against manipulation by the text. My aim, instead, is to develop a discriminating attitude of mind, a readiness to question and to reject anachronistic or unjust assumptions, but a willingness also to accept and build on what is sound in our culture.

Those who claim that there is always a covert political message in teaching literary works of art often disregard their complexity. But I am ready to agree that to claim absence of any political orientation in the classroom only serves confusion. Students should be actively helped to develop criteria based on democratic assumptions about the freedoms and responsibilities of individuals, men and women creating a shared future.

In 1938, democracy was being threatened by fascism in Italy and totalitarian governments in Germany and Russia. This retrospect, this backward look, has not lingered on much that was dark in the intervening years. But in recent years, we have been witnessing the heartening spectacle of the liberation from within of such totalitarian states. We have seen whole peoples effect peaceful nonviolent revolutions, and we apprehensively watch their hazardous gropings toward democracy. Note that, despite their economic sufferings, their demands were first of all for freedom, for the freedom that we enjoy, though often, unfortunately, like some of us, they lacked understanding of the delicate balances of interest such a free society requires.

Yet we should not be complacent over the removal of the crude opposition between democracy and totalitarianism. Much has changed in our own democracy over the past fifty years, especially in terms of the responsibilities accepted by our society toward its members. Nevertheless, we, too, are at a crucial moment in our history. Our democracy is still threatened, not by external totalitarianisms, but by unwise solutions to internal social and economic problems. If short-term financial considerations prevail over concern for long-term human consequences, the foundations for a fully democratic way of life will be destroyed.

The political indifference of many of our citizens, their acceptance of appeals to narrow personal interests, and their vulnerability to the influence of the media are important symptoms. Also, zeal for some, often admirable, social or economic cause seems to blind others to the need to defend our basic democratic values. Much cries out for reform, but an indiscriminately negative attitude may alienate youth from the very democratic means necessary for constructive, humane change.

I am not under the illusion that the schools alone can change society. However, I can reaffirm the belief uttered so many years ago: We teachers of language and literature have a crucial role to play as educators and citizens. We phrase our goals as fostering the growth of the capacity for personally meaningful, self-critical literary experience. The educational process that achieves this aim most effectively will serve a broader purpose, the nurturing of men and women capable of building a fully democratic society. The prospect is invigorating!

Luquillo, Puerto Rico, January 1990
Princeton, New Jersey, April 1995

FOR FURTHER READING

This list is intended as an informal supplement to chapter 6, with no pretensions at inclusiveness. Its purpose is to foster an interdisciplinary approach, to indicate some different ways of looking at human beings and society. Given the general blurring of disciplinary borders in recent years, the titles are loosely grouped in overlapping categories. The works cited do not necessarily reflect my point of view.

A section suggesting a few works on education and teaching methods is included. For the practicing teacher, the journals and other publications of the National Council of Teachers of English (Urbana, Illinois) should be mentioned as sources on teaching methods, on the selection of literary works, and on research in the teaching of literature. The American Library Association (Chicago, Illinois) also issues helpful book lists. Boynton/Cook–Heinemann has published a number of congenial books.

Atwell, Nancie. *In the Middle: Writing, Reading, and Learning with Adolescents*. Portsmouth: Heinemann, 1987.

Clifford, John, ed. *The Experience of Reading: Louise Rosenblatt and Reader-Response Theory*. Portsmouth: Heinemann, 1990.

Cox, Carole, and James Zarrillo. *Teaching Reading with Children's Literature*. New York: Macmillan, 1993.

Dewey, John. *Democracy and Education*. 1916. Dewey, *Middle Works* 9: 1–370.*

———. *Experience and Education*. 1938. Dewey, *Later Works* 13: 1–62.**

Fader, Daniel, and Elton McNeil. *Hooked on Books*. New York: Berkley, Medallion, 1968.

Farrell, Edmund J., and James R. Squire, eds. *Transactions with Literature*. Urbana: NCTE, 1990.

Goodlad, John I. *A Place Called School: Prospects for the Future*. New York: McGraw, 1984.

Heath, Shirley Brice. *Ways with Words: Language, Life and Work in Communities and Classrooms*. Cambridge: Cambridge UP, 1983.

Karolides, Nicholas, ed. *Reader Response in the Classroom: Evoking and Interpreting Meaning in Literature*. New York: Longman, 1992.

Kozol, Jonathan. *Savage Inequalities: Children in America's Schools*. New York: Crown, 1991.

Meier, Deborah. *The Power of Their Ideas: Lessons for America from a Small School in Harlem*. Boston: Beacon, 1995.

Noddings, Nel. *The Challenge to Care in Schools: An Alternative Approach to Education*. New York: Teacher's Coll. P, 1992.

Probst, Robert E. *Response and Analysis*. Portsmouth: Heinemann, 1988.

Rose, Mike. *Lives on the Boundary: The Struggles and Achievements of America's Underprepared*. New York: Free, 1989.

Rosenblatt, Louise M. "The Transactional Theory of Reading and Writing." *Theoretical Models and Processes of Reading.* Ed. R. R. Ruddell, M. R. Ruddell, and H. S. Singer. Newark, DE: Intl. Reading Assn., 1994. 1057–92.

Sizer, T. *Horace's School: Redesigning the American High School.* New York: Houghton, 1992.

Smith, Frank. *Insult to Intelligence: The Bureaucratic Invasion of Our Classrooms.* New York: Arbor, 1986.

Whitehead, Alfred North. *"The Aims of Education" and Other Essays.* 1929. New York: Free, 1967.

Bronowski, Jacob. *Science and Human Values.* Rev. ed. New York: Harper, 1965.

Dewey, John. *Human Nature and Conduct: An Introduction to Social Psychology.* 1922. Dewey, *Middle Works* 14: 1–227.*

———. *Theory of Valuation.* 1939. Dewey, *Later Works* 13: 189–251.**

Edel, Abraham. *In Search of the Ethical: Moral Theory in Twentieth-Century America.* New Brunswick: Transaction, 1993.

Johnson, Mark. *Moral Imagination: Implications of Cognitive Science for Ethics.* Chicago: U of Chicago P, 1993.

Morris, Charles. *Varieties of Human Value.* Chicago: U of Chicago P, 1956.

Pirsig, Robert M. *Zen and the Art of Motorcycle Maintenance.* New York: Bantam, 1975.

Rescher, Nicholas. *Human Interests: Reflections on Philosophical Anthropology.* Palo Alto: Stanford UP, 1990.

Wilson, James Q. *The Moral Sense.* New York: Free, 1993.

Borradori, Giovanna. *The American Philosophers: Conversations with Davidson, Putnam, Nozik, Danto, Rorty, Carrell, MacIntyre, and Kuhn.* Chicago: U of Chicago P, 1994.

Dewey, John. *Art as Experience.* 1934. Dewey, *Later Works* 10: 1–352.**

———. *Experience and Nature.* 1925. Dewey, *Later Works* 1: 1–326.**

Dewey, John, and Arthur F. Bentley. *Knowing and the Known.* 1949. Dewey, *Later Works* 16: 1–294.**

Keller, Evelyn Fox. *Reflections on Gender and Science.* New Haven: Yale UP, 1985.

Kuhn, Thomas. *The Structure of Scientific Revolutions.* 2nd ed. Chicago: U of Chicago P, 1970.

Polyani, Michael. *Personal Knowledge.* New York: Harper, 1964.

Rosenblatt, Louise. *L'idée de l'art pour l'art.* Paris: Champion, 1931. New York: AMS, 1976.

Santayana, George. *Three Philosophical Poets: Lucretius, Dante, and Goethe.* 1910. Cambridge: Harvard UP, 1922.

Searle, John R. *The Construction of Social Reality.* New York: Free, 1995.

Sleeper, Ralph. *The Necessity of Pragmatism.* New Haven: Yale UP, 1986.

Toulmin, Stephen. *Cosmopolis: The Hidden Agenda of Modernity.* New York: Free, 1990.

Benedict, Ruth. *Patterns of Culture.* 1934. Boston: Houghton, 1989.

Boas, Franz. *Anthropology and Modern Life.* New York: Norton, 1962.

Clifford, James. *The Predicament of Culture: Twentieth-Century Ethnography, Literature, and Art.* Cambridge: Harvard UP, 1988.

Geertz, Clifford. *The Interpretation of Cultures.* New York: Basic, 1973.

———. *Local Knowledge.* New York: Basic, 1983.

Goldschmidt, Walter. *The Human Career: The Self in the Symbolic World*. Cambridge: Blackwell, 1990.

Mead, Margaret. *Coming of Age in Samoa*. 1928. New York: Morrow, 1961.

Pinker, Steven. *The Language Instinct: How the Mind Creates Language*. New York: Harper, 1995.

Resaldo, Renato. *Culture and Truth: The Remaking of Social Analysis*. Boston: Beacon, 1989.

Sapir, Edward. *Culture, Language, and Personality: Selected Essays*. Ed. David G. Mandelbaum. Berkeley: U of California P, 1956.

———. *Language: An Introduction to the Study of Speech*. 1921. New York: Harcourt, 1949.

Bateson, Gregory. *Steps to an Ecology of Mind*. New York: Ballantine, 1975.

Bruner, Jerome. *Actual Minds, Possible Worlds*. Cambridge: Harvard UP, 1986.

Csikszentmihaly, M., and Reed Larsen. *Being Adolescent: Conflict and Growth in Teenagers*. New York: Basic, 1984.

Dewey, John. *How We Think*. 1910. Revised and expanded 1933. Dewey, *Later Works* 8: 105–352.**

Erikson, Erik H. *Childhood and Society*. Rev. ed. New York: Norton, 1964.

Gardner, Howard. *Frames of Mind: The Theory of Multiple Intelligences*. New York: Basic, 1983.

Gould, Stephen Jay. *The Mismeasure of Man*. New York: Norton, 1981.

Johnson, Mark. *Moral Imagination: Implications of Cognitive Science for Ethics*. Chicago: U of Chicago P, 1993.

Mead, George Herbert. *Mind, Self, and Society*. 1934. Chicago: U of Chicago P, 1962.

Miller, George, and Philip Johnson-Laird. *Language and Perception*. Cambridge: Belknap–Harvard UP, 1976.

Piaget, Jean. *The Language and Thought of the Child*. Trans. M. Worden. Rev. 3rd ed. New York: Humanities, 1959.

Vygotsky, Lev S. *Mind in Society: The Development of Higher Psychological Processes*. Ed. M. Cole, S. Scribner, V. John-Steiner, and E. Sowderman. Cambridge: Harvard UP, 1978.

————. *Thought and Language*. Ed. and trans. E. Hansmann and G. Vakar. Cambridge: MIT P, 1962.

Bateson, Mary Catherine. *Composing a Life*. New York: Atlantic Monthly, 1989.

Blinder, Alan S. *Hard Heads, Soft Hearts: Tough-Minded Economics for a Just Society*. Reading: Addison, 1987.

Boulding, Kenneth. *The Skills of the Economist*. Cleveland: Howard Allen, 1958.

Dewey, John. *The Public and Its Problems*. 1927. Dewey, *Later Works* 2: 235–372.**

Fleischaker, Samuel. *The Ethics of Culture*. Ithaca: Cornell UP, 1994.

Fox-Genovese, Elizabeth. *Feminism without Illusions: A Critique of Individualism*. Chapel Hill: U of North Carolina P, 1991.

Franklin, John Hope. *Race and History*. Baton Rouge: Louisiana State UP, 1989.

Gates, Henry Louis, Jr. *Loose Canons: Notes on the Culture Wars*. New York: Oxford UP, 1992.

Goffman, Erving. *Relations in Public*. New York: Basic, 1971.

Kelman, Steven. *Making Public Policy: A Hopeful View of American Government*. New York: Basic, 1988.

McCloskey, Donald N. *The Rhetoric of Economics*. Madison: U of Wisconsin P, 1985.

Terkel, Studs. *Working*. New York: Pantheon, 1974.

Walzer, Michael. *Thick and Thin: Moral Argument at Home and Abroad*. Notre Dame: U of Notre Dame P, 1994.

West, Cornel. *Race Matters*. Boston: Beacon, 1993.

Wolfe, Alan. *The Human Difference: Animals, Computers, and the Necessity of Social Science*. Berkeley: U of California P, 1993.

*Dewey, John. *John Dewey: The Middle Works, 1899–1924*. Ed. Jo Ann Boydston. 15 vols. Carbondale: Southern Illinois UP, 1976–83.

**———. *John Dewey: The Later Works, 1925–1953*. Ed. Jo Ann Boydston. 17 vols. Carbondale: Southern Illinois UP, 1981–90.

WORKS CITED

It would be impossible to give a complete list of bibliographical sources for this book, since it represents a distillation of many years of reading and teaching. As indicated in part 4, my most obvious debt is to the works of John Dewey, George Santayana, and Charles Sanders Peirce. In addition to the following list of works cited, see indexed references.

Benedict, Ruth. *Patterns of Culture*. Boston: Houghton, 1934.

Brooks, Cleanth, and Robert Penn Warren. *Understanding Poetry*. 1939. 4th ed. New York: Harcourt, 1976.

Coleridge, Samuel Taylor. *Poetical Works*. Ed. Ernest Hartley Coleridge. 1912. Oxford: Oxford UP, 1967.

Darwin, Charles. *The Origin of Species*. 1859. New York: Random, 1993.

Dewey, John. *Art as Experience*. New York: Minton, Balch, 1934.

———. *Human Nature and Conduct*. New York: Henry Holt, 1922.

Dewey, John, and Arthur F. Bentley. *Knowing and the Known*. Boston: Beacon, 1949.

Dollard, John. *Criteria for the Life History*. New Haven: Yale UP, 1935.

Eddington, Arthur Stanley. *Stars and Atoms*. New Haven: Yale UP, 1927.

Eiseley, Loren C. *The Immense Journey*. New York: Random, 1957.

Farrell, Edmund J., and James R. Squire. *Transactions with Literature*. Urbana: NCTE, 1990.

Frank, Lawrence K. "Some Aspects of Education for Home and Family Life." *Journal of Home Economics* 23 (1931): 213–22.

Freedom and Discipline in English. Rept. of the Commission on English, Coll. Entrance Examination Board. Princeton: CEEB, 1965.

Horney, Karen. *The Neurotic Personality of Our Time*. New York: Norton, 1937.

Huxley, Aldous. "Wordsworth in the Tropics." *Do What You Will*. London: Chatto, 1929. 113–29.

Huxley, Thomas Henry. *Man's Place in Nature*. 1863. Ann Arbor: U of Michigan, 1959.

James, William. *The Principles of Psychology*. 1890. Cambridge: Harvard UP, 1983.

Kallen, Horace M. "Democracy versus the Melting Pot." Nation 18 Feb. 1915: 190–94; 25 Feb. 1915: 217–20. Rpt. in *Culture and Democracy in the United States*. New York: Boni, 1924. 67–125.

Keats, John. *John Keats*. Ed. Elizabeth Cook. New York: Oxford UP, 1990.

LaBrant, Lou L. *An Evaluation of the Free Reading in Grades Ten, Eleven, and Twelve*. Columbus: Ohio State UP, 1936.

Loban, Walter D. *Literature and Social Sensitivity*. Champaign: NCTE, 1954.

Maupassant, Guy de. "Le roman." *Pierre et Jean*. Paris: Conard, 1909.

Ogden, C. K., and I. A. Richards. *The Meaning of Meaning*. 1923. San Diego: Harcourt, 1989.

Ohio State University. University School. Class of 1938. *Were We Guinea Pigs?* New York: Henry Holt, 1938.

Pater, Walter. "Wordsworth." *Appreciations*. London: Macmillan, 1904. 37–63.

Peirce, Charles Sanders. *Collected Papers*. 7 vols. Cambridge: Harvard UP, 1935. [Textual references are to volume and paragraph numbers.]

Plant, James S. *Personality and the Cultural Pattern*. New York: Commonwealth Fund–Oxford UP, 1937.

Purves, Alan C., and Richard Beach. *Literature and the Reader: Research in Response to Literature, Reading Interests, and the Teaching of Literature*. Champaign: NCTE, 1972.

Richards, I. A. *Practical Criticism: A Study of Literary Judgment*. 1929. New York: Harcourt, 1956.

Rosenblatt, Louise M. "The Poem as Event." *College English* 26 (1964): 123–32.

———. *The Reader, the Text, the Poem: The Transactional Theory of the Literary Work*. 1978. Carbondale: Southern Illinois UP, 1994.

———. "Whitman's *Democratic Vistas* and the New 'Ethnicity.'" *Yale Review* 67 (1978): 187–204.

Santayana, George. *Reason in Art*. 1905. New York: Scribner's, 1924.

Smith, Adam. *The Wealth of Nations*. 1776. New York: Random, 1985.

Squire, James R. *The Responses of Adolescents while Reading Four Short Stories*. NCTE Research Rept. 2. Champaign: NCTE, 1964.

Stoll, Edgar Elmer. Othello*: An Historical and Comparative Study*. 1915. New York: Haskell, 1964.

Willis, Margaret. *The Guinea Pigs after Twenty Years*. Columbus: Ohio State UP, 1961.

Wilson, James R. *Responses of College Freshmen to Three Novels*. NCTE Research Rept. 7. Champaign: NCTE, 1966.

Wittgenstein, Ludwig. *Philosophical Investigations*. Trans. G. E. M. Anscombe. 3rd ed. Oxford: Blackwell, 1968.

Wordsworth, William. *Complete Poetical Works*. Boston: Houghton, 1904.

INDEX

absurd, literature of the, 202, 248
adolescents: anthropological studies of, 79; challenges to authority, 78, 83, 164, 195; choices available to, 84, 85, 86, 87, 162, 184–85, 212, 249; conformity of, 193, 194; curiosity of, about adulthood, 82, 181; cynicism of, 177; diversity of, 89; emotional development of, 165; entrance into adulthood, 87, 163, 165; interest in parents, 82, 90; personal focus of, 42; role definition, 86–87; search for order, 42; self-consciousness of, 79, 81, 87, 162, 192, 260; social awareness of, 84; stress of, 78–79, 80, 83, 162, 171, 192; teachers' understanding of, 78, 199. *See also* normality; insecurity/security
adventure, tales of, 18, 204
aesthetic experience, literature as, 22, 23, 28, 29, 32–33, 42–43, 271; neglect of, 294

aesthetic reading. *See* reading, aesthetic
aesthetic stance, 292
African Americans, portrayals of, 38, 183
alienation as literary theme, 248
American literature, 255–57
American studies programs, 257–58
Anderson, Sherwood: *Poor White*, 89; *Winesburg, Ohio*, 40
anthropology, 38; on adolescence, 79; on culture, 162, 244–45; on diversity, 14, 79, 150–51; on human nature, 140, 141–45; influence of, on author, 283
anti-Semitism, 223–24
Aristotle, on tragedy, 197
Arnold, Matthew, 209, 249
art. *See* literature as aesthetic experience
Arthurian legends, 12
artist: aim of, 131; contribution of, 160–61; scientist vs., 127–31

Forster, E. M.: *Howards End*, 208; *A Passage to India*, 107
Frank, Lawrence K., 149n, 191; "Some Aspects of Education for Home and Family Life," 173
Franklin, Benjamin, 193
Freedom and Discipline in English, 30n
Freuchen, Peter: *Eskimo*, 38
futility as literary theme, 250

gender roles: changes in, 86, 122, 182, 189, 210, 217–18; formation of, 140, 145, 193–94. *See also* marriage
Goethe, Johann Wolfgang von, 209; *Faust*, 196; *The Sorrows of Young Werther*, 183
Golding, William: *Lord of the Flies*, 79
Gordimer, Nadine: *July's People*, 89
Gray, Thomas, 243
Guest, Edgar, 92

Hall, James. *See* Nordhoff, Charles
Hardy, Thomas, 113, 194, 252, 264; *Jude the Obscure*, 130
Hawthorne, Nathaniel, 96, 209; *The Scarlet Letter*, 17, 19, 270
Hemingway, Ernest: "The Killers," 78
Herrick, Robert, 264
Hersey, John: *Hiroshima*, 228
Heyerdahl, Thor: *Kon-Tiki*, 18
Homer: *Iliad*, 18; *Odyssey*, 12, 18
Horney, Karen: *The Neurotic Personality of Our Time*, 134-35n
Housman, A. E.: *A Shropshire Lad*, 93
Howard, Sidney: *The Silver Cord*, 41, 222
Hughes, Langston, 209
Hugo, Victor: *Les Misérables*, 90
human nature, 136, 154, 258; interpretation of, 10, 12–14, 20, 137–40, 155; plasticity of, 139–40;

voluntaristic conception of, 14–15, 137–38, 139
human relationships. *See* relationships
Hurston, Zora Neale: *Their Eyes Were Watching God*, 228
Huxley, Aldous, 113; "Wordsworth in the Tropics," 239n
Huxley, Thomas H.: *Man's Place in Nature*, 128n
Hynds, Susan. *See* Beach, Richard

Ibsen, Henrik, 194, 282; *A Doll House*, 115–16, 217–18, 220, 226
"ideal experimentation" (C. S. Peirce), 190, 211
identification with characters, 37, 38, 39–40, 46, 226
imagination, 176–78, 190, 212, 261, 276. *See also* "ideal experimentation"; sympathy
imaginative literature, 264–65. *See also* aesthetic experience; literature
individual: adolescent view of, 167n; complexity of, 138, 143; emphasis on, 87, 146, 218, 246; human rights of, 158–59, 160; maintenance of, 219; as product of environment, 239, 241, 242, 252; variation in, 147
influence of literature on behavior, 187–88. *See also* values, formation of
insecurity/security, emotional, 80, 87, 123, 132–33, 163–64, 192, 212
insight provided by literature, 7, 98, 101, 174, 226, 257, 259
interaction vs. transaction, 26, 276; Dewey on, 291. *See also* transaction between reader and text
interdisciplinary aspects of literary study, 4, 231–32, 258–59